DATE DUE

TENNYSON'S CAMELOT
THE *IDYLLS OF THE KING* AND ITS MEDIEVAL SOURCES

David Staines

As the principal narrative poem of nineteenth-century England, Tennyson's *Idylls of the King* is an ambitious and widely influential reworking of the Arthurian legends of the Middle Ages, which have provided a great body of myth and symbol to writers, painters, and composers for the past hundred years. Tennyson's treatment of these legends is now valued as a deeply significant oblique commentary on cultural decadence and the precarious balance of civilization.

Drawing upon published and unpublished materials, *Tennyson's Camelot* studies the *Idylls of the King* from the perspective of all its medieval sources. In noting the Arthurian literature Tennyson knew and paying special attention to the works that became central to his Arthurian creation, the volume reveals the poet's immense knowledge of the medieval legends and his varied approaches to his sources. The author follows the chronology of composition of the *Idylls*, allowing the reader to see Tennyson's evolving conception of his poem and his changing attitudes to the medieval accounts. The *Idylls of the King* stands, ultimately, as the poet's own Camelot, his legacy to his generation, an indictment of his society through a vindication of his idealism.

David Staines is Associate Professor of English at the University of Ottawa. He received the Ph.D. degree from Harvard University, where he has also taught, introducing Canadian literature courses there. The author of many articles on medieval romance, medieval drama, and Arthurian literature of the Middle Ages and the nineteenth century, he has also edited Responses and Evaluations: Essays on Canada by E. K. Brown *and* The Canadian Imagination: Dimensions of a Literary Culture.

TENNYSON'S CAMELOT

THE *IDYLLS OF THE KING* AND ITS MEDIEVAL SOURCES

TENNYSON'S CAMELOT

THE IDYLLS OF THE KING
AND ITS MEDIEVAL SOURCES

DAVID STAINES

Wilfrid Laurier University Press

Canadian Cataloguing in Publication Data

Staines, David, 1946-
    Tennyson's Camelot : the Idylls of the King and
its medieval sources

Bibliography: p.
Includes index.
ISBN 0-88920-115-3

1. Tennyson, Alfred Tennyson, Baron, 1809-1892. Idylls
of the King.   2. Tennyson, Alfred Tennyson, Baron,
1809-1892 - Knowledge - Folklore, mythology.
3. Arthurian romances - History and criticism.
4. Arthurian romances in literature. I. Title.

PR5560.S82   821'.8   C82-094512-9

Copyright © 1982

WILFRID LAURIER UNIVERSITY PRESS
Waterloo, Ontario, Canada   N2L 3C5

82 83 84 85 4 3 2 1

Cover Design: Polygon Design Limited

for
M. R. S.

Contents

Foreword

by
Charles Tennyson

Two of the great advantages of the system of education at Eton College
eighty years ago—and I am sure that it is the same today—were that
every boy had a room to himself and every boy had a tutor who was one
of the masters and who remained his tutor for the whole of his school
career. His tutor had the duty of looking after him generally, of protect-
ing him (if necessary) from the other masters, and of supplementing the
ordinary curriculum of the school if he thought that in any particular case
it was inadequate. Eighty-odd years ago my tutor was Hugh Vibart
Macnaghten, a saint and a poet who, in spite of being saint and poet, was
much respected and beloved by his pupils. Macnaghten gave a prize
every year for those of his pupils of a certain age who cared to go in for it.
It was called the "Newcastle under Line"—an obscure pun which I will
not stop to elucidate—and eighty years ago the subjects were Four
Books of *The Odyssey*, Four Books of *The Aeneid*, and the whole of the
Idylls of the King. The competitors were entirely free to pursue any
means of study they liked, they had a term and a holiday to prepare for
the examination, which might include any question on any aspect of the
very comprehensive subjects covered. I personally look back on the
competition of 1895 or 1896 as the most valuable item of the whole of my
education, which I suppose covered something like twenty years. In
particular the "Newcastle under Line" for 1895 (or 1896?) gave me an
interest in the *Idylls of the King* and a love for the poem which has
outlasted all changes of critical fashion during the past eighty years and
made the *Idylls* for me the greatest poem of the nineteenth century. And
critical fashion during the last seventy-five years has changed consider-

ably. In 1936 T. S. Eliot said that Tennyson "could not tell a story at all." Thirteen years earlier Harold Nicolson, while admitting that he himself enjoyed the *Idylls* very much indeed, had written that the poem could make no appeal whatever to the modern mind. Now hardly a year passes without the appearance of several laudatory and respectful books on what is rapidly becoming regarded as the greatest poem of the nineteenth century.

Nobody nowadays reads long poems and therefore long poems are not written, which is more than a pity. Our Victorian ancestors were not like this, and I have always been impressed by James Spedding's criticism of Tennyson's volumes of 1842 which ended as follows: "We cannot conclude without reminding Mr. Tennyson, that highly as we value the Poems which he has produced, we cannot accept them as a satisfactory account of the gifts which they show that he possesses . . . Powers are displayed in these volumes, adequate, if we do not deceive ourselves, to the production of a [very] great work; at least we should find it difficult to say which of the requisite powers is wanting. But they are displayed in fragments and snatches, having no connexion, and therefore deriving no light or fresh interest the one from the other . . . If Mr. Tennyson can find a subject large enough to take the entire impress of his mind, and energy persevering enough to work it faithfully out as one whole, we are convinced that he may produce a work, which, though occupying no larger space than the contents of these volumes, shall as much exceed them in value, as a series of quantities multiplied into each other exceeds in value the same series simply added together."

When this review appeared in the *Edinburgh Review*, Spedding found that the Editor had struck out the word "very," which I have included in brackets about half way through my extract from his criticism. When Spedding republished it in volume form in 1879, he reinserted the word "very."

The subject of the *Idylls of the King* fits exactly Spedding's description of what in his view Tennyson required for the completion of his "very great work." In fact the poem occupied Tennyson for nearly fifty years, counting from the date when he wrote his *Morte d'Arthur* and the date when he published the whole series including the last written *Balin and Balan*.

Of course the *Idylls of the King* suffered somewhat from their prolonged period of incubation. There are considerable differences of style between the *Morte d'Arthur* of 1834, published in 1842, and the other idylls, and between the volumes published in 1859, 1869, and 1872. But the differences are very much less than might have been expected, and there is no doubt that Tennyson was wise to give up the idea of an epic narrative, with which in mind he had written the old *Morte* of 1842, and to concentrate on the idyll form, in which he was highly skilled and which enabled him to deal with a vast canvas without having also to deal with the difficulties of connecting narrative—in this case exaggerated by the need to portray in detail the relations of Arthur, Guinevere, and Lancelot. The idyll form enabled him merely to hint at these, though the omission of a further treatment may well strike one as a defect.

Tennyson's poem is highly symbolic—parabolic is the word that he himself preferred. In this it resembles almost all of Tennyson's work. As he himself wrote, "Poetry is like shot silk of many glancing colours and the reader must interpret it according to his ability and his sympathy with the poet."

In *Tennyson's Camelot: The Idylls of the King and Its Medieval Sources*, David Staines deals with Tennyson's poem chronologically, explaining the symbolism in the light of the poet's general views, and explaining why Tennyson dealt with the legends in the curious topsy-turvy way he actually adopted; an Epilogue to this analysis deals with the effect of the *Idylls of the King* on the way in which the Victorian age regarded the Arthurian legends. This is the principal contribution of *Tennyson's Camelot* to the study of the *Idylls of the King* and it is of great value.

The study is followed by a number of very useful appendices. The first appendix sets Tennyson's *Morte* of 1842 against the parallel passages in Malory's *Morte D'Arthur*; the effect of this is to increase one's admiration for Tennyson's adaptation, which is surely one of the greatest poems in the English language. Another appendix gives verbatim the prose drafts from which Tennyson prepared the finished poems. These are often a great help in ascertaining the poet's meaning. They are not accessible to the public in any other form.

Preface

Tennyson was nearly fifty when he began to write his major Arthurian poem, the *Idylls of the King*. From his earliest years the legends of King Arthur, "the greatest of all poetical subjects" as he called them, had fascinated and haunted him. As a child he had been familiar with Malory; throughout his life he read all available medieval writing related to the story of Camelot. The long delay between his early interest in Arthur and his late commitment to a major Arthurian work reflects his inability to find a proper avenue into the medieval legends and an appropriate vehicle for their re-creation.

In his early Arthurian writings, four outlines of a possible treatment of the material and four poems composed in the eighteen-thirties, Tennyson was experimenting with his sources to find a method of handling the medieval subjects. The immensity and power of the myth seemed at times to inhibit his poetic freedom. In some of these early works he attempted to be independent of his sources, yet in his major early Arthurian poem, the *Morte d'Arthur*, he tried to follow closely the narrative structure of his source in Malory. When he finally turned to the *Idylls of the King*, he continued to draw upon Malory; in fact, two of the idylls explicitly acknowledge his medieval master. But he learned to treat his sources in a more free, more independent way. This new relation to the sources reflects his growing confidence that he had found an artistically powerful approach to the Arthurian world. He became, in other words, not a reteller of the familiar stories, but a reshaper of the myth, using it to articulate his own mature vision.

Studying Tennyson's treatment of his medieval sources, I came to realize that the central character, on whom he structured his Arthurian world, is not Arthur, the embodiment of Camelot's ideal values and the ultimate focus of the entire work, but his Queen Guinevere. Tennyson's growing independence from his source parallels his growing use of Guinevere in the development of his Arthurian poem. The idyll devoted to her, *Guinevere*, is the most original in the series, and in it the Queen emerges as a vivid human being while Arthur sinks into the background. Guinevere acquires a new kind and degree of importance quite different from her shadowy and incomplete presentation in Malory and other medieval accounts. But though the prominence of Guinevere permits the poet to create his version of the story of Camelot, it also leads to the ultimately incomplete portrait of Arthur. *Guinevere* presents Arthur as the ideal monarch working God's will on earth, and the idylls written thereafter show Tennyson struggling to infuse his ideal portrait with human qualities. Arthur's unbending and relentless commitment to the Ideal, when contrasted with the graphic delineation of Guinevere's agonized humanity, threatened to make him both a less believable and a less sympathetic hero.

English scholars and critics have been reluctant to acknowledge the importance or the merit of Tennyson's Arthurian poetry, even though Hallam Tennyson, the poet's son, wrote that the *Idylls of the King,* "regarded as a whole, gives his innermost being more fully, though not more truly, than 'In Memoriam.' " Harold Nicolson's important study, *Tennyson* (1923), dismissed much of the later poetry as evidencing a decline in literary sensibility. The effect of Nicolson's judgment was subsequent critical preoccupation with Tennyson's earlier poetry to the exclusion of any adequate appreciation of the later works. Five decades after the publication of Nicolson's volume, Christopher Ricks' *Tennyson* (1972) returned to the practice of casually dismissing the *Idylls* as inferior art.

On the other hand, Jerome H. Buckley's *Tennyson: The Growth of a Poet* (1960) rejected Nicolson's categorical dismissal of the later works and argued for a more coherent understanding of Tennyson's full development as a major poet. Subsequent scholarship has turned with increasing frequency to the *Idylls.* Clyde de L. Ryals' *From the Great Deep* (1967) contradicted Tennyson's own statements about his intentions in the *Idylls* and asserted that Arthur is both hero and villain in his violation of the free will of his associates. John R. Reed's *Perception and Design in Tennyson's Idylls of the King* (1969) offered a different reading of the moral design of the poem; after a preliminary discussion of *The Two Voices* and *Maud,* Reed studied the poet's preoccupation in the *Idylls* with metaphysical questions regarding the relationship of the material to the spiritual world. J. Phillip Eggers' *King Arthur's Laureate* (1971) began its consideration of the *Idylls* from three separate points of view: the poem's sources, contemporary reaction to the poem, and Arthurian literature of Tennyson's contemporaries; the breadth of Eggers' approach prevented his complete analysis of the sources. In a number of short articles and two monographs, *Man and Myth in Victorian England: The Coming of Arthur* (1969) and *Tennyson's Doppelgänger: Balin and Balan* (1971), J. M. Gray presented systematic analyses of corresponding episodes in the *Idylls* and in medieval accounts, though his discussion did not achieve a full perspective on the individual idylls or their role in the complete poem. John D. Rosenberg's *The Fall of Camelot* (1973) has studied the *Idylls* in the context of modern literature and concluded that the poem is "the subtlest anatomy of the failure of identity in our literature." In *Tennyson's Major Poems* (1975) James R. Kincaid has argued that the *Idylls* follows Tennyson's practice of weaving a narrative pattern of comedy and irony so that the complete poem "builds a comic world and then destroys it from within." And A. Dwight Culler's *The Poetry of Tennyson* (1977) affirmed that the structure of Tennyson's Arthurian poem "is apocalyptic rather than elegiac, linear rather than cyclical." Despite such interest in the *Idylls* Kathleen Tillotson's statement in her study, "Tennyson's Serial Poem" (*Mid-Victorian Studies*, 1965), that Tennyson's handling of his sources in the *Idylls* is "a subject on which much remains to be done," still holds true.

The present work approaches Tennyson's Arthurian world through a detailed analysis of his treatment of his sources. More exactly, it studies the way he shaped his source material to create his own Camelot, his re-creation being, in reality, a creation. In noting all the Arthurian literature Tennyson knew and paying careful attention to those works which became central to his Arthurian creation, this study follows the chronology of composition of the *Idylls*, for only in this way can the reader trace Tennyson's evolving conception of his poem and his changing attitude to his sources. The importance of Malory and, to a smaller degree, the other medieval sources available to the poet and Tennyson's dependence upon them alter significantly as the series progresses towards its final form and Tennyson realizes that he has found his own avenue into the Arthurian legends.

As I searched for all of Tennyson's Arthurian readings, I received invaluable assistance from the staffs of the three main repositories of manuscript materials, the Tennyson Research Centre in Lincoln, Trinity College Library, Cambridge, and the Houghton Library of Harvard University. The staff of the Houghton Library was especially helpful in my constant need to examine the Tennyson Notebooks. And on my visits to Lincoln Nancie Campbell answered many questions about Tennyson's personal library; her magisterial two-volume *Tennyson in Lincoln* confirmed many of my own findings.

With the fine teacher's care and insight, F. T. Flahiff introduced me to Tennyson's Arthurian poetry in an undergraduate course in Victorian poetry at the University of Toronto. As this study took its initial shape as a doctoral dissertation Jerome H. Buckley offered encouragement and advice far beyond the duties of a supervisor. To these two scholars I remain deeply indebted. I am also grateful to Larry D. Benson, Morton W. Bloomfield, and B. J. Whiting, my teachers and former colleagues, for their reading of my work; their patience supported while tempering a medievalist's "questionable" interest in Victorian Arthuriana.

To so many students of Tennyson's poetry, myself included, Sir Charles Tennyson was a critic and a friend. Always the epitome of generosity in sharing his knowledge and understanding of his grandfather's writings, he read this study both in its formative stage as an unfinished dissertation and much later in its present form. Shortly before his death in 1977, he wrote the Foreword. My debt to him is evident throughout the book.

A section of Chapter 3, originally published as "Tennyson's 'The Holy Grail': The Tragedy of Percivale" in the *Modern Language Review*, is reprinted with the permission of the editors. Appendix 4, "The Prose Drafts of the *Idylls of the King*," originally published in the *Harvard Library Bulletin*, is reprinted with the permission of the editor. Despite the appearance of John Pfordresher's *Variorum Edition of Tennyson's Idylls of the King*, I have included all the prose drafts because of inaccuracies and omissions in the Pfordresher edition. The drafts in the Harvard College Notebooks are printed with the permission of the Harvard College Library, and the two fragmentary prose drafts of "Gareth and Lynette" in the Tennyson collection of the University of Texas are printed with the permission of the Humanities Research Center Library of the University of Texas. Sir Charles Tennyson and the present Lord Tennyson kindly extended permission to me to quote from unpublished sources.

Tennyson's Camelot was accepted in 1977 by a large European publisher which inexplicably kept postponing publication. In telling contrast Wilfrid Laurier University Press and its Director Harold Remus have shown only courtesy and efficiency.

This book has been published with the help of a grant from the Canadian Federation for the Humanities, using funds provided by the Social Sciences and Humanities Research Council of Canada.

Chapter 1

On the Road to Camelot

What he called "the greatest of all poetical subjects"
perpetually haunted him.[1]

As a young man Alfred Tennyson realized that only one major subject
awaited a full poetic treatment: "I felt certain of one point . . . if I meant
to make any mark at all, it must be by shortness, for the men before me
had been so diffuse, and most of the big things except 'King Arthur' had
been done."[2] He turned to the Arthurian legends with the ardour and
enthusiasm of a young knight on his first quest. The story of King
Arthur, with his ideal vision and his attempt to realize that vision,
permeated the poet's creative imagination. His poetic career was an
attempt to express Arthur's idealism in its many ramifications in a
literary vehicle capable of sustaining the intensity of its subject-matter.

By the early nineteenth century the story of the Round Table, a
mythic treasure for the artists of medieval England, had become a
literary anachronism. For Samuel Taylor Coleridge, the Arthurian
world had no validity; in 1833, the same year that saw Tennyson begin
his *Morte d'Arthur*, Coleridge commented: "In my judgement, an epic
poem must either be national or mundane. As to Arthur, you could not
by any means make a poem national to Englishmen. What have *we* to do
with him? Milton saw this, and with a judgement at least equal to his
genius, took a mundane theme—one common to all mankind."[3] By
daring to employ the Arthurian legends in his poetry, Tennyson brought
about a rebirth of interest in the story of Camelot. At the same time that
he found the appropriate vehicle for the most complete poetic expres-

1 Hallam Lord Tennyson, *Alfred Lord Tennyson: A Memoir* (New York, 1897), II, 125.
2 Ibid., I, 166.
3 *The Table Talk and Omniana of Samuel Taylor Coleridge* (London: G. Bell and Sons, 1923), p. 279.

1

sion of his mind, he established the story of Arthur on a new plateau of respect and significance for the artists of the nineteenth century.

When Tennyson finally began to write his Arthurian epic, he was nearly fifty. His late employment of the myth reflects, not a sudden interest in the legends, but a secure understanding of the medieval world complemented by the discovery of an appropriate method of re-creating Camelot for a Victorian audience. Throughout his life he was drawn to the legends; even in his early twenties he was searching desperately for a proper avenue into the material. Yet his early Arthurian efforts are experiments which anticipate the *Idylls of the King*; such early works reveal his thorough knowledge of medieval Arthuriana, his commitment to a poetic re-creation of the legends, and his constant experimentation with varying degrees of source fidelity. The early material is the road to Camelot, a road which leads directly, though slowly, to the *Idylls of the King*.

Tennyson's lifelong fascination with the story of Camelot was the consequence of the natural bent of his mind and its principal interests. From boyhood, the world of the past exerted a powerful attraction: "for oft / On me, when boy, there came what then I called, / Who knew no books and no philosophies, / In my boy-phrase 'The Passion of the Past.'"[4] Tennyson always experienced passionate yearning for times removed from the present: "it is so always with me now; it is the distance that charms me in the landscape, the picture and the past, and not the immediate to-day in which I move."[5] The predilection for the past asserted itself in the many poems and plays which turn to the past for their subject-matter. Moreover, as the "passion of the past" sent him nostalgically to earlier eras, it also made him aware of their significance. The narrator of *The Lover's Tale* mourned: "The Present is the vassal of the Past"; his assertion reflected the poet's own belief that the past has a causal relationship to the present. The narrator of *Locksley Hall Sixty Years After* understood the importance of the past: "Read the old world's annals, you, and take their wisdom for your friend. / Hope the best, but hold the present fatal daughter of the Past, / Shape your heart to front the hour, but dream not that the hour will last." The present's dependence upon the past allowed the past to function as a mirror which might indicate the moral condition of the present. Tennyson, by nature

---

4 *The Ancient Sage*, 11. 216-219. Unless otherwise indicated, all quotations from Tennyson's poetry are from the Eversley edition of his *Works*, edited in nine volumes by Hallam Lord Tennyson (London: Macmillan, 1907-1908).

5 Quoted by Sir James Knowles, "Aspects of Tennyson," *Nineteenth Century*, 33 (January 1893), 170. *Tears, Idle Tears* presents the fullest expression of this yearning. Frederick Locker-Lampson recalled the poet's comment: "He told me that he was moved to write 'Tears, idle Tears' at Tintern Abbey; and that it was not real woe, as some people might suppose; 'it was rather the yearning that young people occasionally experience for that which seems to have passed away from them for ever.' That in him it was strongest when he was quite a youth" (*Memoir*, II, 73).

nostalgic, turned to the past, not to retreat from the plight of his time, but to discover an adequate barometer of the moral temper of Victorian England; he looked back to find appropriate material to embody themes valid for his own generation.

Tennyson's nostalgic yearning, complemented by his awareness of the didactic significance of the past, made the Arthurian legends a powerful inspiration. He expressed no concern with the question of Arthur's historicity, the problem that had plagued the seventeenth century and prompted Milton to avoid Arthurian material:

> How much of history we have in the story of Arthur is doubtful. Let not my readers press too hardly on details whether for history or for allegory. Some think that King Arthur may be taken to typify conscience. He is anyhow meant to be a man who spent himself in the cause of honour, duty and self-sacrifice, who felt and aspired with his nobler knights, though with a stronger and a clearer conscience than any of them, "reverencing his conscience as his king." "There was no such perfect man since Adam," as an old writer says, "Major praeteritis majorque futuris Regibus."[6]

Arthur became an ideal figure of singular importance to the Victorian age, which shows "the want of reverence now-a-days for great men, whose brightness, like that of the luminous bodies in the Heaven, makes the dark spaces look the darker."[7]

The ideal King of the *Idylls of the King* grew out of Tennyson's extensive study of the medieval legends. Familiar with many accounts of the story of Camelot, the poet wrote a "prefatory MS note about the historical Arthur":

> He lived about 500 A.D. and defeated his enemies in a pitched battle in the Welsh kingdom of Strathclyde: and the earliest allusions to him are to be found in the Welsh bards of the seventh century. In the twelfth century Geoffrey of Monmouth collected the legends about him as an European conqueror in his *History of the Britons:* and translated them from Celtic into Latin. *Morte d'Arthur* by Sir Thomas Malory was printed by Caxton in 1485.[8]

Malory was Tennyson's major source for his conception of Arthur: "the vision of Arthur as I have drawn him . . . had come upon me when, little more than a boy, I first lighted upon Malory."[9] Malory's Arthur is a great warrior, a noble leader of men, an exemplary monarch; at the same time he is a very human ruler, begotten out of wedlock and guilty, though unknowingly, of incest. The earlier chroniclers, who emphasized the blameless nature of Arthur in contrast to Malory's later depiction of a more human and sinful monarch, became another source of Tennyson's King:

6 *Memoir*, I, 194.
7 Ibid., I, 424.
8 Ibid., II, 121.
9 Ibid., II, 128.

He felt himself justified in having always pictured Arthur as the ideal man by such passages as this from Joseph of Exeter: "The old world knows not his peer, nor will the future show us his equal: he alone towers over the other kings, better than the past ones and greater than those that are to be." So this from Alberic,

> "Hic jacet Arturus, flos regum, gloria regni,
> Quem probitas morum commendat laude perenni."

And this from the *Brut ab Arthur*, "In short God has not made since Adam was, the man more perfect than Arthur."[10]

Tennyson, the devoted student of the legends, found in Arthur a character whose life would stand as an example to his Victorian readers of the need for an ideal vision.

Though Tennyson regarded Malory as an almost unlimited reservoir of stories for his study of Arthur, his appreciation of Malory was the product of the literary temper of the early nineteenth century: "I could not read 'Palmerin of England' nor 'Amadis,' nor any other of those Romances through. The 'Morte d'Arthur' is much the best: there are very fine things in it, but all strung together without Art."[11] Yet his estimation of Malory and his recognition of the low literary stature of the legends in his own time did not diminish his enthusiasm. The Arthurian world became his natural haunt. In speaking of his father's employment of classical legend, Hallam Tennyson concluded:

I need not dwell on my father's love of the perfection of classical literary art, on his sympathy with the temper of the old world, on his love of the old metres, and on his views as to how the classical subject ought to be treated in English poetry. He purposely chose those classical subjects from mythology and legend, which had been before but imperfectly treated, or of which the stories were slight, so that he might have free scope for his imagination.[12]

In a similar way Malory provided countless stories, some demanding further development, some adequately treated already, some permitting re-creation in the light of the nineteenth century. Though Malory always remained the major source of the *Idylls,* Tennyson studied all available histories and commentaries which might clarify and expand his knowledge of the Arthurian world.[13] He needed only to find a path into the

10 Ibid., II, 128-129. For Tennyson's familiarity with Joseph of Exeter and the *Brut*, see Chapter 2, footnote 42. Alberic, a thirteenth-century Cistercian, wrote a *Chronicle* of the world from the time of Creation until 1241. For the year 1193, there is a report of the excavation of Arthur's body; the lines quoted here are the inscription found on the tomb. The *Chronicle* was edited by G. W. Leibniz in his *Accessiones Historicae* (Lipsiae, 1698).

11 Ibid., I, 194. In his edition of *Sir Tristrem* (Edinburgh, 1806), Walter Scott expressed a similar attitude to Malory: "*The History of Tristram* was not, so far as I know, translated into English as a separate work; but his adventures make a part of the collection called the *Morte Arthur*, containing great part of the history of the Round Table, extracted at hazard, and without much art or combination, from the various French prose folios on that favourite topic" (p. lxxix).

12 Ibid., II, 13.

13 "On Malory, and later, on Lady Charlotte Guest's translation of the *Mabinogion*, and

legends which would offer him "free scope for his imagination" within the dimensions of the myth.

Before Tennyson found a satisfying method of treating his medieval sources, he experimented with a variety of forms and subjects. In his early Arthuriana he tried every possible means of adapting the medieval stories, from a close fidelity to the text of his source to complete originality with only the slightest connection to a medieval account. His early attempts to depict Arthur and his realm are an important preparation for his final commitment to an Arthurian epic which would occupy so much of his attention from the late eighteen-fifties until the time of his death. The *Idylls of the King* is a cumulative achievement, the culmination of a long poetic career which often turned to the world of Camelot. And the most important preparation for his achievement is the quartet of Arthurian poems and the four outlines of Arthurian material written in the eighteen-thirties.

Four outlines of Arthurian literature are found in the musings of the young poet. A prose sketch from about 1833 emphasizes the splendour and the glory, the beauty and the majesty of Camelot, qualities which would appear to a disciple of Keats:

King Arthur

On the latest limit of the West in the land of Lyonnesse, where, save the rocky Isles of Scilly, all is now wild sea, rose the sacred Mount of Camelot. It rose from the deeps with gardens and bowers and palaces, and at the top of the Mount was King Arthur's hall, and the holy Minster with the Cross of gold. Here dwelt the King in glory apart, while the Saxons whom he had overthrown in twelve battles ravaged the land, and ever came nearer and nearer.

The Mount was the most beautiful in the world, sometimes green and fresh in the beam of morning, sometimes all one splendour, folded in the golden mists of the West. But all underneath it was hollow, and the mountain trembled, when the seas rushed bellowing through the porphyry caves; and there ran a prophecy that the mountain and the city on some wild morning would topple into the abyss and be no more.

It was night. The King sat in his Hall. Beside him sat the sumptuous Guinevere and about him were all his lords and knights of the Table Round. There they feasted, and when the feast was over the Bards sang to the King's glory.[14]

A second fragment, which Hallam Tennyson dated at approximately the same time, concerns itself with an allegorical interpretation of the legends:

K.A.   Religious Faith.
King Arthur's three Guineveres.

on his own imagination, my father said that he chiefly founded his epic" (*Memoir*, II, 121-122). Regarding his knowledge of the Arthurian legends, Tennyson said: "I know more about Arthur than any other man in England" (quoted by James Knowles in a letter appended to the eighth edition of his *The Story of King Arthur and His Knights of the Round Table* [London, 1912], p. viii).
14   Ibid., II, 122-123.

The Lady of the Lake.

Two Guineveres. ye first prim. Christianity. 2^d Roman Catholicism. ye first is put away and dwells apart. 2^d Guinevere flies. Arthur takes to the first again but finds her changed by lapse of Time.

Modred, the sceptical understanding. He pulls Guinevere, Arthur's latest wife, from the throne.

Merlin Emrys, the enchanter. Science. Marries his daughter to Modred. Excalibur, war.

The sea, the people.

The Saxons, the people. } the S. are a sea-people and it is theirs and a type of them.

The Round Table: liberal institutions.

Battle of Camlan.

2^d Guinevere with the enchanted book and cup.[15]

The explicitly allegorical rendering left its influence upon the later Idylls that do move into the realm of allegory, yet the fragment suggests, not that the poet would regard the Arthurian world as the embodiment of allegory, but rather that he was consciously meditating on various literary methods in which the world of Camelot might be presented.

In one of the Harvard Notebooks dating from about the same time as the two preceding sketches, there is a four-page outline of the characters of the Arthurian world that illustrates the poet's attempt to organize in a detailed pattern the various relationships among the many central characters:

> −and there he found ye brauche of an holy herbe that was ye signe of the Sancgraill & no kn^t found such tokens but he were a good lyver−
>
> M. d'A.   4.B.c.5.

Morgause
King Lot's wife of Orkney. Arthur's sister.

her sons.

---

15   Ibid., II, 123-124. Jowett may have been referring to this fragment when he wrote: "Like Milton, he had early been impressed by the Legend of King Arthur, and had intended to weave it into a new form. This was, perhaps, the earliest of his poetical dreams, but it was not one of them which was destined to be carried out. The great work which he had designed was in no respect like the so-called 'Idylls' which have become so familiar to the public. His purpose was to have in some way or other represented in it the great religions of the world: but although it was definitely planned, this poem never saw the light. He offered to show me the rough sketch of it, but on enquiring some years afterwards about it, I found that it had already been destroyed" (*Memoir*, II, 464). In "Alfred Tennyson as a Celticist," *Modern Philology*, 18 (1921), 485-492, Tom Peete Cross shows that the identifications in the fragment are evidence of the poet's familiarity with William Owen's *Cambrian Biography: or Historical Notices of Celebrated Men among the Ancient Britons* (1803) and Edward Davies' *Mythology and Rites of the British Druids* (1809).

Gawayn.
Gaherys.
Agramaynes.
Gareth.

———

son by Arthur.
Mordred.
Morgan le fay. (Arth⁵ sister)
    wife to King Uriens. Sir Uwayne (her son)
Sir Accolon (her paramour)
    (she steals Arth's scabbard as he sleeps & throws
    it into the lake)

———

Dame. Igraine. Arth⁵ mother. Wife of the Duke of
Tintagil (a mighty duke in Cornewaile)
Sir Ector. King Arth: fostʳ fathʳ. Sir Kay.
foster broth.
Gwenever. (the king's daughter of Camyliarde)
                    (Lodegreans)
with Gui − Arth. received the table round & C. knights
    from Lod. the tab. round when complete CL
    knights

———

Pellinore.   Nineve.
    sons.   (one of the damoysels
Percyval of Walys   of yᵉ lake) who
    Lamerak (d⁹)   deceived Merlyn.
        by the cowherd's wife.
Sir Tor.

King Ban ──┬── Elayne
    Launcelot[16]

———

The fourth sketch, also dating from this formative period of the
early thirties, is a draft of a scenario of the Arthurian story. Despite his
poetic experimentation in *The Lady of Shalott, Sir Launcelot and
Queen Guinevere, Sir Galahad,* and the *Morte d'Arthur,* Tennyson was
undecided about the ultimate form for his Arthurian masterpiece. Epic
and musical masque were alternatives. The following draft provides an
interesting contrast to the final achievements of the completed *Idylls:*

First Act.
    Sir Mordred and his party. Mordred inveighs against the King and the
Round Table. The knights, and the quest. Mordred scoffs at the Ladies of the

16 Harvard Notebook 16, watermarked 1833. "4.B.c.5." refers to the fifth chapter of the
    fourth book of Malory according to Caxton's divisions, which were first employed by
    Robert Southey in his 1817 edition of Malory.

Lake, doubts whether they are supernatural beings, etc. Mordred's cringing interview with Guinevere. Mordred and the Lady of the Lake. Arthur lands in Albyn.

Second Act.

Lancelot's embassy and Guinevere. The Lady of the Lake meets Arthur and endeavours to persuade him not to fight with Sir Mordred. Arthur will not be moved from his purpose. Lamentation of the Lady of the Lake. Elaine. Marriage of Arthur.

Third Act.

Oak tomb of Merlin. The song of Nimue. Sir Mordred comes to consult Merlin. Coming away meets Arthur. Their fierce dialogue. Arthur consults Sir L. and Sir Bedivere. Arthur weeps over Merlin and is reproved by Nimue, who inveighs against Merlin. Arthur asks Merlin the issue of the battle. Merlin will not enlighten him. Nimue requests Arthur to question Merlin again. Merlin tells him he shall bear rule again, but that the Ladies of the Lake can return no more. Guinevere throws away the diamonds into the river. The Court and the dead Elaine.

Fourth Act.

Discovery by Mordred and Nimue of Lancelot and Guinevere. Arthur and Guinevere's meeting and parting.

Fifth Act.

The battle. Chorus of the Ladies of the Lake. The throwing away of Excalibur and departure of Arthur.[17]

Significant in this synopsis is the presence of incidents found later in the completed *Idylls*. Hallam Tennyson remarked that in 1859 the poet "did not rush headlong into the other 'Idylls of the King,' although he had carried a more or less perfected scheme of them in his head over thirty years."[18] The "perfected scheme" is not present in the dramatic outline, since a clear focus within the outline is absent. The roles of Mordred and Merlin will be smaller in the *Idylls*; the Ladies of the Lake will not assume such importance; episodes in the early history of Camelot will be added. At the same time other incidents recorded in the later poetry are already present: the important role of Elaine, including the moment when Guinevere tosses the diamonds into the river at the instant Elaine's body appears; the prominence of Nimue and her association with Mordred in the disclosure of the Lancelot-Guinevere relationship; the final meeting of Arthur and his Queen; Arthur's departure from this world. Yet the draft of a drama lacks coherence and unity; it opens with Mordred who would seem more central to the plot than Arthur himself;

17 *Memoir*, II, 124-125.
18 Ibid., II, 125.

Merlin and Nimue seem to be appropriately paired, though the pairing of Mordred and Nimue in the discovery scene is unexplained. The bald outline suggests the poet's desire to incorporate dramatic incidents into an extended treatment of Arthur and his realm, yet it also suggests his search for a focus within these incidents. A satisfactory method for a Victorian treatment of Arthur's world still eluded Tennyson. The final answer is the product of many decades of thought, experimentation, and seeming failure.

Tennyson's first published Arthurian work, *The Lady of Shalott,* is based, not on Malory, but on a medieval Italian novelette entitled "Donna di Scalotta."[19] This short work appeared as Novella LXXXI in Volume One of the *Raccolta di Novelle,* a reprint of the famous thirteenth-century Italian collection known as *Cento Novelle Antiche.*[20] Since Tennyson became acquainted with Italian poetry through Arthur Henry Hallam,[21] he may have been familiar with this Italian work. In any event, in 1825 Thomas Roscoe printed his four-volume collection of translations from the Italian novelists. Entitled "We here learn how the lady of Scalot died for love of Launcelot of the Lake," Novella LXXXI is short and concise:

A daughter of the great Barbassoro became passionately attached to Launcelot of the Lake; but so far from returning her love, he bestowed all his affections on the fair Queen Ginevra. To such a degree did her unhappy attachment arise, that she at length fell a victim to it, and died, leaving a bequest, that as soon as her soul had departed, her body should be transported on board a barge fitted up for the purpose, with a rich couch, and adorned with velvet stuffs, and precious stones and ornaments; and thus arrayed in her proudest attire, with a bright golden crown upon her brows, she was to be borne alone to the place of residence of her beloved. Beneath her silver zone was found a letter to the following tenor; but we must first mention what ought to precede the letter itself. Every thing was exactly fulfilled as she had appointed, respecting the vessel without a sail or oars, helmsman, or hands to guide her; and so, with its lifeless freight, it was launched upon the open waves. Thus she was borne along by the winds, which conveyed her direct to Camelot, where the barge rested of itself upon the banks.

A rumour immediately spread through the court, and a vast train of barons and cavaliers ran out of the palace, followed soon by King Arthur himself. They stood mute with astonishment, on observing the strange vessel there, without a

19 Ibid., I, 91.
20 The first volume of the *Raccolta di Novelle,* edited by G. Ferrario (Milan, 1804), is a reprint of the 1525 edition of the *Libra di Novelle e di parlar gentile, contenente Cento Novelle Antiche.* In Hallam Lord Tennyson's *Materials for a Life of A.T.* (privately printed, no date), IV, 461-462, Novella LXXXI is reprinted from Ferrario's edition with the prefatory statement: "The following is the Italian novella on which 'The Lady of Shalott' was founded."
21 *Memoir,* I, 77. Further evidence suggesting his familiarity with the Italian work is an entry in Trinity College Notebook 23; under the title "Legends," there are two names: "The Lady of Scalot. *Novelle Antiche*" and "Constance, queen of Northumberland. Chaucer."

voice or a hand to stir her out of the dead calm in which she lay. The king was the first to set his foot upon her side, and he there beheld the gentle lady surrounded with the pomp of death. He too first unclasped the zone, and cast his eye over the letter, directed—"To all the Knights of the Round Table, greeting, from the poor lady of Scalot, who invokes long health and fortune for the proudest lances in the world. Do they wish to learn, how I am thus fearfully brought before them? let my last hand witness that it was, at once, for the sake of the noblest and vilest of the cavaliers of the land — for the proud Knight, Launcelot of the Lake. For neither tears nor sighs of mine availed with him, to have compassion on my love. And thus, alas, you behold me dead,—fallen a victim only for loving too true.[22]

Tennyson's treatment of the Italian story shows the attitude towards medieval Arthurian literature that will characterize many of his later Arthurian poems. *The Lady of Shalott* studies the Lady's isolation in the tower and her decision to move into the living world, two subjects absent from the novelette. Whereas the Italian version focuses much of its attention on the Lady's physical appearance in death and her reception at Camelot, such subjects are relegated to a subordinate position in Tennyson's poem.

The Lady of Shalott is an early example of Tennyson's unending study of the nature of the artist. The Lady is an artist, a singer who is isolated and removed from the verdant nature and life that surround and move by her tower. As an artist she weaves, yet she weaves for no practical purpose. Moreover, her subject-matter is not the world, but only "shadows of the world"; her art is an imitation of an imitation, not an imitation of nature. By looking into the mirror with its "blue un-clouded weather," the Lady finds not only isolation from reality but also distortion of reality; even more tragically, though she does exist in this remoteness, she has sufficient self-consciousness to be aware of her plight: "Or when the moon was overhead, / Came two young lovers lately wed; / 'I am half sick of shadows,' said / The Lady of Shalott."[23] The image in the mirror of the two lovers prompts her sudden outburst, just as the figure of Lancelot, whose shield displays a knight kneeling to his lady, becomes the efficient cause of her departure from the tower. Love becomes the power that prevents her pursuit of an existence of stagnation in the manner of the thwarted Mariana. As the poet himself explained, "The new-born love for something, for some one in the wide world from which she has been so long secluded, takes her out of the region of shadows into that of realities."[24]

The Lady of Shalott explores the artist's desire for isolation from the world and the necessity of personal rejection of such isolation. The Arthurian story of Lancelot and the maiden provides a setting for the

22 Thomas Roscoe, *The Italian Novelists* (London, 1825), I, 45-46.
23 Unless otherwise noted, quotations from the four early poems under discussion in this chapter are from Moxon's 1842 edition of Tennyson's *Poems*.
24 *Memoir*, I, 117.

poet's theme, a setting which he can adjust, abuse, or ignore according to his own purpose. The important elements of the poem—the mirror and the web it inspires, the curse, the geographical relationship of the island, the river, and Camelot—have no correspondence in the source. Moreover, the difference between the 1832 and the 1842 versions of the poem emphasizes Tennyson's continuing attempt to distance his poem from its Italian source. The following stanza, taking its inspiration from the crown mentioned in the novelette, is deleted in the revised version because of its lush style:

> A cloudwhite crown of pearl she dight.
> All raimented in snowy white
> That loosely flew, (her zone in sight,
> Clasped with one blinding diamond bright,)
> Her wide eyes fixed on Camelot,
> Though the squally eastwind keenly
> Blew, with folded arms serenely
> By the water stood the queenly
> Lady of Shalott.[25]

The only other stanza entirely deleted in the revised poem gives the contents of the Lady's letter:

> They crossed themselves, their stars they blest,
> Knight, minstrel, abbot, squire and guest.
> There lay a parchment on her breast,
> That puzzled more than all the rest,
> The wellfed wits at Camelot.
> *"The web was woven curiously*
> *The charm is broken utterly,*
> *Draw near and fear not—this is I,*
> *The Lady of Shalott."*[26]

The 1842 version contains no reference to the letter; any references to Arthur and his Queen, so conspicuous in the novelette, are absent from the earlier and the later versions of the poem.

In *The Lady of Shalott,* Arthurian literature is introduced as a valid setting for a study of the artist and the dangers of personal isolation from

25 Both this stanza and the following stanza are from Moxon's 1833 edition of Tennyson's *Poems.* In the *Edinburgh Review,* 77 (April, 1843), James Spedding noted: "The poems originally published in 1832, are many of them largely altered; generally with great judgment, and always with a view to strip off redundancies—to make the expression simpler and clearer, to substitute thought for imagery, and substance for shadow. 'The Lady of Shalott,' for instance (p. 77), is stripped of all her finery; her pearl garland, her velvet bed, her royal apparel, and her 'blinding diamond bright,' are all gone; and certainly, in the simple white robe which she now wears, her native beauty shows to much greater advantage" (pp. 377-378).
26 This stanza was originally the final stanza of the poem. Its deletion may have been influenced by John Stuart Mill's review in *London Review,* 1 (July 1835), 402-424. Mill reprinted the entire poem but omitted the final stanza: "We omit the remaining stanza, which seems to us a 'lame and impotent conclusion,' where no conclusion was required" (p. 413).

the world. Lancelot is not an important figure in himself, but only as a symbol of the life-force in nature which the Lady has denied to herself. The Lady, based on the Lady of the Italian source, bears no resemblance to Malory's Elaine, who will appear as a central figure in one of the earliest idylls. Though familiar with Malory, Tennyson did not seem to know Malory's version of the story: "I met the story first in some Italian *novelle*: but the web, mirror, island, etc., were my own. Indeed, I doubt whether I should ever have put it in that shape if I had been then aware of the Maid of Astolat in *Mort Arthur*."[27] Any details such as the letter which may be found in Malory are also present in the Italian version.

A fuller use of an Arthurian story is suggested in *Sir Launcelot and Queen Guinevere,* "partly if not wholly written in 1830,"[28] though not published until 1842. Composed in the same stanza as *The Lady of Shalott,* except that the fifth and ninth lines are no longer refrains, this section of a much larger anticipated poem is appropriately subtitled "A Fragment"; the extant lines praise the blossoming springtime which serves as a bright backdrop to the youthful and innocent figures of the Queen and her knight. A letter from J. M. Kemble described the projected poem that never appeared:

A companion to *The Lady of Shalott* is in Progress, called the *Ballad of Sir Lancelot;* a most triumphant matter whereof I will give you a sketch; in the Spring, Queen Guinevere and Sir Lancelot ride through the forest green, fayre and amorous: And such a queen! such a knight! Merlin with spindle shanks, vast brows and beard and a forehead like a mundane egg, over a face wrinkled with ten thousand crow-feet meets them, and tells Sir L. that he's doing well for his fame to be riding about with a light o' love &c. Whereupon the knight, nowise backward in retort, tells him it is a shame such an old scandal to antiquity should be talking, since his own propensities are no secret, and since he very well knows what will become of him in the valley of Avilion some day. Merlin, who tropically is Worldly Prudence, is of course miserably floored. So are the representatives of Worldly Force, who in the shape of three knights, sheathed, Sir, in trap from toe to toe, run at Sir L. and are most unceremoniously shot from their saddles like stones from a sling. But the Garde Joyeuse is now in sight; the knight I confess is singing but a loose song, when his own son Sir Galahad (the type of Chastity) passes by; he knows his father but does not speak to him, *blushes and rides on his way!* Voila tout. Much of this is written and stupendous; I regret bitterly that I had not opportunity to take down what there is of it; as it is I can only offer you Sir L.'s song.[29]

The five extant stanzas, the opening of the anticipated work,[30] study the beauty of nature and the beauty of Guinevere; as in *The Lady of Shalott,*

27   Quoted by F. J. Furnivall in his letter of January 17, 1868 to W. M. Rossetti, printed in William Rossetti, ed., *Rossetti Papers 1862-1870* (New York: Charles Scribner's, 1903), p. 341.

28   *Memoir,* II, 122.

29   Reprinted in *The Poems of Tennyson,* edited by Christopher Ricks (London: Longmans, 1969), pp. 502-503.

30   The two-stanza description of the setting prepares for the events of the poem in a manner similar to the opening description of *The Lady of Shalott.* Further proof that

nature is a world of song and colour; Guinevere herself is the apex of this earthly beauty:

> She looked so lovely, as she swayed
> The rein with dainty finger-tips,
> A man had given all other bliss,
> And all his worldly worth for this,
> To waste his whole heart in one kiss
> Upon her perfect lips.

Kemble's letter offers an indication of the story which would have followed this opening. In the spring, Lancelot and Guinevere encounter both Merlin and Galahad on their trip to Garde Joyeuse.[31] Such an incident has no foundation in Malory; moreover, the incident created by Tennyson is a mixture of basic incongruities. In the first place, Malory's Merlin is permanently enchained by Nynyve shortly after Guinevere's arrival in Camelot and before Lancelot's arrival. Thus no encounter of the trio is possible. Secondly, the only journey Lancelot and Guinevere undertake to his castle, the Joyous Garde, follows Lancelot's successful rescue of Guinevere from the stake; though it took place in May, the journey is far from the idyllic and youthful ride of this projected poem. Finally, Malory's Galahad never encounters his father, Lancelot, except during their pursuit of the Holy Grail, when Lancelot, separated voluntarily from Guinevere, seeks in vain the spiritual perfection his own son achieves. Such contrasts suggest the poet's unending practice of ignoring or consciously violating the narrative time-scheme of Malory's stories in order to create a more dramatic or concentrated poetic plot.

The portrait of Merlin suggested by Kemble's letter is substantiated by further stanzas of this poem found in Trinity Notebook 15:

> They came on one that rode alone,
> Astride upon a lob-eared roan,
> Wherefrom stood out the staring bone,
>   The wizard Merlin wise and gray.
> His shanks were thin as legs of pies,
> The bloom that on an apple dries
> Burnt underneath his catlike eyes
>   That twinkled everyway
>
> High brows above a little face
> Had Merlin—these in every place

the two stanzas constitute the intended opening of a longer work is offered by a copy of the poem in the Harvard Tennyson Loose Papers, MS Eng. 952.1.221, perhaps written by Emily Tennyson; in this copy, the subtitle is not "A Fragment," but "Part 1."

31 The verbal mistake Garde Joyeuse for Joyeuse Garde, is Kemble's error; Tennyson refers to this location correctly in the added "Merlin" stanzas of the poem contained in Trinity Notebook 15.

Ten million lines did cross and lace;
Slow as the shadow was his pace,
      The shade that creeps from dawn to dusk.
From cheek and mouth and throat a load
Of beard—a hundred winters snowed
Upon the pummel as he road
      Thin as a spider's husk.

He stopped full butt. "God's death, Sir Knight,
Your fame will flourish pure and bright.
You spare no pains. 'Tis your delight
To seek the Sangraal day and night;
      It is no fable, by my troth;
We know you are the cream and pride
Of knighthood blazoned far and wide,
The talk of the whole countryside.
      Good morrow to you both."

At last, mid lindentufts that smiled
In newest foliage, fresh and wild,—
With haughty towers turret-piled
To Heaven—by one deep moat in-isled
      Shone the white walls of Joyeuse Garde.
Then saw they three

They trampling through the woodland lone
In clanging armour flashed and shone
Like those three suns that flame alone
Chased in the airy giant's zone,
      And burnished by the frosty dark;
And as the dogstar changes hue,
And bickers into green and blue,
Each glittered laved in lucid dew
      That washed the grassy park.

The portrait of Merlin, corresponding to Kemble's account, is a direct anticipation of the Merlin to be drawn by the poet twenty-five years later, yet the time-scheme will be altered, since Merlin's ruin by Vivien will occur before the Grail quest.

Sir Launcelot and Queen Guinevere is an experiment with the Arthurian legends, an attempt to create a highly visualized story involving central figures of the Arthurian world; the poem remains unfinished, perhaps because the poet regarded purely descriptive poetry as unsatisfying and wished to find a proper narrative structure which would include descriptive passages. The spring encounter of Lancelot and Guinevere will become an important episode in the completed *Idylls*; the springtime meeting will be Lancelot's mission from Arthur to conduct the young bride to Camelot.

As Kemble noted, Tennyson conceived of Galahad as "the type of Chastity." Consequently, his poem *Sir Galahad,* completed by September 1834,[32] is a study of Galahad, a virgin knight, the paragon of Chastity. Yet, as in *The Lady of Shalott*, the Arthurian element is not important in itself, but only as a vehicle for transmitting ideas. Tennyson termed the title character "something of a male counterpart to St Agnes,"[33] and one suspects that a female saint, fitted to this theme, would have been equally effective in such a context, were it not for the poet's fascination with Arthur's realm.

    Sir Galahad is a lyrical rhapsody in which the title character reflects on the nature of his chastity. Like his counterpart in Malory, Galahad is a pure knight, a paragon of virtue, the individual whose love for the divine motivates all his actions. The form of Tennyson's poem, a reflective lyric of introspection, serves to distinguish this Victorian Galahad from his medieval prototype. Malory does not give his character any introspective speeches; his Galahad is characterized by his actions and by the words of his associates. Whereas Malory has Galahad's friends praise his innocence and virtue, Tennyson places such sentiments in the mouth of Galahad himself; thus he injects a degree of pride in the knight which is completely absent in his medieval counterpart. The note of pride becomes explicit in the stanza that Tennyson deleted from the final version of the poem:

> Oh power outsoaring human ken!
>   Oh Knighthood chaste and true!
> With God, with Angels, and with men
>   What is it I may not do?
> Not only in the tourney-field
>   The unpure are beaten from the fray,
> Not only the evil customs yield,
>   The very stars give way.
> Lo! those bright stars which thou has made,
>   They tremble fanned on by thy breath:
> Yea Lord! they shine, those lamps of thine
>   In Heaven and in the gulphs of Death.

Galahad's self-analysis introduces an arrogance not found in Malory's knight.

    Secondly, in speaking of his ability to sublimate his desire for human love in his greater love of God, Galahad comments:

> How sweet are looks that ladies bend
>   On whom their favours fall!
> For them I battle till the end,
>   To save from shame and thrall:
> But all my heart is drawn above,
>   My knees are bow'd in crypt and shrine:

---

32 James Spedding wrote of the completed poem in a letter of September 19, 1834, reprinted in *Memoir*, I, 139-140. The original version of the poem is in the Heath Commonplace Book, Fitzwilliam Museum, Cambridge, England.

33 *Memoir*, I, 142.

> I never felt the kiss of love,
> Nor maiden's hand in mine.

Malory's knight engages in only one battle to save maidens from disgrace, a battle undertaken at the command of the voice of God. Tennyson's Galahad, however, gives the impression that, like other knights, he fights often for helpless maidens in distress. Moreover, unlike his medieval counterpart, this Victorian Galahad reflects on his own inexperience in human love, "I never felt the kiss of love, / Nor maiden's hand in mine."

The incidents recounted so vaguely in Tennyson's poem find a degree of correspondence in Malory. "Some secret shrine" of the third stanza may be the desolate chapel in Malory where a voice tells Galahad to end the wicked crimes at the Castle of Maidens. Though Malory's knight never enters a ship alone, he does have a vision of the Holy Grail before he leaves on a ship for Sarras, a vision similar to the vision of Tennyson's knight in the fifth stanza.

Sir Galahad marks a growing dependence upon Malory. The basic character of Galahad is derived from Malory and is presented in terms of that quality, chastity, which makes him the outstanding knight in the Grail quest. Though deriving inspiration from Malory, Tennyson feels no need to depend upon his source for specific details or incidents; he can invent his own episodes or he can elaborate a suggestion found in his source. Like Malory's knight, his Galahad is motivated by love of God; he is pure and honest, devout and sincere. Yet his introspection, his self-analysis, his exuberant joy bordering on arrogance, his ceaseless desire for activity and movement, these qualities make him a distinctly Victorian portrait of a medieval figure and a precursor of the Galahad of the Pre-Raphaelites.

The last of Tennyson's early Arthurian pieces, the *Morte d'Arthur*, completed by October 1834,[34] marks a further development in the poet's attitude towards his source. The poem represents Tennyson's most faithful observance of structural fidelity to Malory. The close relationship of the *Morte d'Arthur* to the appropriate section in Malory is self-evident if the two accounts of Arthur's departure from this world are placed side by side.[35] Except for a few references to the history of Excalibur, the *Morte d'Arthur* is a careful expansion or embellishment

---

34 Ibid., I, 138.
35 For the textual comparison, see Appendix I. For this early poem, Tennyson probably employed the three-volume Wilks edition of Malory which was in his father's library (see Sir Charles Tennyson, *Alfred Tennyson* [London: Macmillan, 1949], p. 32). His father's copy is not in the Tennyson Research Centre, Lincoln. Though the poet also knew the two-volume Walker and Edwards edition of 1816, he received it as a gift from Leigh Hunt (*Memoir*, I, 156) in 1835 after the completion of his poem. For Tennyson's familiarity with Southey's annotated edition of Malory, see preceding footnote 16 and Chapter 2, footnote 12.

of Malory's account of the final moments of Arthur's life. Tennyson focuses on Arthur by removing the extraneous character of Sir Lucan and by omitting references to Guinevere, Lancelot, and Gawain; Bedivere exists only to direct our attention to his dying lord.

The poet's close adherence to the structure of his source, complemented by deliberate verbal echoes of Malory, throws light on the method of his embellishment. Tennyson pays greater attention to the physical landscape. Whereas Malory's Bedivere "hid Excalibur under a tree," Tennyson's knight thinks it "Better to leave Excalibur conceal'd / There in the many-knotted waterflags, / That whistled stiff and dry about the marge." Heightened descriptions exalt the sword into an object of complete wonder. Whereas Malory writes of "that noble sword, where the pomel and the haft were all of precious stones," Tennyson reports that the sword "twinkled with diamond studs, / Myriads of topaz-lights, and jacinth-work / Of subtlest jewellery." Arthur himself is heightened, more vocal, more passionate, more perturbed. Whereas Malory's King is essentially a passive, subdued figure at this final moment, Tennyson's King becomes, for this dramatic scene, an authoritarian, demanding, and regal monarch, aware of and concerned about the plight of his now leaderless realm. Through the added details and through the new life infused into the portrait of the dying King, Tennyson takes an essentially dramatic moment in his source and retells the episode with a degree of embellishment which does not violate the source but enriches it.

The poem departs most forcefully from Malory's account in Arthur's final words:

> The old order changeth, yielding place to new,
> And God fulfils Himself in many ways,
> Lest one good custom should corrupt the world.
> Comfort thyself: what comfort is in me?
> I have lived my life, and that which I have done
> May He within himself make pure! but thou—
> If thou shouldst never see my face again,
> Pray for my soul. More things are wrought by prayer
> Than this world dreams of. Wherefore, let thy voice
> Rise like a fountain for me night and day.
> For what are men better than sheep or goats
> That nourish a blind life within the brain,
> If, knowing God, they lift not hands of prayer
> Both for themselves and those who call them friend?
> For so the whole round earth is every way
> Bound by gold chains about the feet of God.

These lines invite the reader to speculate on the degree to which autobiography enters into the poem. Written shortly after the death of Arthur Hallam, the poem chronicles the death of another Arthur, the mythic King who exists in an idealized presentation which Hallam himself receives in the completed *In Memoriam*.[36] King Arthur's dying words of wisdom reflect the peace and serenity the despairing Tennyson needs in the winter of 1833-34.

The old order does change, yet in the *Morte d'Arthur* change itself is not evil; change in nature is divinely ordained. The poet of the early sections of *In Memoriam* abhors change since it is change that brought about Hallam's death; only through the thematic development within this elegy does the narrator come to see change as an integral and important aspect of human life. The complexity of Tennyson's thoughts, mirrored in the sixteen-year composition of *In Memoriam*, is suppressed in the *Morte d'Arthur*, where change is confronted and its negative powers subdued through the power of prayer. In the prologue to *In Memoriam*, the narrator distinguishes knowledge from wisdom; mere knowledge is earthly in character whereas wisdom is knowledge combined with reverence. Only the wise man realizes the value and the efficacy of prayer; reverence raises knowledge to wisdom and permits a fuller awareness of man's position in this world. The new understanding which Tennyson reaches through the movement of *In Memoriam* stands at the center of King Arthur's final words to Bedivere; it is an understanding which Tennyson senses in 1833, but only through the many years of struggle chronicled in *In Memoriam* will he come to realize and to accept its full meaning.

The theme of the importance of prayer, made even more impressive by the possible autobiographical relevance within the poem, makes the *Morte d'Arthur* an example of the poet's ability to use a myth as a vehicle for his own thoughts or as a framework within which some of his ideas can be mirrored. The seeming autobiographical significance is so veiled that the poem remains basically objective, a substantially accurate rendering of the story as told by Malory, and the basic excellence of the poem is its ability to move into the realm of poetic detachment; "the larger merit of the 'Morte d'Arthur' lies in its independence as a poem, its achievement of an objectivity apart from any personal or private suggestion."[37]

The *Morte d'Arthur* contrasts significantly with the other Arthurian poems. All four are early experimental works. Fascinated with the world of Camelot, Tennyson is trying to create an effective and valid method of utilizing this world in his poetry. *The Lady of Shalott* employs the Arthurian world as a remote objective correlative for the problem of the artist's desire for personal isolation. The projected poem of which

---

36 "And between 'With trembling fingers' and 'When Lazarus left his charnel-cave' he has written the first draft of his 'Morte d'Arthur' " (*Memoir*, 1, 109). The position of the first draft between section 30 and section 31 of *In Memoriam* in Tennyson's manuscript-book suggests the relationship of the two Arthurs.

37 Jerome H. Buckley, *Tennyson: The Growth of a Poet* (Cambridge, Mass.: Harvard University Press, 1960), p. 66.

Sir Launcelot and Queen Guinevere is only a fragment uses the Arthurian characters for basically descriptive and allegorical purposes; no hint of a clear correspondence to Malory is evident. *Sir Galahad*, on the other hand, does not violate the traditional medieval character of Galahad, but it does portray him in a distinctly Victorian manner as an introspective, self-analytical, and ebullient knight. Finally, the *Morte d'Arthur* is the poet's most explicit attempt to follow objectively an Arthurian story and recreate that story through pictorial embellishments without violating the basic structure and substance of Malory's account of the scene.

The supreme importance of the *Morte d'Arthur* within Tennyson's entire Arthurian corpus is evident in the prologue and the epilogue which were added to the poem.[38] In his early Arthurian writings, Tennyson is experimenting with the "greatest of all poetical subjects"; in the prologue, he vaguely admits the cause of his experiment, his own fear of the material, and his consequent search for the proper vehicle for such material.[39] Through the figure of Everard Hall, the "epic" poet, Tennyson offers an ironic commentary on his own dilemma. Like Hall, he would agree that "a truth / Looks freshest in the fashion of the day." Almost in defiance of those critics who will disparage a modern treatment of medieval material, he has Hall comment: "Why take the style of those heroic times? / For nature brings not back the Mastodon, / Nor we those times; and why should any man / Remodel models rather than the life?" More significant, and more explicit, is an earlier draft of these lines which was intended as the opening of the poem:

> Why, what you ask—if any writer now
> May take the style of some heroic age
> Gone like the mastodon—nay, why should he
> Remodel models rather than the life?
> Yet this belief was lately half-unhinged
> At Edward Allen's—on the Christmas-Eve.[40]

38 Edward FitzGerald wrote: "The 'Morte d'Arthur' when read to us from manuscript in 1835 had no introduction or epilogue; which was added to anticipate or excuse the 'faint Homeric echoes,' etc. (as in the 'Day-Dream'), to give a reason for telling an old-world tale" (*Memoir*, I, 194); the statement does suggest that the prologue and the epilogue were not part of the poem's original conception. In *A Bibliography of the Writings of Alfred, Lord Tennyson* (London: privately printed, 1908), T. J. Wise noted: "The fifty-two Introductory Lines (styled The Epic), and also the thirty-one Supplementary Lines, do not appear in this, the first, version of the *Morte d'Arthur*. They were added when the Idyl was reprinted in the *Poems* of 1842" (I, 77). The "first version" is a forgery to which Hallam Tennyson referred unsuspectingly (*Memoir*, I, 189-190). For a complete discussion of this forgery, see John Carter and Graham Pollard, *An Enquiry Into the Nature of Certain Nineteenth Century Pamphlets* (London: Constable, 1934), pp. 295-297.
39 The same attitude prompted Tennyson to speak of *Demeter:* "I will write it, but when I write an antique like this I must put it into a frame—something modern about it. It is no use giving a mere *réchauffé* of old legends" (*Memoir*, II, 364).
40 In Harvard Notebook 21, a copy of the poem, not in the poet's handwriting, begins with these lines.

What Hall failed to achieve is the task Tennyson assigns himself. The
prologue offers a proper guide to a reading of his Arthurian poetry. The
validity of his Arthurian work is its ability to touch "the distance into
fresh results."

The epilogue stresses the powerful impact of the figure of Arthur,
the great mythic King, on the poet:

> where yet in sleep I seem'd
> To sail with Arthur under looming shores,
> Point after point, till on to dawn, when dreams
> Begin to feel the truth and stir of day,
> To me, methought, who waited with a crowd,
> There came a bark that, blowing forward, bore
> King Arthur, like a modern gentleman
> Of stateliest port; and all the people cried,
> "Arthur is come again: he cannot die."

The hope and faith which are embodied in the figure of Arthur stir the
imagination of the poet to a new personal peace and joy. The hope of
return, which Arthur left as a legacy to Bedivere, must satisfy the
dreaming Tennyson just as it satisfies the inhabitants of his dream. In
this hope and in its beneficial effect on the dreamer, Tennyson expresses
man's need for an ideal and the necessity of the renewal of such an ideal,
a theme which will assume dominant importance in the completed
Idylls.

Tennyson's idealism found a natural champion in Arthur, the King
who does not die. Arthur's future return, a fundamental premise of the
medieval legend, aroused the interest of the young poet:

He cried aloud for some "soldier-priest, no sabbath-drawler of old saws," to set
the world right. But however gloomy his own view and that of his contemporaries was then as to the present, my father clearly saw the "Day-beam,
New-risen o'er awaken'd Albion." Indeed now, as always, he was one of those
"on the look-out for every new idea, and for every old idea with a new application, which may tend to meet the growing requirements of society"; one of those
who are "like men standing on a watch-tower, to whom others apply and say, not
'What of the night?' but 'What of the morning and of the coming day?' "[41]

In King Arthur, Tennyson found a fictional embodiment of this
"soldier-priest." The concept of Arthur's return stands behind Tennyson's original interest in the legend; the idea forms the conclusion of the
Morte d'Arthur and forms the basis of some early lines on Avalon:

> And she, how fast she sleeps! What is it? truth
> Or glamour? fairies come from fairyland
> To fetch the king to Avalon
>
> And what is Avalon? Avalon is an isle
> All made of apple-blossom in the West,

41 *Memoir*, I, 66-67.

> And all the waves are fragrant & the winds
> About it & the fairies live upon it
> And there are those have seen it far away
> Shine like a rose upon the summer sea
> And thither goes the king & thence returns
> And reigns hereafter: some hold he cannot die.[42]

Lastly, the humorous parson of the prologue of the *Morte d'Arthur* bores his audience with his comments on "the general decay of faith / Right thro' the world." Though Tennyson is creating a satiric portrait in the parson, there is validity to his criticism of Victorian society: "there was no anchor, none, / To hold by." When Tennyson comes to employ the Arthurian world in the *Idylls,* the idealism of Arthur will become an example to the poet's generation of the need for faith and idealism. Bedivere's plight will become a mirror of the predicament of the nineteenth century:

> For now I see the true old times are dead,
> When every morning brought a noble chance,
> And every chance brought out a noble knight.
> Such times have been not since the light that led
> The holy Elders with the gift of myrrh.
> But now the whole ROUND TABLE is dissolved
> Which was an image of the mighty world;
> And I, the last, go forth companionless,
> And the days darken round me, and the years,
> Among new men, strange faces, other minds.

The *Morte d'Arthur* is Tennyson's most complete employment of Malory until he turns to a realized conception of the *Idylls* in the mid-eighteen-fifties. His experimentation ends with a close adherence to a medieval source, an adherence embellished by vivifying descriptions and overlaid with contemporary significance. The relevance of the Arthurian story is both personal and universal, personal in its parallel to the death of Hallam and universal in its parallel to the absence of any real religious faith within Victorian society. Through the prologue and the epilogue, Tennyson hopes that such relevance will be noted: "Perhaps some modern touches here and there / Redeemed it from the charge of nothingness."

42 Trinity Notebook 28, which also contains drafts of lines from *Aylmer's Field, Sea Dreams,* and *Reticence.* These lines on "Avalon" must date from a time before the composition of the *Morte d'Arthur,* which refers to Arthur's ultimate destination as "Avilion." In the final version of *The Palace of Art,* there is a similar reference to Arthur: "Or that deepwounded child of Pendragon / Mid misty woods on sloping greens / Dozed in the valley of Avilion / Tended by crowned queens." In the 1832 version of this stanza, the valley has the spelling used in Trinity Notebook 28: "Or mythic Uther's deeply-wounded son / In some fair space of sloping greens / Lay, dozing in the vale of Avalon / And watched by weeping queens." The "Avalon" fragment probably dates from about the same time as the fragment *Sir Launcelot and Queen Guinevere.* For a further indication of Tennyson's interest in Arthur's "death," see Appendix 2.

Unfortunately, contemporary criticism failed to perceive the "modern touches"; the majority of reviewers were favourable towards the 1842 edition, but many ignored the *Morte d'Arthur* despite its prominent position as the opening poem of the second volume. One review, written by the poet's friend John Sterling, commented about this major Arthurian poem: "The miraculous legend of 'Excalibur' does not come very near to us, and as reproduced by any modern writer must be a mere ingenious exercise of fancy."[43] Such criticism only confirmed the tentative nature of Tennyson's approach to the Arthurian world.[44] The fears which he expressed ironically in the prologue are now substantiated. Like the character in *The Epic*, he must dream about Arthur and create an appropriate method whereby the Arthurian legends will look "freshest in the fashion of the day." Never again will he return to that degree of close fidelity to his source which he practises in the *Morte d'Arthur;* contemporary criticism seems to imply that, with such a degree of fidelity, "nothing new was said."

In these four early poems Tennyson moves from a vague and free employment of Arthurian literature to a close textual fidelity to Malory. In addition, he focuses his attention on those three major concerns of the Arthurian world which will dominate his ultimate achievement in the *Idylls*. In *Sir Launcelot and Queen Guinevere* he studies the love of this couple, admittedly only a nascent love here, but nonetheless present. In *Sir Galahad* the chastity of the knight is a prelude to a brief description of the Holy Grail, a theme that will vex his imagination for many years. In the *Morte d'Arthur* he turns complete attention to the figure of Arthur as ideal ruler, the symbolic embodiment of the perfection of the old

43 John Sterling, "Review of 'Poems,' " *Quarterly Review*, 70 (September 1842), 401. Few reviewers offered more than a token response to the *Morte d'Arthur*, if indeed they bothered to single out the poem for attention. James Spedding, *Edinburgh Review*, 77 (April 1843) reported that such poems as the *Morte d'Arthur* "could derive no additional interest from any comment of ours" (p. 390). Richard Monckton Milnes, *Westminster Review*, 28 (October 1842) echoed Sterling's thought, though he was less critical and more inclined to accept the poem as "gracefully linking on the old English story to present English domestic life" (p. 373). Apart from these casual remarks, the *Morte d'Arthur* escaped the attention of the critics.

44 In his *Diary*, edited by H. Allingham and D. Radford (London: Macmillan, 1907), William Allingham noted: T. told me that he had planned out his Arthuriad, and could have written it all off without any trouble. But in 1842 he published, with other poems, the 'Morte d'Arthur,' which was one book of his Epic (though not the eleventh), and the review in the *Quarterly* disheartened him, so that he put the scheme aside. He afterwards took it up again, but not as with the first inspiration. This unlucky article in the *Quarterly* was written by John Sterling, who was then thirty-six years old, just three years older than Tennyson: "... This [the review], it will be observed, chimes in with the doubts expressed by the Poet himself in the lines written by way of prologue. Blame or doubt in regard to his own writings always weighted more with Tennyson than praise. He often said that he forgot praise and remembered all censure. Sterling's review, meant to be friendly, was a thin pretentious piece and of no value whatever: a pity it should have chanced to prove so mis-effectual!" (pp. 314-315).

order. Out of these three areas will come a focal point which will provide him with a coherent structure for his final treatment of Arthur and his Round Table. The four early poems are a prelude to that later achievement. With unusual perception and foresight, James Spedding, in response to the two volumes of 1842, noted the drift of Tennyson's creative power:

If Mr. Tennyson can find a subject large enough to take the entire impress of his mind, and energy persevering enough to work it faithfully out as one whole, we are convinced that he may produce a work, which, though occupying no larger space than the contents of these volumes, shall as much exceed them in value, as a series of quantities multiplied into each other exceeds in value the same series simply added together.[45]

Tennyson has already found such a subject in the world of Camelot.

45 *Edinburgh Review*, p. 391.

Chapter 2

1859: The Four Women

Enid, Vivien, Elaine, Guinevere

Ye know me then, that wicked one, who broke
The vast design and purpose of the King.[1]

In the figure of Guinevere, Tennyson would find his avenue into the
world of the Arthurian legends. Yet her presence in *Sir Launcelot and
Queen Guinevere* did not alert him to her future importance. A poetic
treatment of the account of Nimue's seduction of Merlin and an adaptation of the story of Enid and her jealous husband Geraint would precede
his direct confrontation with Arthur's Queen; when that confrontation
occurs, Guinevere becomes the structural principle who gives the unity
and coherence to his Arthurian world that were absent in the early
outlines.

The world of Camelot continued to occupy Tennyson's thoughts;
his lack of self-confidence in his handling of Arthurian material led him
to experiment with other poetic material. *The Princess* represented, not
a dismissal of Arthurian stories, but an attempt to find an appropriate
form for a larger vessel which would contain the account of Arthur and
his realm;[2] it grew by accretion into a large vessel of seven sections with
intercalary lyrics and a preface and conclusion. Each section is an
individual episode within the larger framework that chronicles the plight

---

1 All quotations from the four idylls under discussion in this chapter are from Moxon's
   1859 edition of the *Idylls of the King*.
2 Sir Charles Tennyson described *The Princess* as "a complete change from anything
   that he had done before and on a much larger scale. He had been tempted in the thirties
   and early forties to try his hand at a long work, and had thought of composing an epic
   on King Arthur and the Round Table. But he had refrained, partly from lack of
   self-confidence, partly because he felt that a small vessel built on fine lines might float
   further down the stream of time than a big raft" (p. 218).

24

of a woman's university operating against the basic laws of Nature. The emphasis falls on the element of drama:

What distinguishes it from all Tennyson's earlier work is the persistent use of a dramatic method, which gives it a liveliness and power not present in anything that he had previously written. Scene after scene, particularly in the later sections, are so written that they could with hardly any change be translated into dramatic form.[3]

The dramatic method, however, is a continuation of the method that formed the basis of the *Morte d'Arthur*. Despite some critical dissatisfaction with the seeming irrelevance of the content of that earlier poem, Tennyson seemed satisfied with its style and pursued the creation of an essentially dramatic method in his poetry.

After the publication of *The Princess*, Tennyson undertook a trip to Cornwall in the summer of 1848; the legendary haunts of King Arthur might offer him further inspiration for his great work. Hallam Tennyson commented that at that time his father "began to study the epical King Arthur in earnest... He thought, read, talked about King Arthur."[4] Edward FitzGerald also noted the poet's meditative return to Arthur: "now the Princess is done, he turns to King Arthur—a worthy subject indeed—and has consulted some histories of him, and spent some time in visiting his traditionary haunts in Cornwall."[5] Sir Charles Tennyson saw the increasing popularity of *The Princess* as an encouraging factor in his decision, not only to visit Cornwall, but also to embark finally on a long Arthurian poem:

Another reason for this visit was the revival of his desire to treat the Arthurian legends ("the greatest of all poetic subjects" he called them) in a long poem. The success of *The Princess* had made him feel that his powers were now at last adequate for this long-cherished project, and perhaps he was stimulated by the news that his old enemy, Bulwer Lytton, was bringing out an epic poem on the subject which he intended to be his masterpiece.[6]

A highlight of the trip was Tennyson's brief encounter with Stephen Hawker, the elderly vicar of Morwenstow. Their conversation often turned to the subject of Cornwall and King Arthur, and Tennyson took

3 Sir Charles Tennyson, p. 222.
4 *Memoir*, II, 125.
5 Edward FitzGerald, *Letters and Literary Remains of Edward FitzGerald* (London: Macmillan, 1902), I, 276.
6 Sir Charles Tennyson, pp. 224-225. Though Lytton's project may have hastened Tennyson's return to his Arthurian work, Lytton's poem had no influence upon Tennyson since it is Arthurian in name only. In the preface to his *King Arthur*, Lytton wrote: "In taking my subject from Chivalrous romance, I take, then, the agencies from the Marvellous that it naturally and familiarly affords—the Fairy, the Genius, the Enchanter; not wholly, indeed, in the precise and literal spirit with which our nursery tales receive those creations of Fancy through the medium of French Fabliaux, but in the larger significations by which in their conceptions of the Supernatural, our Fathers often implied the secrets of Nature" (*King Arthur* [London, 1849], I, viii-ix).

his departure from this knowledgeable man with "his arms full of Arthurian books and manuscripts lent him by the vicar."[7]

The trip to Cornwall reaffirmed the poet's intention to write a great Arthurian work. The terrain of Cornwall, rugged and desolate, complemented his abiding fascination with the world of Arthur and his vision. The late forties saw Tennyson augment *The Princess* with the series of intercalary lyrics; at the same time he was preparing the publication of the series of elegies he would later name *In Memoriam*.

The 1850 publication of *In Memoriam* marked the end of the sixteen-year composition of the elegy. With this achievement widely acclaimed by the critics[8] and with the poet's acceptance of Queen Victoria's offer of the Laureateship, the Arthurian world beckoned him even more strongly. The non-Arthurian poetry of the fifties, especially *Maud*, was not so much a prelude to his ultimate Arthurian poem, but rather an interruption of that unceasing fascination with Camelot.[9] The fifties marked Tennyson's final commitment to an Arthurian epic poem. The project he had always anticipated was now beginning to assume its final shape.

When Tennyson returned to the creation of a major Arthurian poem after a twenty-year pause, he chose to begin with a story about Merlin, a legendary figure who had always interested him. In the projected poem of which *Sir Launcelot and Queen Guinevere* is only a fragment, Merlin, the figure of "worldly Prudence," was to have a major role. In the Arthurian scenario the third act focuses on Merlin both as a prophetic figure and as a man subordinated to Nimue. Interestingly, when Tennyson published his two socially hortatory and prophetic poems, *The Third of February, 1852* and *Hands All Round*, in the *Examiner* of February 7, 1852, he signed them with the pseudonym "Merlin." His new Arthurian poem chooses an incident involving Merlin, though it reduces the role of the prophetic man to a secondary one.

Vivien, "begun in February and finished on March 31st, 1856,"[10] is a study of the corrosive power of lust, the destructive nature of wanton

7 Sir Charles Tennyson, p. 229. For the poet's diary account of his trip, see *Memoir*, I, 274-276.
8 For an account of critical reaction to *In Memoriam*, see Edgar F. Shannon, Jr., *Tennyson and the Reviewers* (Cambridge, Mass.: Harvard University Press, 1952), pp. 141-153.
9 Sir Charles Tennyson noted: "Alfred had already begun work on a poem about the enchantment of Merlin, but he laid this aside for *Maud*, the composition of which occupied him during the last six months of 1854" (p. 282). Though the form of *Maud* differs from the form of the *Idylls*, Tennyson's concern in *Maud* with the individual and his relationship to society and to an appropriate code of behaviour foreshadows similar themes in the *Idylls*.
10 Eversley edition, V, 478. In the 1857 trial-edition of *Enid and Nimuë: The True and the False*, Vivien is still called Nimue; because of the awkward diphthong and consequent preference for the smoother sounding Vivien, Tennyson changed the name in the 1859 edition of the *Idylls*. For consistency, I refer to her only as Vivien.

sensuality. The title suggests the proper centre of the poem, the female agent who achieves her goal of ruining Merlin's nobility. The sage of Arthur's Round Table, the man who brought Arthur to his regal position, is relegated to the subordinate role of a passive recipient of the taunts and actions of a clever seductress.

Malory's account of Merlin's tragedy is succinct and brief;[11] its unadorned plot provided the poet with a bare outline for his story. Tennyson made no attempt to be faithful to the outline. The active Merlin of Malory, unable to restrain his lustful desire for Nimue, became the passive Merlin of Tennyson, sorely besieged by an insistent woman. In this way the poet reversed the roles of the two protagonists and embellished the plot so that the completed poem was his own creation with only a tenuous relationship to Malory.

Tennyson found further inspiration for his poem in the section of the medieval French *Romance of Merlin* which Southey translated in the introduction to his 1817 edition of Malory.[12] This commentary offered a more vivid depiction of the seduction, the centre of Tennyson's poem; here the figure of Vivien began to approach the dramatic dimensions of Tennyson's lurid creature:

When Viviane heard this, for her great treason, and the better to delude and deceive him, she put her arms round his neck, and began to kiss him, saying, that he might well be hers, seeing that she was his: You well know, said she, that the great love which I have in you, has made me leave father and mother that I may have you in my arms day and night.

Yet even this account pales by contrast with Tennyson's Vivien, a fundamentally original creation. Tennyson may have drawn further inspiration from the ornamental "S" at the opening of Southey's fourth book of Malory; the "S" is formed by an enormous serpent winding itself around the ankle and across the knees of a naked man.[13] Yet we

11 For this and subsequent idylls, Tennyson employed the two-volume Walker and Edwards edition of Malory which he received from Leigh Hunt (*Memoir*, I, 156). Volume I is now in the Tennyson Research Centre, Lincoln; it contains numerous marginal markings by the poet. With the exception of the second volume of the Wilks edition, which has a few minor marginal markings, Tennyson's copy of the Wilks edition seems relatively unused.

12 Though Southey's edition is not part of the poet's surviving library, there seems little doubt that the annotated edition was familiar to him. For evidence of his knowledge of Southey's edition, see chapter 1, footnote 16. The introductory selection from the *Romance of Merlin* refers to Viviane, whereas the Wilks and the Walker and Edwards editions refer to Nimue and Southey's edition of Malory's text refers to Nynyve. Moreover, only in the introduction does the seduction occur in the Forest of Broceliande, the exact spelling of Tennyson's setting. For the pertinent section from Southey's introduction, see Appendix 3. In her "Note on the Forest of Broceliande, and the Fountain of Baranton" in her edition of the *Mabinogion* (London, 1840), Lady Charlotte Guest includes this section of Southey's introduction (I, 216-218), though she employs the spelling of "Breceliande."

13 The same ornamental "S" also appears at the beginning of the sixth, eighteenth, and

should be wary of seeing Vivien only in the
light of the abundant serpent imagery which
surrounds her character. Animal imagery in
general forms her portrait; in addition to her
serpentine qualities she is described as a
kitten, a "gilded summer fly," a kid, and a
cageling.

 In essence, Tennyson's poem is the
most original idyll of the completed series,
with the exception of *Guinevere*. Tennyson
has taken a relatively minor character in
Malory, Nimue, and made her the central

The ornamental "S" which
opens Malory's fourth book
in Southey's edition.

focus of a poem; he has given her an importance totally alien to Malory's
world. Vivien is a woman unrelated to her medieval counterpart; in
Malory's version, Merlin is the active pursuer of a disdaining and
frightened woman; his complete infatuation leads to his abdication of his
social position in Camelot and to his plan to travel "with her evermore
wheresoever she went." Tennyson's woman is a disgraceful wanton,
the wilful deceiver of a passive Merlin. She is totally and knowingly evil,
without any trace of a moral conscience. Even the *Romance of Merlin*
gives her a small degree of moral feeling: "often time she regretted what
she had done, for she had thought that the thing which he taught her
could not be true, and willingly would she have let him out if she could."
Tennyson's Vivien is permitted no such moment of remorse or regret;
she is the personification of falsehood, the embodiment of active evil.
She is the poet's own creation denied even the goodness that is found in
Malory's Nimue in a later scene where Pelleas is united with Nimue in
love; when Tennyson comes to create his own version of the Pelleas
story, he omits the deadly enchantment that the Lady of the Lake casts
on the false Ettarde and he fails to extend to Pelleas the last love of
Nimue that Malory includes in his account. In an effort to preserve the
unmitigated evil his Vivien represents, Tennyson ignores the redeeming
moments of her portrait that are recorded by Malory.

 Tennyson's Merlin is similarly divorced from his medieval counterpart. Though both Merlins are sages, Tennyson's figure becomes a
morally spotless wizard destroyed by the too potent evil of Vivien.
Tennyson has removed any indication that Merlin is infatuated with
Vivien and subservient to her desires. The Victorian Merlin has a
complete awareness of her evil nature and her evil purpose:

> And smiling as a Master smiles at one
> That is not of his school, nor any school

nineteenth books of Southey's edition, though Vivien has, of course, no role in these
books.

> But that where blind and naked Ignorance
> Delivers brawling judgments, unashamed,
> On all things all day long.[14]

Merlin is not infatuated with this woman; his surrender to her evil genius is less a reflection of his character than an indication of the potency of her attraction. With clever subtlety she insinuates herself into that one area of his potential weakness: "the old man, / Tho' doubtful, felt the flattery, and at times / Would flatter his own wish in age for love."

The central episode of the idyll, the seduction of Merlin, is based, however vaguely, upon an incident mentioned in Malory; the details that surround this incident and the many events mentioned by the characters during the episode are further inventions by the poet. In Malory there is no confrontation between Nimue and Arthur, no justification for the opening incident of Tennyson's poem:

> the King
> Had gazed upon her blankly and gone by:
> But one had watch'd, and had not held his peace:
> It made the laughter of an afternoon
> That Vivien should attempt the blameless King.

Merlin's journey to Brittany is an attempt to escape the wily Vivien, who "follow'd, but he mark'd her not"; Malory has Merlin set out for Cornwall so that he can dote without interruption upon his beloved Nimue. Tennyson's protagonists differ from their medieval counterparts, both by their natures and by the new setting in which they operate.

The verbal strife between Merlin and Vivien reaches its climax in her accusations regarding the decreasingly virtuous conduct of the knights of the Round Table. Here again Tennyson's freedom with regard to his source is evident. The first accusation centres on the wife of Sir Valence and her supposed infidelity; Sir Valence is a non-existent medieval knight bearing no correspondence to any possible counterpart in Malory.[15] The second accusation refers to Sir Sagramore's supposed violation of his intended wife, "To crop his own sweet rose before the hour." Although Sir Sagramore, a relatively minor knight, is frequently mentioned in Malory, no incident in which he is involved bears even remotely on this story. The third accusation refers to Percivale's infatuation with a young maiden. In Malory, Percivale meets a young woman who promises to direct him to Galahad, the goal of his quest;

14 For a detailed account of the changes between the trial-edition of 1857 and the 1859 edition of the *Idylls of the King*, see Richard Jones, *The Growth of the Idylls of the King* (Philadelphia, 1895). Any changes relevant to this study are noted in the appropriate footnotes.

15 In Malory there are two knights who have the epithet "valyaunte," Vyllars and Synounde. Neither of these minor figures has any correspondence to the knight Vivien describes.

overcome by her beauty, he places himself in her power; in a pavilion the lady has set up, he becomes the victim of her enchantment and "proferred her love, and prayed her that she would be his love" (Part III, Chapter lvii). After he agrees to be her "true servant, and to do nothing but that I shall command you," his sinful desire almost reaches its fulfillment:

and then sir Percivale laid him down by her naked, and by adventure and grace he saw his sword lie upon the ground all naked, in whose pommel was a red cross, and the sign of the cross therein, and bethought him of his knighthood, and on his promise made beforehand unto the good man. Then he made a sign of the cross on his forehead, and therewithal the pavilion turned upside down; and then it changed unto a smoke and a black cloud, and then he was dread, and cried out aloud [III, lvii].

Percivale's sudden rescue from the brink of iniquity leads him to "rove himself through the thigh, that the blood started about him." At this moment, he discovers that the woman is "the master fiend of hell; the which hath power over all devils." The incident does form the basis of Vivien's allusion to Percivale's "horrid foulness," though here again the poet takes only the bare outline of the story. Malory's episode finds a new setting:

> A sober man is Percivale and pure;
> But once in life was fluster'd with new wine,
> Then paced for coolness in the chapel-yard;
> Where one of Satan's shepherdesses caught
> And meant to stamp him with her master's mark;
> And that he sinn'd, is not believable;
> For, look upon his face!

The fourth and final accusation, which remains unanswerable, refers to Lancelot's growing love for the Queen. Merlin is forced to acknowledge the adulterous relationship, but he adds: "Sir Lancelot went ambassador, at first, / To fetch her, and she took him for the King; / So fixt her fancy on him: let him be." Tennyson returns to the idea, unsubstantiated by Malory but already suggested in *Sir Launcelot and Queen Guinevere,* that Guinevere's love for Lancelot arose from her initial glimpse of the knight in his role as Arthur's ambassador before she met her bridegroom. Moreover, the reference to the relationship between the Queen and Lancelot is a further indication of Tennyson's freedom from his source, since Malory's Lancelot does not appear until Merlin has been destroyed by Nimue. Thus these four accusations emphasize the originality of the poem; only one of them has any possible substantiation in Malory, and that solitary accusation, Percivale's temptation, has been re-created in a new setting.

    Vivien is a depiction of the potency of lust in its ability to destroy the life of the intellect. The basic incident of the poem comes from the

Arthurian world; its importance, however, lies not in its Arthurian source, but in its plot, a plot that offers Tennyson a mode of studying the conflict between an intellectual being and a sensual being. The Arthurian background that surrounds the entire poem colours and intensifies what is basically a dramatic confrontation of two opposed personalities. The poem is a violation of the characters and incidents as recorded by Malory; the Arthurian world here exists to be re-created in the light of the poet's own purpose. Malory has offered Tennyson the names, the incident, and the setting for a dramatic and original study of the potency of falsehood as personified in a creature of unbridled sensuality.

Enid is not a movement towards a great Arthurian work, but a dramatic answer to the negative horror of Vivien; Vivien's destructive nature demanded a positive response, a female character who embodied the ideal of truth absent in the earlier poem. For a proper antidote to Vivien's deceptions, Tennyson chose the figure of Enid, a paragon of virtue and truth. He found the story of Enid and her patient submission to the jealous suspicions of her husband Geraint in Lady Charlotte Guest's translation of the *Mabinogion*.[16] *Enid* was begun immediately after the completion of *Vivien*,[17] but Tennyson's progress with this idyll was slow. His source was a lengthy narration of incidents that often bore slight causal relationships; his task was to condense his source in such a fashion that the completed poem would focus on Geraint and Enid and thereby provide a suitable contrast to the story of Merlin and Vivien. The summer of 1856 offered the poet a conducive milieu for his proposed poem:

early in July the whole family set off for Wales, where Alfred was anxious to gather impressions for the Geraint story, which had been sadly interfered with by the events of the last two months.

During the days of preparation for the journey, he bought a Welsh dictionary and he and Emily set about the works of the Bards. The party visited Llangollen, Dolgelly, Barmouth, Harlech, Tan-y-bwlch, Llanidloes, Brecon, Caerleon, Raglan, and other places in between. Wherever he went Alfred tried to find a schoolmaster or other scholar who would help him with the language, and made a point of hunting out some person with antiquarian knowledge—often the local chemist or cobbler—who would go with him to places of historic interest. In those days almost every little town or village seemed to have an aged harper, and they delighted in getting these old men to play them Welsh airs and talk to them of the ancient lays and ballads.[18]

16 *Mabinogion*, II, 67-141. In Harvard Notebook 27 (no date), there is an alphabetical listing of books in Tennyson's own handwriting which contains the 1840 edition of the *Mabinogion* under "M." In Harvard Notebook 26 (no date), six pages of Welsh vocabulary are followed by the opening lines in Welsh of the *Mabinogion's* "Dream of Macsen Wledig."

17 *Vivien* "was finished by March 31st, and 'Geraint and Enid' begun on April 16th" (*Memoir*, I, 414).

18 Sir Charles Tennyson, p. 301. H. G. Wright's "Tennyson and Wales," *Essays and Studies*, 14 (1929), 71-103, shows how certain Welsh landscapes may have had specific influence on scenes in the idyll.

By the end of September Tennyson returned to his new home at Farringford where he began to work in earnest on the Geraint story.

Enid represents the truth that Vivien lacks, the true beauty that Vivien feigns, the love that for Vivien can only be lust. In her notes, Lady Guest commented:

Throughout the broad and varied region of Romance, it would be difficult to find a character of greater simplicity and truth than that of Enid the daughter of Earl Ynywl. Conspicuous for her beauty and noble bearing, we are at a loss whether most to admire, the untiring patience with which she bore all the hardships she was destined to undergo, or the unshaken constancy and devoted affection which finally achieved the triumph she so richly deserved.

The character of Enid is admirably sustained throughout the whole Tale: and as it is more natural, because less overstrained, so, perhaps, it is even more touching than that of Griselda, over which, however, Chaucer has thrown a charm that leads us to forget the improbability of her story.

There is a triad, in which Enid's name is preserved as one of the fairest and most illustrious ladies of the Court of Arthur. It runs thus,—

"Tair Gwenriain Llys Arthur: Dyfir wallt euraid; Enid ferch Yniwl Iarll; a Thegau Eurfronn: Sef oeddent Tair Rhiain Ardderchawg Llys Arthur." —T. 108

The Bards of the Middle Ages have frequent allusions to her in their Poems; and Davydd ap Gwilym could pay no higher compliment to his Lady-love than to call her a second Enid.[19]

Here, indeed, is the antithesis of Vivien.

Enid is a study of two personalities who are so portrayed as to stand in direct contrast to the two personalities portrayed in *Vivien*. Whereas Vivien is a demonically active being, ever working the ruin of her victim, Enid is an angelically passive being, ever thinking of her ability to aid her husband. Similarly, the lethargic passivity of Merlin contrasts with the relentless activity of Geraint. Yet Geraint's activities should not blind the reader to the fact that Enid, the title figure, is central to the poem; though the initial combat with the Sparrow-Hawk is caused by the insult done to the Queen, all the subsequent action is prompted, either consciously or unconsciously, by Enid. Her voice, "Clear thro' the open casement of the hall," leads Geraint to exclaim, "Here, by God's grace, is the one voice for me." Her concern for the growing public disfavour towards her husband prompts the tearful outburst that leads Geraint to his suspicious treatment of his wife. Moreover, the minor characters are always motivated by Enid. The original mistreatment of Yniol by Edyrn is the result of Yniol's refusal to grant Edyrn the hand of his daughter. Later, when the converted Edyrn encounters the wounded Geraint, it is "the voice of Enid" that stays his lance. Likewise, the evil actions of Limours are prompted by his lust for Enid, a lust only further inflamed

19 *Mabinogion*, II, 164-165. Translated, the triad states: "Three fair maidens of Arthur's court: Dyfir the golden-haired, Enid the daughter of Earl Yniwl, and Tegau the golden-breasted. These were the three splendid maidens of Arthur's court."

by Yniol's refusal to grant Limours Enid's hand in marriage. In this idyll, as in *Vivien*, the title character is the cause of the action. Tennyson's treatment of the *Mabinogion* is a combination of fidelity to a source of the type already displayed in the *Morte d'Arthur* and freedom with regard to characters and incidents already exemplified in the originality of *Vivien*. His first task is the condensation of the bulky episodic structure of the *Mabinogion* account. Since the episodic pattern would lead to a tale of adventures rather than a dramatic study of characters, Tennyson reduces the number of characters and tightens the interdependence of the remaining episodes. After he completes the tightening, he remains comparatively faithful to the narrative pattern of his source.

The Welsh source falls naturally into two major divisions, corresponding to the later separation Tennyson introduced into his completed idyll.[20] The first recounts the events leading up to the marriage of Geraint; the second, the trials of the patient Enid during the journey forced upon her by her suspicious husband. The primary action of the first section concerns the knight known as the Sparrow-Hawk (Edyrn, son of Nudd), whose insulting behaviour to Guinevere inflames Geraint's revengeful wrath; subsidiary to this is the story of Yniol's deprivation of his nephew's rightful inheritance. Tennyson combines the good character of the nephew and the evil character of the Sparrow-Hawk into the single knight Edyrn; the amalgamation creates one interesting and important character out of two relatively minor characters. In addition, by making Edyrn's seizure of Yniol's property a malicious act provoked by Yniol's refusal to grant Edyrn his daughter in marriage, Tennyson whitens the originally corrupted character of Yniol and removes any moral taint from the family which fostered the spotless perfection of Enid.

The second section of the Welsh tale is a long series of loosely related episodes. Aroused by Enid's tears, and consequently suspicious of her devotion to him, Geraint embarks on a series of adventures that tend to be redundant and extravagant in the manner of a loose medieval romance. First, in three encounters he defeats a total of twelve knights; Tennyson wisely reduces this section to two brief encounters with a total of six knights. These combats, however, represent only the beginning of Geraint's journey. In a town where the couple lodges they receive a visit from Earl Dwrm, whose lust for Enid leads to his unsuccessful plot to abduct her during the night. The following day Geraint encounters Gwiffert Petit, the Little King, whom he subsequently defeats; the sudden arrival of Arthur and his retinue provides treatment for the grievous wound Geraint received. Upon leaving Arthur's camp Geraint

---

20   In 1873 the poem is divided into two sections; not until 1886 do the two sections receive separate titles.

and Enid find a dead knight and his bewailing lady; Geraint proceeds to attack the three giants, the knight's assassins, and achieves victory despite a new and serious wound. At this moment a new knight, Earl Limours, finds the seemingly lifeless Geraint and the moaning Enid and conducts the pair to his palace where he brutally mistreats Enid; his striking of her revives Geraint from his swoon, and the ensuing fight leads to the Earl's death. Geraint and Enid make a hasty departure from the palace and are met at once by an armed knight, the Little King, who was on his way to rescue them. The Little King conducts them to the court of his sister-in-law, where Geraint recovers completely. In the subsequent and final episode Geraint arrives at a magic realm where he defeats a knight and destroys the magic enchantments.

To alleviate the dreary repetition of the narration and to introduce greater interdependence among the episodes, Tennyson again reduces the number of characters by assigning the actions of extraneous characters to more important figures. In this way he retains the basic structural pattern and tone of his Welsh source, while he presents a tightened and interwoven development of the episodes. The role of the Little King is divided between Arthur and Edyrn; Geraint's initial encounter with the Little King is omitted, and the final meeting between Geraint and the Little King becomes the reunion of Geraint and the converted Edyrn; in addition, Edyrn leads Geraint to Arthur's camp where the King's medical advisers offer the assistance given in the source by the court of the Little King's sister-in-law. The roles of Limours and Earl Dwrm follow closely their roles in the *Mabinogion,* although Tennyson inexplicably reverses the names of the two characters. Limours remains the wild, lustful Earl of the *Mabinogion;* Tennyson does add to his character the fact that Limours was Enid's first rejected suitor, in order to link his appearance in the poem's later section with the earlier history of Enid. Doorm, Tennyson's spelling of the Welsh Dwrm, receives a larger and more sinister development in the poem; he represents the bestiality associated with the wildness of uncivilized man. Doorm lacks any culture, any refinement, any self-control; his hall, Tennyson's addition to the source, is the world of the stable or the sty rather than the court; his women are described in language that recalls the serpentine aspects of the equally horrid Vivien:

> While some, whose souls the old serpent long had drawn
> Down, as the worm draws in the wither'd leaf
> And makes it earth, hiss'd each at other's ear
> What shall not be recorded—women they,
> Women, or what had been those gracious things,
> But now desired the humbling of their best,
> Yea, would have helped him to it.

Doorm's realm is a world without order: he rules through brute force: "I compel all creatures to my will." The expanded treatment of Doorm is a deliberate anticipation of the later appearance of Arthur, who comes to "weed this land." It is especially fitting that Edyrn, once as lawless as Doorm, should announce to Geraint:

> Now, made a knight of Arthur's Table Round,
> And since I knew this Earl, when I myself
> Was half a bandit in my lawless hour,
> I come the mouthpiece of our King to Doorm
> (The King is close behind me) bidding him
> Disband himself, and scatter all his powers,
> Submit, and hear the judgment of the King.

The world of Doorm is marked by the lawlessness and brutality that Arthur has come to eradicate; Doorm is a concrete verification of the necessity of Arthur's mission.

The structural technique of condensation is complemented by a number of minor omissions. In order to focus intensely on the relationship of Geraint and Enid, Tennyson leaves out extraneous descriptions and incidents not crucial to the Enid plot. His source delights in long lists of the royalty assembled at Caerleon-upon-Usk; Tennyson dismisses this material with the statement: "For Arthur on the Whitsuntide before / Held court at old Caerleon upon Usk." The stag hunt which sets the scene for the meeting of Guinevere and Geraint and which receives extended treatment in the source is relegated to a minor background incident and is completely ignored after the appearance of the knight, the damsel, and the dwarf. Unlike his source, Tennyson does not return to the stag hunt after the insulting behaviour of the dwarf; the hunt has served its initial purpose, to bring together Geraint and Guinevere; it has no further value. Finally, Tennyson begins the story, not with the court at Caerleon, but with Enid's growing concern with Geraint's luxuriating uxoriousness; here is the centre of the story, placed with emphasis at the outset of the poem.

Within the new structure created by the condensation, Tennyson adheres closely to the episodic movement of his source. Except for the beginning "in medias res," the idyll follows the plan of the source with a textual fidelity somewhat reminiscent of his treatment of Malory in his *Morte d'Arthur*. For example, the first appearance of Geraint is similar in both versions:

And one of them went, and she found but two horses in the stable, and Gwenhwyvar and one of her maidens mounted them, and went through the Usk, and followed the track of the men and the horses. And as they rode	But rose at last, a single maiden with her, Took horse, and forded Usk, and gain'd the wood; There, on a little knoll beside it, stay'd

thus, they heard a loud and rushing sound; and they looked behind them, and beheld a knight upon a hunter foal of mighty size; and the rider was a fair-haired youth, bare-legged, and of princely mien, and a golden-hilted sword was at his side, and a robe and a surcoat of satin were upon him, and two low shoes of leather upon his feet; and around him was a scarf of blue purple, at each corner of which was a golden apple.

And his horse stepped stately, and swift, and proud; and he overtook Gwenhwyvar, and saluted her. "Heaven prosper thee, Geraint," she said, "I knew thee when first I saw thee just now. And the welcome of heaven be unto thee. And why didst thou not go with thy lord to hunt?" "Because I know not when he went," said he. "I marvel, too," said she, "how he could go unknown to me." "Indeed, lady," said he. "I was asleep, and knew not when he went; but thou, O young man, art the most agreeable companion I could have in the whole kingdom; and it may be, that I shall be more amused with the hunting than they; for we shall hear the horns when they sound, and we shall hear the dogs when they are let loose, and begin to cry." So they went to the edge of the Forest, and there they stood. "From this place," said she, "we shall hear when the dogs are let loose."

Waiting to hear the hounds; but heard instead
A sudden sound of hoofs, for Prince Geraint,
Late also, wearing neither hunting-dress
Nor weapon, save a golden-hilted brand,
Came quickly flashing thro' the shallow ford
Behind them, and so gallop'd up the knoll.
A purple scarf, at either end whereof
There swung an apple of the purest gold,
Sway'd round about him, as he gallop'd up
To join them, glancing like a dragon-fly
In summer suit and silks of holiday.
Low bow'd the tributary Prince, and she,
Sweetly and statelily, and with all grace
Of womanhood and queenhood, answer'd him:
"Late, late, Sir Prince," she said, "later than we!"
"Yea, noble Queen," he answer'd, "and so late
That I but come like you to see the hunt,
Not join it." "Therefore wait with me," she said;
"For on this little knoll, if anywhere,
There is good chance that we shall hear the hounds:
Here often they break covert at our feet."

Tennyson's respect for the detailed description and the pattern of the incidents of his source is evident; he follows the narrative pattern of the *Mabinogion* and incorporates many of its details into his account. The similarities between the *Mabinogion* and the poetic version are less verbally close than those between Malory and Tennyson's *Morte d'Arthur;* now, more than twenty years after the composition of that early

Arthurian poem, Tennyson eschews close verbal fidelity. At the same time many minor details, especially descriptive details such as the pair of golden apples, are retained. Moreover, as in the *Morte d'Arthur*, Tennyson indulges in his favourite technique of descriptive expansion; where his source merely mentions a particular object or setting, he expands the source by painting the setting in detail or by giving an object a new life through a heightened description. The trip to the town of the Sparrow-Hawk is now seen through Geraint's eyes; the poet expands his source appropriately to capture a stranger's reaction to a new landscape:

And the road they took was below the palace of Caerlleon, and across the ford of the Usk; and they went along a fair, and even, and lofty ridge of ground, until they came to a town, and at the extremity of the town they saw a Fortress and a Castle. And they came to the extremity of the town.

By ups and downs, thro' many a
   grassy glade
And valley, with fixt eye following
   the three.
At last they issued from the world of
   wood,
And climb'd upon a fair and even
   ridge,
And show'd themselves against the
   sky, and sank.
And thither came Geraint, and
   underneath
Beheld the long street of a little town
In a long valley, on one side of which,
White from the mason's hand, a
   fortress rose;
And on one side a castle in decay,
Beyond a bridge that spann'd a dry
   ravine:
And out of town and valley came a
   noise
As of a broad brook o'er a shingly
   bed
Brawling, or like a clamour of the
   rooks
At distance, ere they settle for the
   night.

Similarly the *Mabinogion* introduces Yniol's castle with a paucity of detail: "And at a little distance from the town he saw an old palace in ruins, wherein was a hall that was falling to decay." Tennyson seizes this opportunity for a characteristically expanded description:

He look'd and saw that all was ruinous.
Here stood a shatter'd archway plumed with fern;
And here had fall'n a great part of a tower,
Whole, like a crag that tumbles from the cliff,
And like a crag was gay with wilding flowers:
And high above a piece of turret stair,
Worn by the feet that now were silent, wound
Bare to the sun, and monstrous ivy-stems

> Claspt the gray walls with hairy-fibred arms,
> And suck'd the joining of the stones, and look'd
> A knot, beneath, of snakes, aloft, a grove.

Such descriptions are heightened realizations of moments left undeveloped in the source; without violating the source Tennyson's expansions intensify the original story by vivification of the external setting.

These two basic attitudes to his source, the technique of condensation and the fidelity to the plot outline, are completed by a third attitude which violates the source and makes the story a distinctly Tennysonian creation. Whereas the *Morte d'Arthur* asserts its distinctly nineteenth-century creation by the expanded use of dialogue and introspection, *Enid* becomes a new work by the small but extremely important additions Tennyson introduces into the story. The most vital, indeed crucial, addition is the growing suspicion of Guinevere's adulterous behaviour; in the *Mabinogion* there is no reference to Guinevere's love for Lancelot. Tennyson, on the other hand, makes this issue central to his version of the story. At the beginning Guinevere oversleeps the hunt: "Lost in sweet dreams, and dreaming of her love / For Lancelot, and forgetful of the hunt." The *Mabinogion* offers no reason or excuse for her late awakening. More importantly, Geraint's departure from the court has a new motivation; in the *Mabinogion*, Geraint's elderly father summons home his son "to protect his possessions, and to become acquainted with his boundaries." Tennyson, however, makes Guinevere's behaviour the cause of Geraint's sudden departure:

> But when a rumour rose about the Queen,
> Touching her guilty love for Lancelot,
> Tho' yet there lived no proof, nor yet was heard
> The world's loud whisper breaking into storm,
> Not less Geraint believed it; and there fell
> A horror on him, lest his gentle wife,
> Thro' that great tenderness for Guinevere,
> Had suffer'd, or should suffer any taint
> In nature.

Even the final happy ending is marred by the telling addition:

> Then, when Geraint was whole again, they past
> With Arthur to Caerleon upon Usk.
> There the great Queen once more embraced her friend,
> And clothed her in apparel like the day.
> And tho' Geraint could never take again
> That comfort from their converse which he took
> Before the Queen's fair name was breathed upon,
> He rested well content that all was well.

Tennyson's version of the Geraint story moves within a new background created by the prominence bestowed upon Guinevere's behaviour. It is Geraint's devotion to Guinevere that launches the plot of the story; it is a young Geraint's adoration of Guinevere that makes him so adamant that his new bride be clothed by the Queen herself:

> I vow'd that could I gain her, our kind Queen,
> No hand but hers, should make your Enid burst
> Sunlike from cloud—and likewise thought perhaps,
> That service done so graciously would bind
> The two together; for I wish the two
> To love each other: how should Enid find
> A nobler friend?

The harsh reality that confronts Geraint is the growing knowledge of the true nature of Arthur's Queen.

Enid follows the progress of Geraint both as a suspicious and later repentant husband and as a devout and later suspicious servant of the Queen. In the idyll the ideal order of Camelot is damaged even before it has established itself completely. Arthur has not subdued the realm to his pattern of the law and order; he must bring Doorm to subjection. Yet the seeds of destruction are already in evidence; a youthful and idealistic Geraint is suddenly thrown into terror by a rumour of Guinevere's adultery; earlier he asserted that Enid could have no "nobler friend" than Guinevere; his wish is fulfilled:

> and the Queen herself,
> Grateful to Prince Geraint for service done,
> Loved her, and often with her own white hands
> Array'd and deck'd her, as the loveliest,
> Next after her own self, in all the court.
> And Enid loved the Queen, and with true heart
> Adored her, as the stateliest and the best
> And loveliest of all women upon earth.

Geraint's faith in Arthur and his realm is destroyed by a mere rumour. Though his rash reaction is indicative of his overly suspicious nature,[21] the reaction does draw attention to the fact that his harsh treatment of Enid begins after his departure from Camelot, which is necessitated by Guinevere's loose behaviour. The story of Enid's plight is cast in a new

---

21 Tennyson makes Geraint a very suspicious person; Geraint confesses to Enid's parents:

> I came among you here so suddenly,
> That tho' her gentle presence at the lists
> Might well have served for proof that I was loved,
> I doubted whether filial tenderness,
> Or easy nature, did not let itself
> Be moulded by your wishes for her weal;
> Or whether some false sense in her own self
> Of my contrasting brightness, overbore
> Her fancy dwelling in this dusky hall.

This passage has no substantiation in the source. Tennyson adds the detail in order that Geraint's response to the rumour of the adultery will seem natural to a man of his suspicious temperament.

light, since it now exists within the framework of the romantic intrigue at
the centre of Arthur's realm.

Begun as a contrast to *Vivien, Enid* adds a new contrast to Guinevere herself. Enid is a paragon of virtue, of love, of selflessness, those
qualities totally absent in the lustful sensuality Vivien personifies. The
Mabinogion shows Enid as a woman second only to Guinevere in
goodness and beauty; Tennyson uses this fact as a beginning; his treatment of the story follows the goodness of Enid as it is tested in the light of
Guinevere's misconduct. By the end of the idyll the goodness and purity
of Enid stand in contrast, not only to the character of Vivien, but also to
the character of Guinevere. A happy but ominous detail concludes this
study of Enid: "But Enid, whom her ladies loved to call /Enid the Fair, a
grateful people named / Enid the Good." The adjective "Fair" is no
longer Enid's epithet. "Fair" has been superseded by the much more
virtuous "Good." The shift in evaluation is a decisive movement which
a grateful people would be unable to make in the case of Guinevere, their
Queen.

In *Enid* Tennyson shows fidelity to the story in the *Mabinogion;* his
additions and minor changes serve to bring the story into a new light.
The plot offered him an excellent contrast to his completed study of
Vivien, yet it also gave him an opportunity to expand his brief study of
the ideal Order Arthur set out to establish. The contrast in the foreground between Enid and Vivien parallels the contrast in the background between the realm in very early decay and the realm on the verge
of ruin; in *Enid* Arthur's order is not fully organized, yet sin already
exists as its centre; in *Vivien* the destruction of Merlin is only part of the
large decay operating in Camelot; whereas Geraint remains uncertain
about Guinevere's behaviour, Merlin cannot deny Vivien's accusation
about the Queen's adultery.

Tennyson's fidelity to the *Mabinogion* and his simultaneous freedom with its materials stand in contrast to the close fidelity displayed in
the *Morte d'Arthur*. The intervening years have given him increased
confidence to treat his source with an originality dictated by his own
particular purpose; *Vivien* is almost completely original, being only
loosely related to a small incident recorded by Malory; *Enid* is more
closely related to its source, though the finished idyll receives a different
emphasis and tone with the introduction of Guinevere's adultery.

In addition, *Enid* exhibits Tennyson's increased familiarity with
Arthurian literature and his willingness to incorporate added details
from other sources. Geraint's marriage is performed by Dubric, a name
not mentioned in the *Mabinogion* or in Malory; Dubric reflects Tennyson's familiarity with the legends of Arthur in the chronicle tradition.[22]

22 Both Geoffrey of Monmouth's *Historia Regum Britanniae* and Layamon's *Brut*
    describe the Whitsunday assembly at Caerleon where Dubric is Archbishop. Sir

Another added detail is the account of Geraint's death, which is not recorded in the *Mabinogion:* "fell / Against the heathen of the Northern Sea / In battle, fighting for the blameless King."[23] This detail reflects Tennyson's familiarity with the account of Geraint's death in Llywarch Hen's elegy.[24] No longer yoked by a feeling of absolute reverence for his source, Tennyson freely adapts the *Mabinogion* account to his own purpose and embellishes it with details gathered from other medieval works. A medieval tale of knightly adventure with the usual delight in accumulated incidents has become a study of two characters caught in the slightly decayed world of Camelot.

Printed together in a trial-edition in 1857, these two idylls, originally titled *Enid and Nimuë: The True and the False,* exist as a separate work in their own right, but they also exist, more powerfully, as part of an incomplete context suggested by the framework that Tennyson adds to the story of Enid. With the creation of *Vivien* Tennyson showed an awareness of the idyll structure that would form the individual pattern within a much larger whole. The path he would choose seems to be asserting itself during the completion of the two idylls. Unlike Malory's version, which takes place shortly after the marriage of Arthur and Guinevere, Tennyson's presentation of Merlin's seduction occurs at a much later time in the history of the realm. What primarily separates Tennyson's account of the Enid story from his Welsh source is the superimposition of the rumour of Guinevere's adultery. Guinevere has only a minor role in the idyll, but her sin, or at least the rumour about it, makes her an unseen presence throughout the poem. Tennyson chose to set the Enid story within the context of the Queen's adultery; he has deliberately placed the sequence at a time when the rumour is only arising, at a time markedly earlier than the time chosen for Merlin's seduction. The contrast of Vivien and Enid is a prelude to the subsequent contrast of Enid and Guinevere; by the end of her idyll Enid receives the rightful homage that should be, but cannot be, accorded to Guinevere.

Charles Tennyson notes the poet's familiarity with these works (p. 296). Tennyson's library included J. A. Giles' *Six Old English Chronicles* (London, 1848), which includes a translation of Geoffrey, and the three-volume edition of Layamon's *Brut* edited by Sir Frederick Madden in 1847. Harvard Notebook 18 contains the poet's transcription of seventeen lines from the second volume of Madden's edition of Layamon.

23   "Against the heathen of the Northern Sea" was added in 1859; "In battle" was "At Longport" in the 1857 trial-edition.

24   "With the help of local schoolmasters in Wales my parents learned some Welsh, and now read together the *Hanes Cymru* (Welsh History), the *Mabinogion* and *Llywarch Hen*" (*Memoir*, I, 416). The relevant passage about Geraint's death is appended in the notes to the *Mabinogion* (II, 151): "At Llongborth was Geraint slain, / A valiant warrior from the woodlands of Devon, / Slaughtering his foes as he fell." Lady Guest added that "the Rev. T. Price supposes it to be Langport, in Somersetshire." This detail is also found in T. Price, *Hanes Cymru* (Crughywel, 1842), p. 276.

Even before the 1857 trial-edition, Tennyson was "already meditating a successor to the two Arthurian stories which he had completed,"[25] and the proper successor was the natural product of these two poems. Having studied the ennobling power of a good woman in *Enid* and the degrading horror of a base woman in *Vivien,* Tennyson can now turn to Guinevere, the woman who should share the exalted stature of an Enid, but who sadly veers in the direction of a Vivien. When Tennyson begins his third idyll, he has carefully prepared the proper position for the Queen: "the Queen who sat betwixt her best / Enid, and lissome Vivien, of her court / The wiliest and the worst." Guinevere partakes of both the ennobling goodness associated with Enid and the destructive sensuality associated with Vivien. From this dual association the poet creates a portrait of a complex woman at war with her own being and acutely conscious of the nature of that war.

Guinevere took its initial shape from the passage: "But hither shall I never come again, / Never lie by thy side; see thee no more, / Farewell!"[26] From its inception the idyll existed as a dramatic rendition of the final meeting of Arthur and Guinevere,[27] a meeting that does not occur in Malory. Unlike *Vivien* the idyll is not an expansion of a brief moment in a source, nor does it, like *Enid,* condense and alter a particular plot. *Guinevere* is a creation, not a re-creation, yet this creation exists, not wholly independently of Malory, but seemingly as an integral section of the basic plot of the history of Camelot. Though inventing the scene, Tennyson takes care to find a setting from Malory; once again he finds an undeveloped moment:

And when queen Guenever understood that her lord, king Arthur, was slain, and all the noble nights, sir Mordred and all the remnant, then she stole away, and five ladies with her: and so she went to Almesbury, and there she let make herself a nun, and wore white clothes and black: and great penance she took, as ever did sinful lady in this land, and never creature could make her merry, but lived in fastings, prayers, and alms-deeds, that all manner of people marvelled how virtuously she was changed. Now leave we queen Guenever in Almesbury, that was a nun in white clothes and in black, and there she was abbess and ruler as reason would; and turn we from her, and speak we of sir Launcelot du Lake [III, clxx].

Since the time of this setting prevents a final meeting of Arthur and his Queen, Tennyson again adjusts the chronology of Malory's plot and reworks the causal relationship of the final events of the story.

In Malory, Mordred and Aggravayne scheme to entrap Lancelot in Guinevere's bedroom. Their plot suceeds, Lancelot flees in the ensuing

25   Sir Charles Tennyson, p. 303.
26   In her journal entry of July 9, 1857, Emily Tennyson noted in regard to this passage: "A. T. has brought me two lines that he has made of Guinevere which may be the nucleus of the parting of Arthur and Guinevere" (*Materials*, II, 185).
27   On June 8, 1859, Emily referred to the idyll as "his parting of King Arthur and Queen Guinevere" (*Materials*, II, 193).

combat, and Arthur is forced to sentence his adulterous wife to death at the stake. Lancelot's sudden rescue of the Queen, her flight to Lancelot's castle, the Pope's subsequent reconcilement of Arthur and Guinevere—these incidents precede Arthur's war against Lancelot. During the war occur Mordred's usurpation of the realm, Arthur's prompt return, Mordred's death, and Arthur's own passing. At this juncture in the chronology Guinevere steals away to Almesbury.

Tennyson alters Malory's chronology in order to create his own version of the demise of Camelot. Having already written a poem about Arthur's passing, he sets out to study the final meeting of the King and Queen, which must precede the war against Modred, the opening of his *Morte d'Arthur*. Consequently, Guinevere's flight to Almesbury is now motivated by Modred's scheming; his discovery of the lovers necessitates the final parting of Lancelot and Guinevere, a brief scene which is a prelude to the long confrontation of Arthur and Guinevere, the dramatic centre of the idyll.

Following Malory's example, Tennyson makes Modred the engineer of the disclosure scene that entraps the lovers. Though Tennyson's villain is also motivated by jealousy of Lancelot, he assumes a new character through the emphasis on his bestiality; Tennyson surrounds him with the animal imagery already associated with Vivien. Modred has a "foxy face"; he is a "subtle beast," a "green caterpillar," a "worm." Modred is another agent of evil; he unmasks the frailties and sins of human beings; his aims are selfish and perverted; he is an Iago in an Arthurian setting.[28]

In *Guinevere* Tennyson is secure in his own conception of his Arthurian project; *Vivien* and *Enid* offer him the confidence and assur-

---

28 In the 1859 volume, Tennyson maintains the blood relationship between Arthur and his sister, Lot's wife (named Morgawse in Malory); Modred is, therefore, Arthur's nephew, though the poet makes no suggestion that Modred is Arthur's illegitimate son by Morgawse, a fact often reiterated by Malory. Thus Edyrn grew "To hate the sin that seem'd so like his own / Of Modred, Arthur's nephew," and Lancelot is described in *Guinevere* as "reverencing king's blood in a bad man." Modred is introduced in *Guinevere* as "he nearest to the King, / His nephew." Later, Arthur says: "Where I must strike against my sister's son, / Leagued with the lords of the White Horse and knights, / Once mine, and strike him dead."

With the re-creation of Morgawse as Bellicent in *The Coming of Arthur* and with Tennyson's desire to cast in doubt the blood relationship between Arthur and Bellicent, the blood relationship between Arthur and Modred is severed. Bellicent cannot swear that Arthur is her brother; Modred is the son of Lot and Bellicent. The 1870 edition of the *Idylls* deletes Edyrn's comment about Modred and the early introduction of Modred in *Guinevere;* Arthur now says: "Where I must strike against the man they call / My sister's son—no kin of mine, who leagues / With Lords of the White Horse, heathen, and knights, / Traitors—and strike him dead." Lancelot's comment, "reverencing king's blood in a bad man," is not deleted since Modred, being the son of Lot, still has king's blood. Similarly, the doubtful relationship between Arthur and Bellicent will change Arthur's address to Gawain in *Elaine*; "Gawain, rise, / My nephew, and ride forth," to read, "Wherefore, rise, / O Gawain, and ride forth" in the 1870 edition.

ance he lacked in the eighteen-thirties; the details of *Guinevere* bear
only a token relationship to Malory. The development of the idyll is the
development of themes and details present in Tennyson's earlier Arthurian poems. Malory offers him a setting for the idyll, but the tone, the
form, and the inspiration come from his earlier poems.

In Malory, Guinevere is a shadowy, secondary, and seemingly
unimportant figure. In the early tales, she is Arthur's Queen; her appearances are brief and desultory; in the later tales, her appearances are
somewhat more frequent, though her character is only vaguely developed. As her adultery becomes known, Malory offers a few brief
glimpses, most notably in the episode of the poisoned apple, of a spoiled,
childish woman who becomes petulant when her wishes are not satisfied. Her sin aids in the destruction of Arthur's realm, yet her sin seems
more important than her own character; she remains the undistinguished
agent of that sin.

In her idyll Guinevere makes her first appearance at the moment of
her repentance; she is a penitent, weeping woman living in grief and
self-imposed solitude at Almesbury. The opening gives way to the poet's
depiction of past events, those actions that precipitated her plight. Even
the younger Guinevere now described by the poet is not the innocent
virgin of pre-Camelot days but rather a confused and frightened Queen
already conscious of her sin and its effects; there is no portrait of the
Queen at a time when her life was pure and happy. Burdened by her
sense of guilt, she suffers the agonies of awaiting her own unmasking.
She exists in a state of morbid fear where even sleep offers no escape
from frightening reality; before its discovery her sin has begun to inflict
its own punishment. Her guilt is contrasted with the strength and dignity
she can never abandon; it is Guinevere who decides that the potential
power of "smouldering scandal" necessitates her permanent separation
from Lancelot; she takes the initiative in devising the scheme for their
final parting. Modred's treachery reveals only more clearly her queenly
nobility; when Lancelot accepts the blame for their sin, she asserts her
own painful awareness:

> Would God, that thou could'st hide me from myself!
> Mine is the shame, for I was wife, and thou
> Unwedded: yet rise now, and let us fly,
> For I will draw me into sanctuary,
> And bide my doom.

A resolute woman, she would rather accept the direct consequence of
the discovery than flee to another country; her guilt prevents her from
aligning herself any longer with Lancelot; her ensuing sorrow leads to
the portrait of the contrite woman at Almesbury.

The poet relates with deliberate care the initial impact of the Queen
on the nuns:

And when she came to Almesbury she spake
There to the nuns, and said, ''mine enemies
Pursue me, but, O peaceful Sisterhood,
Receive, and yield me sanctuary, nor ask
Her name, to whom ye yield it, till her time
To tell you'' and her beauty, grace and power,
Wrought as a charm upon them, and they spared
To ask it.

Even in her sinful state Guinevere's ''beauty, grace and power'' have a
profound effect on those around her; in the same way the seemingly
miraculous power of Enid's beauty had such effect on the evil figures
who confronted her.

Tennyson's creation of a childlike and innocent novice as Guinevere's sole companion serves to bring the Queen's true nature into
sharper focus. By preventing the Queen from forgetting even momentarily the confusion she has brought to the Round Table, the novice
becomes a scourge; her incessant talk becomes a form of further mortifi-
cation for an already contrite woman. The world of Almesbury, represented by the novice, is a world of half-truth which contrasts with the
more complex consciousness of the Queen. At Almesbury ''they talk . . .
about the good King and his wicked Queen,'' but such a simplification
ignores the complexity of the relationship Tennyson creates. Guinevere
is guilty by her own admission, yet her sin, as she alone realizes, is more
complex than the novice can ever imagine. The novice tells Guinevere:

But let my words, the words of one so small,
Who knowing nothing knows but to obey,
And if I do not there is penance given—
Comfort your sorrows; for they do not flow
From evil done; right sure am I of that,
Who see your tender grace and stateliness.

Her advice recalls the behaviour of the patient Enid, the obedience of a
laudable but simple girl like the novice. Guinevere, however, is a complex woman; she is aware of the powers of good and evil that exist within
her own being. She answers the novice: ''O closed about by narrowing
nunnery-walls, / What knowest thou of the world, and all its lights / And
shadows, all the wealth and all the woe?'' Tennyson's Queen is conscious of the complexity of human life, of ''all its lights / And shadows.''

The novice's long discussion of the world of Camelot prior to
Guinevere's arrival places the Queen in the role of Eve; Camelot becomes a world of pristine innocence, of pre-lapsarian perfection, a world
destroyed by ''the coming of the sinful Queen.'' If the discussion makes
Guinevere realize more painfully the world her sin has threatened, the
novice's account of the bardic version of Arthur's origin must make her
more conscious of the man to whom she is married. In a most important

departure from Malory, Tennyson ignores the human origin of Arthur
and offers a new account:

> For there was no man knew from whence he came;
> But after tempest, when the long wave broke
> All down the thundering shores of Bude and Boss,
> There came a day as still as heaven, and then
> They found a naked child upon the sands
> Of wild Dundagil by the Cornish sea;
> And that was Arthur; and they foster'd him
> Till he by miracle was approven king.[29]

Malory's King has become more than a king; he is a saviour, not merely
a human saviour, but a saviour "well-nigh more than man." Arthur is a
mystical figure of almost divine proportions, a fact that must intensify
the complexity of Guinevere's relationship with him.

Before Arthur's arrival at Almesbury, Tennyson creates a full
character in the Queen, a woman obsessed by awareness of her guilt but
also conscious of the complexity of her sin and of the circumstances that
accompanied it. She is repentant:

> But help me, heaven, for surely I repent.
> For what is true repentance but in thought—
> Not ev'n in inmost thought to think again
> The sins that made the past so pleasant to us:
> And I have sworn never to see him more,
> To see him more.

Yet when she is alone, her thoughts turn back unwillingly to those
"golden days" when she first met Lancelot, Arthur's ambassador, a
scene already described by Merlin in *Vivien*. If Arthur's golden world
was Camelot before Guinevere's arrival, her golden world was the
Maytime before her introduction to Arthur. She entered Camelot as a
reluctant woman, disappointed at the sight of a King whom she found
"cold, / High, self-contain'd, and passionless." This description of
Arthur does not necessarily contradict the novice's mystical portrait,
but it does add a new characterization which reflects both the nature of
Arthur and the nature of the Queen who thought him such a man.

Arthur's climactic appearance is the fullest and most direct presentation of the King in Tennyson's poetry. In the *Morte d'Arthur* Tennyson depicts a dying King uttering words of wisdom to his lone companion; his dependence upon Malory and his uncertainty about the proper
treatment of Arthurian material do not allow him to move inside what
remains a distinguished but one-sided portrait of the King. In *Enid*

29   In Malory, Uther's love for the married Igrayne is aided by Merlin, who devises the
      secret union of Igrayne and Uther; the consequence of the union is Arthur, who grows
      up under the guidance of his foster-father, Sir Ector.

Arthur's address to Geraint, a eulogy on Edyrn's conversion, reveals a youthful monarch about to complete the establishment of order throughout his realm; there is even a degree of humility in his opening comment:

> Prince, when of late you pray'd me for my leave
> To move to your own land, and there defend
> Your marches, I was prick'd with some reproof,
> As one that let foul wrong stagnate and be,
> By having look'd too much thro' alien eyes,
> And wrought too long with delegated hands,
> Not used mine own.

Humility is absent from Arthur when he confronts his Queen at Almesbury. In this developed portrait of a strong King, a portrait created through his own words, Arthur becomes an agent of the divine will; his mission is to bring order out of chaos, to raise a base world to its proper height; he seeks to make this earth a paradise, a perfect realm where the animal nature of man is in total obedience to the higher faculty of the intellect; ultimately, Arthur sees himself less as an agent of the divine than as the divine force itself. Consequently, the oath he makes his knights swear is an oath of allegiance to their King, not to their King as a representative of God:

> I made them lay their hands in mine and swear
> To reverence the King, as if he were
> Their conscience, and their conscience as their King,
> To break the heathen and uphold the Christ,
> To ride abroad redressing human wrongs,
> To speak no slander, no, nor listen to it,[30]
> To lead sweet lives in purest chastity,
> To love one maiden only, cleave to her,
> And worship her by years of noble deeds,
> Until they won her; for indeed I knew
> Of no more subtle master under heaven
> Than is the maiden passion for a maid,
> Not only to keep down the base in man,
> But teach high thought, and amiable words
> And courtliness, and the desire of fame,
> And love of truth, and all that makes a man.

Malory has the oath emphasize the obligations of the knights to the outside world:

then king Arthur established all his knights, and gave them lands, that were not rich of land, and charged them never to do outrage nor murder, and always to flee treason; also by no means to be cruel, but to give mercy unto him that asked mercy, upon pain of forfeiture of their worship and lordship of king Arthur for

---

30 When Tennyson tried to bring out more effectively the human side of Arthur's character in the 1873 edition, he added after this line the following attempt to humanize the King: "To honour his own word as if his God's."

evermore; and always to do ladies, damsels, and gentlewomen, succour, upon pain of death: also that no man take no battles in a wrong quarrel for no law, nor for worldly goods. Unto this were all the knights sworn of the round table, both old and young; and every year they were sworn at the high feast of Pentecost [I, lix].

This oath, which arises out of the senseless fighting and the wars that precede it, establishes modes of behaviour that will act as a proper guide for future conduct. The emphasis falls on the noble and gracious courtesy of each knight to other human beings. In Tennyson's oath, however, the emphasis falls on the role of the King, whose very person is the cause of the new Order; the oath is the creation of a being who demands and merits reverence to the degree that the individual conscience should be identical with the conscience of the King. Far from being the objective code of Malory's oath, it is highly personal, the creation of a new world according to the designs of one being.

In addition, unlike the medieval version, the oath pays special attention to the role of the passions, which become a cause of evil in man. The "base," that indefinable region which seems to contain the specifically human area that aligns man to the beast, is the evil that must be subordinated if man is to realize the highest calling of his nature. Arthur's oath is a deliberate attempt to turn man's mind upward to the realm of the intellect and thereby to subjugate man's sensuality.

The quality of the oath colours Arthur's relationship with Guinevere. Though he wanted his wife to be "a helpmate, one to feel / My purpose and rejoicing in my joy," his treatment of Guinevere is as proud, as egocentric, and as necessarily strict as his treatment of his knights. Her sin is not her betrayal of their marriage through infidelity; her sin is her betrayal of his vision; she has "spoilt the purpose of my life." From Guinevere Arthur demanded a dedicated obedience similar to his own strict adherence to the pursuit of his mission. Her sin, grounded in sensuality, is a denial of the higher calling within man; consequently, her adultery brings about the destruction of Camelot.

Arthur's behaviour would seem to indicate that Guinevere is correct in her estimation of his "passionless" nature; his own words, however, contradict such a conclusion: "For think not, tho' thou would'st not love thy lord, / Thy lord has wholly lost his love for thee. / I am not made of so slight elements." Arthur has risen above the flesh and subordinated it to the higher and nobler end of man. His defeat rests in his failure to find a woman capable of sharing this exalted commitment. In their final confrontation Arthur still fails to reach a level of true communication with his wife; assuming the role of a divine force he pardons her: "And all is past, the sin is sinn'd, and I, / Lo! I forgive thee, as Eternal God / Forgives: do thou for thine own soul the rest." Arthur remains the divine agent whose mission is to bring the fallible world to a level of paradisal perfection. His mission is thwarted by his wife's sin; he understands her failing but cannot realize the complexity of her nature.

More fully than her husband Guinevere comes to realize the depth of her failing; she is more aware of human frailty; in the past she

> Would not look up, or half-despised the height
> To which I would not or I could not climb—
> I thought I could not breathe in that fine air
> That pure severity of perfect light—
> I wanted warmth and colour which I found
> In Lancelot.

Guinevere is a human being, a woman of soul and sense, a person either frightened or unable to reach "that fine air" inhabited by the higher being of her husband. Her sin and her repentance have brought her to a sudden new understanding: "'now I see thee what thou art, / Thou art the highest and most human too, / Not Lancelot, nor another." Experience brings her to a realization of her sin and to an acceptance of the proper path she should have chosen:

> Ah my God,
> What might I not have made of thy fair world,
> Had I but loved thy highest creature here?
> It was my duty to have loved the highest:
> It surely was my profit had I known:
> It would have been my pleasure had I seen.
> We needs must love the highest when we see it,
> Not Lancelot, nor another.

Arthur is the highest human being, the worthy centre of Guinevere's love and obedience. Her sensuality asserted itself to the degree that she failed to see her proper mode of existence; the "warmth and colour" offered by Lancelot blinded her to the higher calling, which, if she had accepted it, would have become, not a mere duty, but a true pleasure. By subjugating her base desires and controlling her passions, she would have realized "the highest and most human" capability of her own being. Her sin is the failure of mortals to realize the full capacity of their humanity.

Guinevere asserts a frail humanity in contrast to Arthur's seemingly cold dogmatism, yet her acceptance of his chastisement is a further indication of the rectitude of his position. Arthur's only failing is his necessarily limited understanding of the complexity of her sin. From his perfected position he looks down upon her and condemns her actions; she alone has the full perspective, since she is conscious of the two other positions struggling within her soul; not capable of the simplistic obedience of Enid, yet capable of having the same ennobling effect upon those around her, capable of basking in sensuality as Vivien does, but capable also of realizing its base and ignoble aspects, she stands in the centre of the world, a microcosm of the problems that confront human nature and an example of its folly and frailty.

In *Guinevere* Arthur, the ideal King, does not grow or change; the ultimate failure of his mission brings him no new insight. The only potential change in his character would come through the agency of his Queen; he can make an admission:

> and mine own flesh,
> Here looking down on thine polluted, cries
> "I loathe thee:" yet not less, O Guinevere,
> For I was ever virgin save for thee,
> My love thro' flesh hath wrought into my life
> So far, that my doom is, I love thee still.
> Let no man dream but that I love thee still.

Beyond this Arthur does not progress; he remains in his exalted realm where he is incapable of realizing fully the problems of man's fallen nature.

Arthur's appearance in the idyll focuses solely on his significance as the ideal ruler alerting mankind to the possibility of human perfection. In later idylls Tennyson will need to draw attention to the human aspect of "the highest." The depiction of Arthur at the end of his earthly mission in *Guinevere* needs to be augmented by a delineation of Arthur's humanity, yet the vivid presentation of the final meeting of Arthur and his Queen becomes a hindrance to the poet in any future attempt to focus in detail on the personal relationship of Arthur and Guinevere, the one element of Tennyson's Arthurian world that will never be adequately studied.

Unlike her husband Guinevere becomes a character of growth and development; from her human level she rises to a new understanding of the height to which a mortal may ascend. Her initial reaction to Arthur, "cold, / High, self-contain'd, and passionless," grows through her experience and her repentance to the degree that she proclaims with complete faith: "We needs must love the highest when we see it."

Guinevere is the idyll that asserts most clearly the unique Arthurian world Tennyson is creating out of his study of Malory and out of his own thematic interests. In the final meeting of Arthur and Guinevere, a scene not even suggested by Malory, Tennyson paints his conception of the King and Queen of Camelot. Arthur is now an almost divine force trying to lead mankind to the highest realization of its capability; his higher instincts properly dominate the lower instincts of his being. Guinevere is not Malory's vague figure of a queen; she is a passionate and intelligent woman conscious of the complexities of humanity and ultimately aware of the necessity of a proper response to the highest calling. Arthur's perfection prevents him from personal growth; Guinevere's fallen nature is portrayed in its arduous path of sin and in its subsequent realization of the necessity of pursuing the vision exemplified by her husband.

Vivien and *Enid* were only preludes to Tennyson's confrontation
with the figure of Guinevere; his achievement in this third idyll will lead
him to create his large study of Camelot along the pattern and the themes
this idyll suggests. In the future he will again return to Malory for further
plot and background material, but the basis of his Arthurian poetry will
be his own conception of the complexity of human nature which is most
forcefully expressed in this idyll.

Just as Guinevere is the centre of Tennyson's re-creation of the
medieval Arthurian world, so too her idyll is the centre of an understanding of his Arthurian world. Guinevere's sin, her rejection of Arthur's
vision, stands ominously behind the world of *Enid;* her adultery will
become the ultimate cause of the tragedy of the Grail quest; her sin will
drive Pelleas to madness and will offer Tristram and Isolt a warrant for
their adultery; the senseless behaviour of the knights in *Balin and Balan*
will stem from the Queen's faithlessness; only in *Gareth and Lynette*,
the springtime idyll in which the full glory of Arthur's vision is realized,
will the Queen have no role whatsoever. Tennyson's lifelong attempt to
depict the world of Camelot becomes a depiction of the tragedy that
ensues when mankind fails to "love the highest when we see it."

Elaine, the fourth member of the quartet of women whose names
furnish the titles of the 1859 idylls, allowed Tennyson to return to the
story of the Lady of Shalott and to re-create that episode in the light of
Malory's version. Though he often searched for proper subjects in
Malory that he could treat in the light of his conception of Camelot, the
plot of *Elaine* represented a ready vehicle, already employed in a different form in *The Lady of Shalott* and appropriate for its new position.[31]
Since *Vivien* and *Enid* were originally composed as a self-contained
pair, Tennyson may have believed that *Guinevere* required a
companion-piece to complete a quartet of idylls for subsequent publication.[32] The story of Elaine, the only maiden in Malory whose love for

31 Emily's journal recorded many of Tennyson's readings in Malory for possible additions to his Arthurian poem. The absence of any references to the Elaine story before
its composition and the absence of references to any other episodes under consideration at this time suggest that the poet was aware of the possibility of returning to this
particular story. His awareness may have been influenced by Woolner's note to Emily
of June 7, 1858: "I most earnestly wish you could persuade him to do the Maid of
Astolat, not only for the extreme beauty of the subject, but for the sake of introducing
much of Sir Lancelot, he being a character of such terrible importance to the 'Guenevere' poem, and the immense suggestions arising from the poor lady's death" (Amy
Woolner, *Thomas Woolner R. A. Sculptor and Poet: His Life in Letters* [London:
Chapman and Hall, 1917], p. 149). Tennyson began to write the idyll in July, 1858
(*Memoir,* I, 427-428).
32 Edward Lushington wrote to Tennyson about the first pair of idylls: "My tenderness
for your fame will not let me be silent when I fear anything that may cast a shade upon
it, and few things can be more certain to me than that these two poems, coming out
by themselves, would not receive their due of admiration. It would be quite different if
they were, as I hope they will be, supported by others of varied matter and interest,
giving more completeness and beauty of circular grouping and relation. Such a work I

Lancelot is described in detail, became an excellent companion to the idyll that depicted the passion of Guinevere for Lancelot and its ultimate consequence.

In addition, a full treatment of the story of Elaine allowed Tennyson to develop the figure of Lancelot, who remained an indistinct and colourless character in *Guinevere*.[33] In that idyll Lancelot had no existence apart from his role as Guinevere's lover; he lacked the personal strength of character he displayed in Malory. When the medieval Lancelot expressed concern about the shame of their adultery, a petulant and childish Guinevere dismissed his wise comments as the babbling lies of a false knight.[34] Tennyson, however, deprived Lancelot of this degree of selfless consideration in order to focus on Guinevere as the wiser and more perceptive member of the adulterous union. In *Guinevere* it was the Queen who continually feared disclosure and who sought the necessary termination of their relationship. A re-creation of the Elaine story offered Tennyson the occasion to do justice to the character of Lancelot.

The outline of the plot of *Elaine* is found in Malory. Tennyson's attitude to his source follows the pattern observed in the *Morte d'Arthur* and, in a more modified manner, in *Enid;* unlike *Vivien* and *Guinevere,* two highly original idylls, *Elaine* observes a close fidelity to the plot of the source. The fidelity, however, is often more apparent than real; Tennyson's increasing freedom with regard to source material, noted in the contrast between the marked fidelity of the *Morte d'Arthur* and the combination of fidelity and freedom in *Enid*, is further extended in this idyll. *Elaine* displays a free handling of plot material juxtaposed with a still prevalent desire to follow, however randomly, certain structural patterns and incidents of the source outline.[35] The consequence is that

want you to produce, and believe you can, which would surpass all you have written yet" (quoted by Henry Craik, "Tennyson and Lushington," in *Tennyson and His Friends,* edited by Hallam Lord Tennyson [London: Macmillan, 1911], p. 95). A note by F. T. Palgrave on the flyleaf of his copy of *Enid and Nimuë: The True and the False,* now in the British Museum, reads: "These two Idylls it was A. T.'s original intention to publish by themselves. Six copies were struck off, but owing to a remark upon *Nimue* which reached him, he at once recalled the copies out: giving me leave, however, to retain the present: which is, so far as I am aware, the single one remaining. From this change of purpose & delay grew the idea of publishing *four* as 'Idylls of the King': a felicitous accident for English literature!"

33   If Tennyson had decided to return to the Elaine story before the composition of *Guinevere,* he may have deliberately refrained from developing Lancelot in that idyll in order to develop him fully in *Elaine*.

34   For an example of such an attitude, see Malory's account of the poisoned apple episode which opens with such a verbal exchange between Guinevere and Lancelot.

35   As in *Enid,* where Tennyson incorporates details from his knowledge of other Arthurian works, he adds material here from his other readings. Lancelot's long enumeration of the wars he fought with Arthur is a close paraphrase of Nennius' account of Arthur's twelve major battles; Nennius' *History of the Britons* is also in Giles' *Six Old English Chronicles*.

Elaine is a creation of alternating freedom and fidelity, of moments zealously borrowed from Malory and moments invented by the poet. Following the pattern established in the three earlier idylls, Tennyson begins *Elaine* in the middle of the story; the solitary figure of Elaine is guarding Lancelot's shield. The events that form the background to the scene become the substance of the first half of the poem; the major episode is the tournament that sends Lancelot away from Camelot and its Queen. In Tennyson's invented episode of the diamonds and their history, love of Guinevere is Lancelot's inspiration in the tournament. This departure from the source leads immediately to a close commitment to the source in the description of the Queen's sickness; as in Malory, Guinevere cannot attend the tournament; her sickness prompts Lancelot to feign suffering from an ancient wound in order to stay with her.[36] Arthur's departure for the tournament introduces a scene present in both the medieval and the Victorian accounts:

So, when the king was departed, the queen called sir Launcelot unto her and thus she said, "Sir Launcelot, ye are greatly to blame, thus to hold you behind my lord; what trow ye what your enemies and mine will say and deem? nought else but see how sir Launcelot holdeth him ever behind the king, and so doth the queen, for that they would have their pleasure together, and thus will they say," said the queen unto sir Launcelot, "have ye no doubt thereof."

"Madam," said sir Launcelot to the queen, "I allow your wit, it is of late come sith ye were wise" [III, cxii-cxiii].

No sooner gone than suddenly she began.
　　　"To blame, my lord Sir Lancelot, much to blame.
Why go you not to these fair jousts? the knights
Are half of them our enemies, and the crowd
Will murmur, lo the shameless ones, who take
Their pastime now the trustful King is gone!"

Then Lancelot vext at having lied in vain:
"Are you so wise? you were not once so wise,
My Queen, that summer, when you loved me first."

At this juncture Tennyson again departs from his source and extends the scene in order to continue and complete the characterization of Guinevere which began in her idyll. Lancelot's upbraiding remarks force the Queen's response:

Arthur, my lord, Arthur, the faultless King,
That passionate perfection, my good lord—
But who can gaze upon the Sun in heaven?
He never spake word of reproach to me,
He never had a glimpse of mine untruth,

36　Malory comments on the Queen's sickness: "So king Arthur made him ready to depart to these jousts and would have had the queen with him, but at that time she would not go she said, for she was sick, and might not ride at that time" (III, cxii). Tennyson removes any possible ambiguity and makes her sickness wholly feigned.

He cares not for me: only here to-day
There gleam'd a vague suspicion in his eyes:
Some meddling rogue has tamper'd with him—else
Rapt in this fancy of his Table Round,
And swearing men to vows impossible,
To make them like himself: but, friend, to me
He is all fault who hath no fault at all:
For who loves me must have a touch of earth;
The low sun makes the colour: I am yours,
Not Arthur's, as you know, save by the bond.

Here is the intermediate stage of Guinevere's personal development, before her realization that "we needs must love the highest when we see it," yet after her initial reaction to Arthur's "passionless" nature. At this moment Guinevere sees the passion within her husband directed towards his mission, the establishment of a perfect Order; she needs that "warmth and colour" which she mentions during her repentance. The portrait of the Queen is now complete; having seen her as a repentant woman and having heard her own description of her innocent childhood before she came to Camelot, we now see a woman trapped in the consequences of her sin; afraid only of those "vermin voices" spreading tales about her adultery, she has yet to realize that the potency of such voices will awaken a conscience momentarily silenced by the intensity of her love for Lancelot.

The opening section of the idyll is less a beginning to the Elaine story than the completion of Tennyson's study of Guinevere. Satisfied with his presentation of the Queen, Tennyson turns back to Malory to begin his account of Lancelot and Elaine. He describes Lancelot's decision to enter the tournament under an assumed disguise, but he alters the original story by making Guinevere the instigator of the disguise; as in her own idyll Guinevere assumes control in their relationship.

Lancelot's arrival at Astolat introduces a further change into the poetic account. Unlike Malory, who has Arthur and his knights stay in the town, Tennyson sends Lancelot alone into the unknown world of the castle. The extended treatment of his stay finds more details that have been altered from the source. An "old, dumb, myriad-wrinkled man," Tennyson's expansion of the minor figure in Malory who drives Elaine down the Thames to Camelot, is a vivid reminder of the heathen world that existed "till our good Arthur broke / The Pagan yet once more on Badon hill." The Baron's sons, Torre and Lavaine, correspond to their counterparts in Malory, Tirry and Lavayne, but both characters are given strokes of individuality absent in the source; Torre is a man of moody behaviour, and Lavaine's close affection for his sister Elaine is developed at length; in addition, Lavaine accompanies Lancelot of his own volition, not at the behest of his father.

The scene at Astolat is Tennyson's attempt to develop the initial motivation of Elaine's love for Lancelot. Malory dismisses the scene with brevity:

This old baron had a daughter at that time, that was called the fair maid of Astolat, and ever she beheld sir Launcelot wonderfully; and she cast such a love unto sir Launcelot, that she could not withdraw her love, wherefore she died; and her name was Elaine la Blaunch [III, cxiii].

Tennyson develops the reasons for Elaine's infatuation, and such reasons, in turn, develop the character of Lancelot. In his depiction of Elaine's rapture over Lancelot's manners and appearance, Tennyson dramatizes the implications of Guinevere's statement to the novice: "For manners are not idle, but the fruit / Of loyal nature, and of noble mind." Lancelot's arrival at Astolat supports the Queen's comment: "Marr'd as he was, he seem'd the goodliest man, / That ever among ladies ate in Hall, / And noblest." Lancelot is the knight whose nobility stands second only to Arthur's; his personal warmth, which so captured the Queen's affection that her frail nature could not withstand his charm, exhibits itself clearly in his evening at Astolat. Tennyson, however, introduces a new and significant element into the portrait of Lancelot; the renowned knight is, indeed, marred: "The great and guilty love he bare the Queen, / In battle with the love he bare his lord, / Had marr'd his face." Lancelot is already a guilt-ridden figure similar to the Guinevere presented in the early section of her idyll. Like the Queen he is a being at war with himself; plagued by divided loyalties he is conscious of the agony his sin has caused, even before he fully realizes the evil of his action. As in his depiction of Guinevere, Tennyson never presents Lancelot as a being at peace with himself; again, he introduces the character when he is already suffering under the consequences of his behaviour.[37]

Employing the technique of condensation already used in *Enid*, Tennyson unites the home of the rich burgess where the two knights stay before the tournament and the hermit's home where they retire after Lancelot's defeat. The tightening is accompanied by the omission of many details from the source about the combat; only two knights, Lancelot and Lavaine, are named. Tennyson ignores the catalogue of knights and their adventures found in Malory in order to focus on the protagonist and his companion.

Lancelot's defeat in the tournament heralds the poet's return to a close fidelity to his source:

37 In "Tennyson and W. G. Ward and Other Farringford Friends," Wilfrid Ward wrote: "I recall her [Julia Cameron] bringing Tennyson to my father's house while she was photographing representatives for the characters in the 'Idylls of the King,' and calling out directly she saw Cardinal Vaughan (to whom she was a perfect stranger), 'Alfred, I have found Sir Lancelot.' Tennyson's reply was, 'I want a face well worn with evil passion' " (*Tennyson and His Friends*, pp. 231-232).

And therewith he groaned piteously, and rode a great gallop away from them, until he came under a wood's side; and when he saw he was from the field nigh a mile, that he was sure he might not be seen, then he said, with a high voice, "O gentle knight, sir Lavaine, help me, that this truncheon were out of my side, for it sticketh so sore, that it almost slayeth me." "O, mine own lord," said sir Lavaine, "I would fain help you, but it dreads me sore; and I draw out the truncheon, that he shall be in peril of death."—"I charge you," said Sir Lancelot, "as ye love me, draw it out." And therewith he descended from his horse, and so did sir Lavaine; and forthwith sir Lavaine drew the truncheon out of his side: and sir Lancelot gave a great shriek, and a marvellous ghastly groan, and his blood burst out nigh a pint at once, that at the last he sunk down upon his buttocks and swooned, pale and deadly [III, cxvi].

He spoke, and vanish'd suddenly
        from the field
With young Lavaine into the poplar
        grove.
There from his charger down he slid,
        and sat,
Gasping to Sir Lavaine, "draw the
        lance-head:"
"Ah my sweet lord Sir Lancelot,"
        said Lavaine,
"I dread me, if I draw it, you will
        die."
But he "I die already with it: draw—
Draw"—and Lavaine drew, and that
        other gave
A marvellous great shriek and
        ghastly groan,
And half his blood burst forth, and
        down he sank
For the pure pain, and wholly
        swoon'd away.

The similarity of the accounts shows that Tennyson did create his idyll with the text of Malory before him, yet at the same time he felt no pressure to observe the degree of indebtedness displayed in his *Morte d'Arthur*. Almost heedless of his source, he condenses, adds, and eliminates; at the same time he readily retains details from his source, details for a sentence or details for an incident. In this way Tennyson observes a seeming fidelity and justice to Malory while he simultaneously creates his own Arthurian world.

The remainder of the poem follows the outline of Malory's story, though changes already noted must alter the significance of certain subsequent events. Arthur's ignorance of Lancelot's identity adds suspense and tension; Gawain's mission to deliver the diamond becomes a search, not only for the knight, but also for the identity of the knight.[38] Thus the role of Guinevere receives added importance, since she is the source of the truth about Lancelot's disguise. As originator of the

38 This is Gawain's first appearance in Tennyson's Arthurian poetry; his subsequent appearances create a completely unflattering portrait. Tennyson's decision to paint a bad character for Gawain may have been instrumental in his decision to sever the connection between Bellicent (Gawain's mother) and Arthur. For a history of Gawain in English literature, see B. J. Whiting, "Gawain: His Reputation, His Courtesy, and His Appearance in Chaucer's 'Squire's Tale,' " *Mediaeval Studies*, 9(1947), 189-234.

disguise plot she is the ultimate cause of the severe wounds which Lancelot's kin inflict upon him.

Elaine continues to follow the structural pattern of Malory's account as Tennyson continues to shift between moments of source fidelity and moments of originality. Elaine's appearance at Winchester reveals further fidelity to Malory:

So as the fair maid Elaine came to
Winchester, she sought there all
about, and by fortune sir Lavaine
was ridden to play him and to
enchase his horse. And anon as
Elaine saw him, she knew him, and
then she cried aloud unto him: and
when he heard her, anon he came
unto her, and then she asked her
brother, "How fareth my lord, sir
Launcelot?"—"Who told you,
sister, that my lord's name was Sir
Lancelot!" [III, cxix].

and before the city-gates
Came on her brother with a happy
 face
Making a roan horse caper and
 curvet
For pleasure all about a field of
 flowers:
Whom when she saw, "Lavaine,"
 she cried, "Lavaine,
How fares my lord Sir Lancelot?"
He amazed,
"Torre and Elaine! why here? Sir
 Lancelot!
How know you my lord's name is
 Lancelot?"

The moment of resemblance leads to another moment of originality where the poet abridges and tightens the subsequent events of Malory's plot. In Malory, Lancelot is wounded by Sir Bors, his trusted friend; Bors is eliminated from the poetic account so that his reappearance here is unnecessary; though Bors did add a touch of pathos in his loyalty to Lancelot and in his sorrow on learning of the disguised knight's identity, the elimination of his character allows further concentration on Elaine and Lancelot. As in his treatment of the *Mabinogion* Tennyson handles his source so as to centre his attention on the title figure and her beloved. Moreover, though she performs the ministerial healing as she did in Malory, Elaine now becomes the prime, indeed almost sole agent in Lancelot's recovery: "her fine care had saved his life."

Tennyson's enlargement of the character of Elaine through his concentration upon her role necessitates his alteration of her final encounter with Lancelot. Whereas Malory's Elaine openly tells Lancelot, "I would have you unto my husband" (III, cxxiii), the Victorian Elaine, a more reticent and demure maiden, is too frightened to avow openly her love. At the same time the poet makes Lancelot more courteous and noble; he prolongs Lancelot's departure for Camelot: "And Lancelot saw that she withheld her wish, / And bode among them yet a little space /

Till he should learn it." Lancelot's courtesy is emphasized again by the rebuke Elaine's father gives him: "Too courteous are you, fair Lord Lancelot. / I pray you, use some rough discourtesy / To blunt or break her passion." Lancelot's one discourteous act, his deliberate failure to wave good-bye, is the direct result of this request.

Tennyson's alteration of the departure scene precedes another moment of fidelity; in Elaine's instructions to her father and brother regarding her funeral Tennyson returns to a close adherence to his source:

And then she called her father, sir Bernard, and her brother sir Tirre; and heartily she prayed her father, that her brother might write a letter like as she would indite it. And so her father granted it her. And, when the letter was written, word by word, as she had devised, then she prayed her father that she might be watched until she were dead.

"And while my body is whole let this letter be put into my right hand, and my hand bound fast with the letter until that I be cold; and let me be put in a fair bed, with all the richest clothes that I have about me. And so let my bed, with all my rich clothes, be laid with me in a chariot to the next place whereas the Thames is; and there let me be put in a barge, and but one man with me, such as ye trust to steer me thither, and that my barge

So when the ghostly man
    had come and gone,
She with a face, bright as for sin
    forgiven,
Besought Lavaine to write as she
    devised
A letter, word for word; and when he
    ask'd
"Is it for Lancelot, is it for my dear
    lord?
Then will I bear it gladly;" she
    replied,
"For Lancelot and the Queen and all
    the world,
But I myself must bear it." Then he
    wrote
The letter she devised; which being
    writ
And folded, "O sweet father, tender
    and true,
Deny me not," she said—"you
    never yet
Denied my fancies—this, however
    strange,
My latest: lay the letter in my hand
A little ere I die, and close the hand
Upon it; I shall guard it even in death.
And when the heat is gone from out
    my heart,
Then take the little bed on which I
    died
For Lancelot's love, and deck it like
    the Queen's
For richness, and me also like the
    Queen
In all I have of rich, and lay me on it.
And let there be prepared a
    chariot-bier
To take me to the river, and a barge
Be ready on the river, clothed in
    black.

be covered with black samite over
and over. Thus, father, I beseech you
let be done.''

So her father granted her faithfully
that all this thing should be done like
as she had devised. Then her father
and her brother made great dole; for,
when this was done, anon she died
[III, cxxiii].

I go in state to court, to meet the
  Queen.
There surely I shall speak for mine
  own self,
And none of you can speak for me so
  well.
And therefore let our dumb old man
  alone
Go with me, he can steer and row,
  and he
Will guide me to that palace, to the
  doors.''
    She ceased: her father
promised; whereupon
She grew so cheerful that they
  deem'd her death
Was rather in the fantasy than the
  blood.
But ten slow mornings past, and on
  the eleventh
Her father laid the letter in her hand,
And closed the hand upon it, and she
  died.

In addition to the poet's habit of expanding his source through added description, the only important distinction between the two accounts is the prominence Tennyson gives to the position of the Queen. Like Enid, Elaine aspires to equal the Queen in richness and beauty, yet unlike Enid she never realizes the falsity of her impression of Guinevere. Her unreciprocated, indeed rejected love for Lancelot so blinds her that she refuses to recognize the truth about the Queen, even when her own father reveals it to her.

Tennyson's depiction of the ensuing confrontation between Lancelot and Guinevere at Camelot, expanded from the brief account in the source, is meant to form a parallel to their meeting at the beginning of the idyll. The Queen's petulant jealousy, revealed in her conversation with Sir Bors in Malory's account, is now more dramatic since it asserts itself in her meeting with Lancelot. Malory's jealous Queen is now a woman whose distraught emotional state has been caused by uncertainty about that one relationship which both sustains and destroys her. In the crisis Guinevere expresses the guilt that will bring her to repentance: ''I for you / This many a year have done despite and wrong / To one whom ever in my heart of hearts / I did acknowledge nobler.''

When the body of Elaine appears at Camelot, Tennyson significantly alters the group of knights who remove the maiden from her bier. Percivale and Galahad, the prominent figures in the Grail quest, replace Malory's trio of Kay, Braundiles, and Aggravayne. Such an alteration shows that Tennyson is already conscious of the Grail story that awaits his treatment.

Elaine's will shows one final moment of close adherence to the source:

Most noble knight, my lord, sir Launcelot du Lake, now that death hath made us two at debate for your love. I was your lover, that men called the Fair Maiden of Astolat; therefore unto all ladies I make my moan.

Yet for my soul that ye pray, and bury me at the least, and offer me my mass penny. This is my last request: and a clean maid I died, I take God to my witness. Pray for my soul, sir Launcelot, as thou art a knight peerless [III, cxxiv].

Most noble lord, Sir Lancelot of the
   Lake,
I, sometime call'd the maid of
   Astolat,
Come, for you left me taking no
   farewell,
Hither, to take my last farewell of
   you.
I loved you, and my love had no
   return,
And therefore my true love has been
   my death.
And therefore to our Lady
   Guinevere,
And to all other ladies, I make moan.
Pray for my soul, and yield me burial.
Pray for my soul thou too, Sir
   Lancelot,
As thou art a knight peerless.

The major distinction is the additional reference to the Queen. Unlike Malory, Tennyson continually emphasizes her pre-eminence among all the ladies of the court, a pre-eminence made tragic by her failure to live up to the demands of her position.

The idyll ends with the most significant addition to the source, the soliloquy of a mentally tormented Lancelot. Arising out of increased awareness of his plight, the soliloquy takes the place of the final confrontation between Lancelot and Guinevere, a scene Tennyson chose to leave out of his poem.[39] Lancelot's analysis of his situation, his remorse, and his desire for a change in his behaviour reflect a conscience disturbed by guilt, a conscience in a perturbed state of mind similar to the Queen's anxiety in the early section of her idyll. Malory's Lancelot, confronted by Guinevere's remorse for her petulant behaviour, answers: "but madam, ever I must suffer you, but what sorrow that I endure, ye take no force" (III, cxxiv). Tennyson's knight sees his

39   "I asked my father why he did not write an Idyll 'How Sir Lancelot came unto the hermitage, and how he took the habit unto him; how he went to Almesbury and found Queen Guinevere dead, whom they brought to Glastonbury; and how Sir Lancelot died a holy man'; and he answered, 'Because it could not be done better than by Malory.' My father loved his own great imaginative knight, the Lancelot of the *Idylls*" (Eversley edition, V, 486-487).

dilemma as "love's curse"; he begins an introspective study of the dilemma. Like his medieval counterpart Lancelot is the obedient servant of the Queen, her partner in adultery, and her slave in their passion; this aspect of his character, already seen in *Guinevere,* is now subordinate to his guilty remorse. The resulting conflict within his mind forms the basis of the portrait: "I needs must break / These bonds that so defame me: not without / She wills it: would I, if she will'd it? nay, / Who knows?" Like Guinevere, he is a character trapped by sin and aware of its consequences; like her, he sees the need for repentance and contrition; like her, he will die in a state of holiness. A complete depiction of his movement into repentance would lessen the power of Guinevere's similar movement which forms the basis of her idyll. Consequently, Tennyson contents himself with giving Lancelot the soliloquy as a foreshadowing of his future.

In *Elaine* Lancelot achieves a personality and depth of character equal to the depth of character Guinevere achieves in her idyll. No longer the wooden figure of *Guinevere,* he is a knight of striking appearance and manners, a man of passion and love, a man guilty of sin, and, most importantly, a sinner whose conscience is asserting its moral awareness. The struggling conscience, which brought a new life to Malory's Guinevere, brings a similar life to Malory's Lancelot:

He [Lancelot] does both right and wrong, but a conflict precedes and either a calm of soul or a pang of conscience follows either. Malory occasionally sketched Lancelot in this manner, but never succeeded in making him so. Lancelot loves the Queen here just as truly and intensely as in Malory, but he realizes that his love is sinful and he struggles against it, vainly, it is true, but sincerely and remorsefully none the less.[40]

Although Elaine is less important in her own being than in her ability to reveal Lancelot's character, she is a member of the female quartet; at the same time, however, she resists any categorization in relation to the other women. She is initially described as "Elaine, the fair," an epithet which has been carefully applied to Enid, yet she never follows Enid's progression from "Fair" to "Good," even though her innocence would seem to align her with Enid. Elaine's unrequited love leads to her self-destruction. Elaine stands in contrast to Guinevere, who also loves Lancelot; she lacks the Queen's sensuality and nobility, though her appearance in death, a "Fairy Queen," gives her a final dignity appropriate to a queen. Moreover, the contrast to Guinevere is ironically strengthened by her attitude towards Lancelot, which should have been adopted by Guinevere in her relationship with her husband. Elaine worships Lancelot above the King:

40 A. J. App, *Lancelot in English Literature* (Washington: Catholic University of America Press, 1929), p. 168.

"Yet in this heathen war the fire of God
Fills him: I never saw his like: there lives
No greater leader."
                    While he [Lancelot] utter'd this,
Low to her own heart said the lily maid
"Save your great self, fair lord."

Elaine fails to perceive that she is offering the Queen's lover the form of
reverence the Queen herself has failed to offer Arthur.

Elaine cannot occupy any simple category in relation to the female
trio. She is a complex composite of the qualities and attitudes of the
other women; she exists to clarify them, and each woman becomes an
individual study developed and heightened by reflections generated by
the others.

As a complete work *Elaine* does remain faithful to Malory's story,
but the fidelity, often close indeed, is continually undercut by the new
motivations and character studies added by Tennyson. Unlike *Guinevere, Elaine* is not a work of complete originality; its originality lies in the
shades of meaning superimposed upon a seemingly parallel treatment of
Malory's story. Undoubtedly Tennyson wanted to employ his source
with sincere fidelity; the moments of adherence suggest his hesitancy to
distance himself from a source when the plot is not of his own invention;
each moment of fidelity, however, is separated by periods of expanded
treatment, tightened structure, or invented scenes which present those
moments of fidelity in a new and often unmedieval light.

Elaine is a realized character who exists to show the destructive
power of the adultery, destructive both of her own being and of Lancelot's ability to overcome his sin. The power of a potentially great love
between Lancelot and the maid is destroyed by the Queen. Lancelot
himself admits the quality of the maid's love: "Ah simple heart and
sweet, / Ye loved me, damsel, surely with a love / Far tenderer than my
Queen's." The plight of Elaine, her foolishly misapplied affection, is
located in the general perspective of the court; her dilemma and her
subsequent death are causally related, however distantly, to Guinevere:

And peradventure had he seen her first
She might have made this and that other world
Another world for the sick man; but now
The shackles of an old love straiten'd him,
His honour rooted in dishonour stood,
And faith unfaithful kept him falsely true.

Elaine remains the victim of her unreciprocated love. By emphasizing
Lancelot's affection for the Queen as the reason for the absence of
reciprocation, Tennyson suggests that Elaine is also a victim of the
adultery that lies at the centre of Arthur's Order.

Elaine is a completion and a beginning. It shows the destructive
power of Guinevere's sin as it reaches out to a distant and innocent

human being. Guinevere's behaviour served as Vivien's vindication of her lustful activity, gave rise to rumours that motivated Geraint's suspicious jealousy, and became, for Arthur, the ultimate cause of the destruction of his realm. Now the sin leads to a girl's death. Guinevere is both an individual member of the female quartet and an ominous background to the other three idylls.

At the same time *Elaine* is a beginning. No longer focusing its primary attention on the title figure, the idyll takes a character from Malory and retells her story in the light of the particular world already created in preceding idylls. Malory furnished Tennyson with a world where he found a vehicle for his own ideas and ideals.

The quartet of idylls becomes the foundation of Tennyson's long-anticipated Arthurian poem. The original title of the volume, *The True and the False*, is changed to *Idylls of the King* to show that the poems form only a segment of a larger whole.[41] In addition, Tennyson places the phrase, "Flos Regum Arthurus," on the title-page to emphasize the importance of King Arthur to the world of the four idylls.[42]

The complete work will require many additions, but the work has begun. The 1859 volume marks the beginning of Tennyson's realization of his early dream to create an Arthurian masterpiece that will be an appropriate document for his own age. Malory, who offered the initial inspiration to the young poet, can now be freely employed to offer the impetus for more stories which develop further Tennyson's study of man's ceaseless but seemingly unsuccessful pursuit of the ideal.

41 In Tennyson's personal copy of the trial title-page of the volume (now in the University of Virginia Library), the title reads: *"The True and the False"*; underneath the title is printed *"Four Idylls of the King."* Tennyson has crossed out both the first title and the first word of the added sub-title.

42 The trial title-page shows that Tennyson originally intended to place the phrase, "God has not made, since Adam was, the man more perfect than Arthur," from the *Brut G. ab Arthur* on the title-page; he has crossed out the passage in favour of "Flos Regum Arthurus" from Joseph of Exeter. Both passages are quoted in Sharon Turner's *The History of the Anglo-Saxons* (London, 1836), I, 284. Tennyson would also be familiar with the Joseph of Exeter passage since the surviving fragment of the *Antiocheis* from which the phrase is taken is printed in its entirety in Thomas Warton's *History of English Poetry* (London, 1824), I, clxvi.

Chapter 3

1869: The Holy Grail

The Coming of Arthur, The Holy Grail,
Pelleas and Ettarre, The Passing of Arthur

> As to Macaulay's suggestion of the Sangreal, I doubt
> whether such a subject could be handled in these days,
> without incurring a charge of irreverence. It would be
> too much like playing with sacred things. The old writ-
> ers *believed* in the Sangreal.[1]

Even before the publication of the 1859 volume, Tennyson was studying other stories in Malory as possible episodes for his Arthurian poem.[2] A full decade passed, however, before he began another idyll. His hesitation was nurtured by an often paralyzing awareness of the grandeur and the power of the Arthurian world. In 1862 he wrote: "I have thought about it and arranged all the intervening 'Idylls,' but I dare not set to work for fear of a failure and time lost."[3] Though the story of Arthur and his realm remained the grand project of his poetic career, he feared that his own exalted conception might never find an adequate poetic realization. Even the proper closing to his plan caused anxiety; the *Morte d'Arthur* offered a natural conclusion, but he also sensed the beautiful propriety of the closing of *Guinevere:* "I could hardly light upon a finer

---

1 *Memoir*, I, 456-457.
2 In her journal Emily noted on May 24, 1859: "A.T. read the 1st Act of Macbeth and
   next night some of the Morte d'Arthur where Sir Lancelot behaves so courteously to
   Sir Palamedes, and where Arthur goes to see La belle Isoude (with a view to a poem on
   Tristram and Isolt)" (*Materials*, II, 218). On June 28, 1859 she noted: "A.T. read 'Sir
   Pelleas and Ettare' to Mrs. Cameron and myself (with a view to a new poem)"
   (*Materials*, II, 220). Early in 1861 he was reading Malory's account of the Gareth story
   with a view to a further episode (*Memoir*, I, 471).
3 *Memoir*, II, 126.

close than that ghost-like passing away of the King."[4] Once again the poet undertook another trip to Cornwall for further inspiration.[5] Such hesitation and anxiety indicate his fear that the ideal he set for himself would never be realized.

The poet's major fear, the reason for the delayed continuation of the *Idylls of the King*, was the story of the Holy Grail. Tennyson had already approached this subject in *Sir Galahad*, a comparatively light and energetic monologue; avoiding a confrontation with the meaning and significance of the Grail, *Sir Galahad* is a study of the committed nature of Galahad but avoids being a study of the nature of his particular commitment. In 1859 Tennyson said that he had made a poem on Lancelot's quest of the Grail: "in as good verses as I ever wrote, no, I did not write, I made it in my head, and it has now altogether slipt out of memory."[6] It is significant that this treatment of the Grail story focuses on Lancelot, a knight whose sin prevents his ultimate vision of the sacred vessel. Tennyson himself could not accept the medieval belief in the supernatural reality of the Grail; hence, as early as 1859, he imagined the Grail quest through the eyes of a knight who does not achieve the final vision.

Though Tennyson regarded the Grail quest as a necessary part of an Arthurian work, he did not know how to incorporate the episode into a modern poem. Immediately after the publication of the 1859 volume, he wrote to the Duke of Argyll to decline the suggestion that he take up the Grail as his next subject; he "shunned handling the subject, for fear that it might seem to some almost profane"; at that time, he confessed: "As to the *Sangreal*, as I gave up the subject so many long years ago I do not think that I shall resume it."[7] His refusal to incorporate the Grail episode reflects his desire to find a proper treatment of the subject.

The early sixties marked a major revival of interest in the Grail story.[8] F. J. Furnivall edited a two-volume edition of Henry Lovelich's fifteenth-century poem on the Grail with its French prose source printed

---

4 Ibid., II, 126.
5 Palgrave wrote: "Following the publication of the first four 'Idylls of the King' in 1859, when he was intending to write further Idylls, this was, perhaps, specially entitled to be named Tennyson's Arthurian journey" (*Memoir*, I, 461).
6 *Memoir*, I, 457.
7 Ibid., I, 459. The Duke of Argyll wrote: "By the bye Macaulay, when I last saw him, was in great hopes that you would pursue the subject, and particularly mentioned the Legend of the 'Sangreal' as one capable of being made much of in your hands, as also the latter days and death of Lancelot" (*Materials*, II, 236).
8 The late fifties had shown some interest in the Grail story, or, more accurately, in Galahad's quest. William Morris' two poems which employ Galahad as their central character, *Sir Galahad: A Christmas Mystery* and *The Chapel in Lyoness*, were published in 1858; in the same year *Arthur's Knights, an adventure from the Legend of the Sangrale*, a long anonymous poem in blank verse with a pastoral setting, was published.

beside it; he sent a copy of each volume to Tennyson. In the first volume, the editor commented:

Any one who does not find the "thing" "ful swete" can pass it by; enough for me to know that our great Victorian poet has glanced over these pages with interest; I trust he will accept them as a slight acknowledgement of the debt of gratitude all English-reading men now owe him, for the perfect words, and noble and beautiful thoughts, that are the delight of many a working-man in his workshop, as I well know, as well as of the Queen in her palace.[9]

More important was Furnivall's 1864 edition of the French prose *Queste del Saint Graal,* the long treatise that had served as Malory's source for his account of the Grail. In his preface the editor again referred to Tennyson:

Again, as to Arthur's relation to Guinevere, I cannot feel that the modern representation is the truest one. To any one knowing his Maleore,—knowing that Arthur's own sin was the cause of the breaking up of the Round Table, and Guinevere's the means only through which that cause worked itself out,— having felt Arthur's almost purposed refusal to see what was going on under his own eyes between his queen and Lancelot, so as to save a quarrel with his best knight till it was forced on him; having watched with what a sense of relief, as it were, Arthur waited for his wife to be burnt on her second accusal,—then, for one so primed to come on Mr. Tennyson's representation of the king, in perfect words, with tenderest pathos, rehearsing to his prostrate queen his own nobleness and her disgrace; the revulsion of feeling was too great; one was forced to say to the Flower of Kings, "if you really did this, you were the Pecksniff of the period." I quite admit that any one and especially Mr. Tennyson, (who is to me personally more than all the other English poets put together, save alone Chaucer,) has a right to take Arthur's nobleness from the early legend, and Guinevere's sin from the later one, and combine them together as he will, (and whatever he has done or may do with them the English world will be grateful;) but I desire to point out that the early legend, which says nothing of Arthur's sin, says nothing of Guinevere's sin with Lancelot either.[10]

An eminent authority on medieval literature, Furnivall accepted Tennyson's version of the Arthurian story; he perceived the alteration of Malory for the creation of two important patterns: the purification of Arthur's character and the increased importance of Guinevere's disloyalty to her husband. At the same time the publication of these two major

9 Henry Lovelich, *Seynt Graal, or the Sank Ryal: The History of the Holy Graal,* edited by F. J. Furnivall (London, 1861-1863), I, xii. The front flyleaf of the first volume of Tennyson's copy has the inscription: "To Alfred Tennyson from the Editor Oct. 31, 1861." The front flyleaf of the second volume has the inscription: "To Alfred Tennyson Esq. With the Editor's Homage Jan. 26, 1864." Both volumes are in the Tennyson Research Centre, Lincoln.

10 Walter Map, *La Queste del Saint Graal,* edited by F. J. Furnivall (London, 1864), pp. vi-vii. The front flyleaf of the poet's copy has the inscription: "Alfred Tennyson Esq. from the Editor Xmas, 1864." The volume is also in the Tennyson Research Centre. For further comments by Furnivall about Tennyson's Arthurian world, see his article, "Mr. Hutton and Tennyson's 'King Arthur,'" *Notes and Queries*, series four, 11 (1873), 3-4.

versions of the Grail quest failed to offer Tennyson any indication of a method of incorporating the story into his scheme.

Meanwhile, three other English poets were working on poetic treatments of the Grail story. In 1863 George MacDonald published *The Sangreal*, an account in six short sections of Galahad's successful quest and his death; though not a monologue, the poem is reminiscent of Tennyson's earlier poem in its emphasis on Galahad's momentary self-doubts.[11] In 1864, Tennyson's friend Hawker, the Vicar of Morwenstow, brought out *The Quest of the Sangraal*, which recounts the preparation and initial actions of four knights in search of the Grail: Tristan, Perceval, Galahad, and Lancelot of the Lay. Hawker's originality lies in his allotment of symbolic geographical designations to each knight: to Galahad, the east, "the Source and Spring of Life and Light"; to Tristan, the west, "the symbol and the Scene of populous Life . . . the Realm and Region of the Set of Sun"; to Lancelot, the north, "the Lair of Demons"; to Perceval, "the happy South: the Angels' Home." Despite his wide knowledge of Arthurian literature, Hawker created a poem that was less an Arthurian work than a heavy and rough paean to the rugged scenery of Cornwall.[12] In 1868 Thomas Westwood published *The Quest of the Sancgreall*, a six-part poem relating the vows, various legends about the Grail, and the vision achieved by Galahad, Perceval, and Bors.[13] The poet's prefatory statement, "The following Legends, with the exception of the 'Sword of Kingship,' in no wise pretend to be a close rendering of the Arthurian romance, to which I have only adhered intermittently, and when it suited my purpose," appropriately reflects the form of his work; the pentecostal setting and the legend of King Evelake take their inspiration from Malory; the carnal temptations suffered by Lancelot and his son Galahad are invented by the poet; the final scene at Sarras follows Malory with such fidelity that Galahad commands Bors to return to Camelot to find "Sir Lancelot, my sire, and in God's name / Bid him remember this unstable world." Westwood's poem may have been read by Tennyson, though it obviously exerted no influence, not only because of the poor quality of its verse, but also because of its treatment of Malory, which could offer no new thoughts to a poet still seeking a path into the world of the Grail.

In the year of the publication of Westwood's poem Tennyson did find the path he had been seeking:

Sept. 9th.   A. read me a bit of his "San Graal," which he has now begun.
Sept. 11th.   He read me more of the "San Graal": very fine . . .
Sept. 14th.   He has almost finished the "San Graal" in about a week (he had

11   "The Sangreal" first appeared in *Good Words*, 4 (June 1863), 454-455.
12   R. S. Hawker, *The Quest of the Sangraal* (Exeter, 1864).
13   Thomas Westwood, *The Quest of the Sancgreall, The Sword of the Kingship, and Other Poems* (London, 1868).

seen the subject clearly for some time). It came like a breath of inspiration. I was
pleased to think that the Queen and the Crown Princess wished him to write it.[14]

Emily's account indicates that the poet came upon a method which
would allow him to handle a subject for which he felt both reverence and
fear. The "breath of inspiration" asserts itself in the form of the idyll;
unlike its predecessors and its followers, the idyll is related, not by an
omniscient narrator, but by a character within the story. Moreover, this
character is not Galahad, the subject of his earlier poem, nor Lancelot,
the subject of the mentally prepared treatment of the Grail story, but
Percivale, an Arthurian character until now absent from Tennyson's
plans for an Arthurian work.

Percivale is both the path for Tennyson into his creation of the work
and the path for the reader into a proper understanding of the completed
poem. In the earliest versions of the Grail story Percivale is the successful quester; indeed, he is the original hero of the quest. In the later forms
of the story, exemplified by the *Queste del Saint Graal,* Galahad becomes the hero of the story, and Percivale is "little more than an extra
and slightly soiled Galahad."[15] Following this conception of Percivale,
Tennyson chooses Percivale rather than Galahad because of his hesitation to portray directly the highest form of manhood; his disinclination to
offer a direct portrait of Arthur leads to a similar disinclination with
regard to Galahad, an equally perfect and enlightened being. Moreover,
by making Percivale the poem's focus, he makes the failed quest the
poem's centre. Instead of emphasizing the glory of Galahad, the poem
emphasizes the ultimate folly of the quest. The entire story, with its
glory and its failings, is seen through the human eyes of the failing
Percivale.

Malory's account of the Grail quest[16] is a study of a higher calling for
the knights of the Round Table, a study of human worthiness to accept
the call of Christ and repudiate the ways of the world. Although one
hundred and fifty knights leave the court, only three attain the vision of
the Grail: Galahad, Percivale, and Bors. Malory's account focuses on

14 *Memoir,* II, 57.
15 Charles Moorman, " 'The Tale of the Sankgreall': Human Frailty," *Malory's Originality,* edited by R. M. Lumiansky (Baltimore: The Johns Hopkins Press, 1964), p. 197.
16 Though Tennyson owned the three-volume edition of Malory edited by Thomas
Wright (London, 1858), which he received as a gift from Julia Cameron in 1859 (the
title-pages of the first two volumes are inscribed: "Alfred Tennyson from Julia
Margaret Cameron Aug. 16th, 1859."—both volumes are now in the Tennyson Research Centre), he seemed to continue to employ the Walker and Edwards edition;
consequently, I shall continue to refer to this edition. Tennyson's familiarity with the
stories he would incorporate into his poem predates his acquisition of Wright; in
addition, the few marginal markings in his copy of Wright occur beside some of the
lines he borrows from Malory, especially in his early *Morte d'Arthur;* such markings
suggest that someone, not necessarily the poet, traced Tennyson's employment of
Malory by reading this edition.

the purity of these men, their worthiness for the quest, and their response to the gift of divine grace. At the same time Malory pays special attention to Lancelot as the sinful man incapable, however great his desire, of achieving the quest; Lancelot is the most worthy of the unworthy and he receives only a glimpse of the holy vessel, an intimation of the spiritual world that is closed to his impurity. At the end of their long search the chosen trio of knights reaches the spiritual city of Sarras; even this city cannot satisfy Galahad, whose prayer for death is answered. After Galahad's assumption into heaven, Bors and Percivale depart to a hermitage, where Percivale becomes a hermit; Bors remains there until Percivale's death, fourteen months later, whereupon he returns to Camelot.

Tennyson's poem employs Malory's account of the Grail quest as a resource rather than a source; it is indebted to Malory for the basic idea of the quest motif, for the account of the origin of the Grail, for the names of the characters, and for their practical relationship to each other; beyond these factors the indebtedness is, at best, negligible. *Guinevere*, the most original of the series, is the poet's creation; *Elaine*, an idyll whose strong degree of indebtedness is overlaid with moments of originality, is the poet's re-creation. *The Holy Grail* unites indebtedness with originality to create a new version of the Grail story, a quest specifically suited to the nineteenth century. Unlike *Vivien*, the idyll is not an attempt to use a particular Arthurian story in a special context; it must do justice to the reverent subject-matter, yet at the same time make that theme valid in an age which no longer accepts the religious outlook of the medieval period. *The Holy Grail* achieves a precarious balance; with inspiration derived from Malory, Tennyson eschews any necessary fidelity to the medieval account and creates his own version of the Grail quest. A contrast between Malory's account and Tennyson's version will not reveal any important causal connections, but it will set off more clearly the new form of quest that has arisen out of the poet's knowledge of Malory and his own freedom and security in regard to that knowledge.

The Holy Grail does not portray the quest for the Grail as much as it studies the various figures who respond to the Grail. Their responses are the subject-matter of the poem:

He pointed out the difference between the five visions of the Grail, as seen by the Holy Nun, Sir Galahad, Sir Percivale, Sir Lancelot, Sir Bors, according to their different, their own peculiar natures and circumstances, and the perfection or imperfection of their Christianity. He dwelt on the mystical treatment of every part of his subject, and said the key is to be found in a careful reading of Sir Percivale's vision and subsequent fall and nineteenth century temptations.[17]

Percivale's vision is the key to the poem; it is coloured, rarefied, and explained through its contrast with the four other quests. Each vision

17 *Memoir*, II, 63.

reflects upon the other visions, and the final commentary, anticipated by the consequences of the quests, is appropriately proclaimed by the King.

Adapting the pattern already employed in *Guinevere,* Tennyson creates the interrogating figure of Ambrosius, a monk cut off from the world by his religious environment. The dialogue between Percivale and Ambrosius centres at once on the importance of Percivale's sister, a nameless holy nun.[18] In Malory the Grail swept through the hall at Camelot; its fleeting presence motivated the knights' vows to make the quest. Tennyson, however, makes a woman the instigator of the quest. Thus, following the pattern of the earlier set of idylls, Tennyson has a woman as the initiator, if not the centre, of the poem. In the religious realm Percivale's sister offers the inspiration that Guinevere should offer in the realm of the court:

> So now the Holy Thing is here again
> Among us, brother, fast thou too and pray,
> And tell thy brother knights to fast and pray,
> That so perchance the vision may be seen
> By thee and those, and all the world be heal'd.[19]

Whereas her counterpart in Malory serves only to guide the three questers in the final stages of their journey, Tennyson's nun becomes the source of the entire action of the quest. Her movement into the ascetic life, occasioned by a human love "rudely blunted," leads her to forsake the world for the cloister. Accepting her special and restricted vocation, she advises Galahad alone to make a similar commitment. The knights, however, misunderstand her dedication; they regard her command "to fast and pray" as their calling to the ascetic life; her singular dedication to the Grail becomes a model for emulation. Tennyson's general comment is significant in this context: "Faith declines, religion in many turns from practical goodness to the quest after the supernatural and marvellous and selfish religious excitement. Few are those for whom the quest is a source of spiritual strength."[20] The tragic and unintended effect of the nun's active commitment to the Grail is the rash quest of the knights and the ultimate dissolution of the Round Table.

Tennyson connects the world of Guinevere's sin with the world of the nun's cell:

> And yet,
> Nun as she was, the scandal of the Court,

18   There is no correspondence between Malory's portrait of Percivale's sister and Tennyson's nun except the incident when she offers Galahad a belt fashioned of her hair. In Malory, however, this is one of the final actions of the quest immediately before the final vision; shortly after the episode, she dies.
19   All quotations from the four idylls under discussion in this chapter are from *The Holy Grail and Other Poems* (London: Strahan, 1870).
20   Eversley edition, V, 487.

> Sin against Arthur and the Table Round,
> And the strange sound of an adulterous race,
> Across the iron grating of her cell
> Beat, and she pray'd and fasted all the more.

Had it not been for this sin, the world Arthur envisioned would have been conducive to the reappearance of the Grail:

> And when King Arthur made
> His Table Round, and all men's hearts became
> Clean for a season, surely he had thought
> That now the Holy Grail would come again;
> But sin broke out.

Though the nun's vision motivates the action of the poem, the Queen realizes that the nun is only the efficient cause of the tragic quest; the ultimate cause is the Queen, who "wail'd and shriek'd aloud, / 'This madness has come on us for our sins.' "

The nun's sanctity and purity are paralleled in the spiritual perfection of Galahad, the only other character who sees the Grail and whose life must be a commitment to it. Galahad is the perfect spiritual knight, the man destined to sit in the Siege Perilous; he represents the highest calling of man in a spiritual dedication. Tennyson accepts such a capacity within Galahad and consequently limits his presence in the poem. The pure knight of Malory is now more elevated and isolated, with the result that his achieved quest teaches that "few are those for whom the quest is a source of spiritual strength."

Tennyson elevates Galahad by denying that Lancelot is Galahad's father. Just as he severs the connection between Arthur and Modred, which may tarnish the character or lineage of the King, so he shatters the traditional conception of Galahad's parentage:

> Sister or brother none had he; but some
> Call'd him a son of Lancelot, and some said
> Begotten by enchantment—chatterers they,
> Like birds of passage piping up and down,
> That gape for flies—we know not whence they come;
> For when was Lancelot wanderingly lewd?

Galahad becomes the spiritual equivalent of the more human Arthur. The distinction between the two men becomes the divine calling Galahad receives: "But I, Sir Arthur, saw the Holy Grail, / I saw the Holy Grail and heard a cry— / 'O Galahad, and O Galahad, follow me.' "[21] The fact that the vision never failed Galahad is further proof of the necessity of his commitment. Such a vision has one destination: "And hence I go; and one will crown me king / Far in the spiritual city."

---

21 Galahad is the only knight who addresses the King as "Sir Arthur"; the appellation is a further indication of the equality of Galahad and Arthur in their realization of their own spirituality.

Galahad becomes the king of the spiritual city, while Arthur attempts to create the spiritual city in his earthly sphere. Galahad is given the role that Arthur strives to realize in this world. Arthur can sympathize with his spirituality and he can accept Galahad's special commitment as certified by the vision he is given:

> "Ah, Galahad, Galahad," said the King, "for such
> As thou art is the vision, not for these.
> Thy holy nun and thou have seen a sign—
> Holier is none, my Percivale, than she—
> A sign to maim this Order which I made."

Only Galahad and Percivale's sister are summoned to the higher calling outside the earthly realm; by the folly of their quests the other knights show their own impurity, the necessity of their personal fulfillment within this world, and the sanctified but select road that awaits the chosen few who are summoned beyond this present existence.

Having established Galahad and Percivale's sister on the highest plateau of human purity and spiritual commitment, Tennyson focuses on Percivale. Malory's Percivale is an impure knight whose adventures and misconduct purify and prepare him for the final vision; he does achieve union with God through the Grail and ends his life, not by returning to Camelot, but by becoming a hermit. Tennyson violates Malory and Arthurian tradition by denying Percivale a complete vision; moreover, Percivale now returns to Camelot to relate the failure of his quest to an understanding and disappointed King. Thus the poet retains Percivale's pre-eminent stature, second only to Galahad; at the same time he denies him the fulfillment of the quest. The dual action in his presentation of Percivale suggests clearly Tennyson's particular treatment of the Grail story.

For Percivale the quest of the Grail becomes self-exploration. His desire to find the Grail is the rash, somewhat proud ambition of a naïve and innocent young knight. His enthusiasm blinds his reason to the continuing dictates of his conscience: "This Quest is not for thee." His journey is a series of impressionistic temptations which emphasize the isolation of the pure quester's journey. The pleasures of the senses, the delights of the home, the grandeur of wealth, and the influence of political power, all these earthly satisfactions do tempt Percivale; his eagerness to embrace them is always answered by their necessary disappearance and his lament, "And I was left alone." What distinguishes the quest of Percivale from Galahad's quest is the degree of their aloneness. To the worthy knight, the Grail, a vision given by God, is never absent; to the unworthy knight, a feeling of aloneness is always present. To Percivale, the vision is a sight to be reached; to Galahad, the vision is a sight to be re-attained in a permanent union. Percivale fails to realize that such a vision is a divine gift; his quest becomes an indication

of his presumption: "I knew / That I should light upon the Holy Grail."
Through the admonishment of a wise hermit Percivale learns the necessity of humility, and it is his growth in humility that permits him to
witness Galahad's transformation in a scene reminiscent of Arthur's
parting from the world: "And with exceeding swiftness ran the boat / If
boat it were—I saw not whence it came." Like Bedivere, Percivale is
stranded on this side of eternity and must commit himself to his own
environment. Though he has learned the lesson of humility, the newly
acquired virtue does not necessitate his union with the Grail. Still failing
to realize that the Grail is a divine gift, Percivale does not learn the
proper lesson from the vision that is denied to him.

    After Percivale recounts the particular vision he witnessed, Am-
brosius asks: "O brother, saving this Sir Galahad / Came ye on none but
phantoms in your quest, / No man, no woman?" Percivale's reply is an
account of his experience of human love: "The Princess of that castle
was the one, / Brother, and that one only, who had ever / Made my heart
leap." Unlike his sister who finds her human love "rudely blunted,"
Percivale is given a second opportunity for the fulfillment of his love.[22]
His true beloved, now a widowed princess, needs a husband for herself
and a lord for her kingdom; her people cry out: "Wed thou our Lady, and
rule over us, / And thou shalt be as Arthur in our land." Percivale is
summoned to the highest earthly commitment, to "be as Arthur" in this
realm; his refusal indicates the blindness that afflicts his being as a
consequence of his wrong commitment to the Grail. His partial glimpse
of the Grail prevents him from appreciating and accepting his proper role
within this world; his only desire is for the isolation of the cloister. Upon
returning to Camelot Percivale has a brief but telling interchange with his
King:

> So when I told him all thyself hast heard,
> Ambrosius, and my fresh but fixt resolve
> To pass away into the quiet life,
> He answer'd not, but, sharply turning, ask'd
> Of Gawain, "Gawain, was this Quest for thee?"

Arthur's silence and his abrupt movement are his moral verdict on
Percivale's behaviour; the Round Table has lost the presence of another
knight; Arthur will rightfully lament: "Another hath beheld it afar off, /
And leaving human wrongs to right themselves, / Cares but to pass into
the silent life."

22 The incident has no foundation in Malory. The account of Percivale's temptation (III,
    lvi-lvii), a possible source of Vivien's accusation to Merlin about Percivale, concerns
    his seduction by a disguised devil; in *The Holy Grail* Tennyson invents a story which
    recounts, not a temptation, but a calling to a true and valid earthly commitment. The
    episode does have a partial analogue in the role of Condwiramurs, Parzival's wife, in
    Wolfram's poem; Tennyson's familiarity with the German poem seems doubtful.

For Percivale the Grail quest is both beneficial and detrimental; it instills humility in him, yet it removes him from the practical affairs of this world. His new self-awareness lacks proper perspective; he becomes a victim of his own vision. As a victim he is basically a tragic hero. His capacity to "be as Arthur" is destroyed by his ultimately selfish "resolve / To pass away into the quiet life."

Tennyson's treatment of the Grail story is his study of "Percivale's vision and subsequent fall and nineteenth century temptations." The poem is Percivale's tragedy, his inability to adapt to his awareness of the limits of human capability. To brand Percivale "a vain, self-centered, irresponsible knight . . . guilty of the sin of pride"[23] is to overlook Arthur's comment: " '—and ye, / What are ye? Galahads?—no, nor Percivales' / (For thus it pleased the King to range me close / After Sir Galahad)." Though a still somewhat proud Percivale recounts Arthur's address, the passage does emphasize the high position Percivale merits. A knight second only to Galahad in spiritual perfection, he is the most worthy of those men who are denied the complete vision. By denying him the spiritual realm Malory opened to him, Tennyson makes Percivale a knight related to, but finally separated from, the world where Galahad must live. The offer of an earthly kingdom where "thou shalt be as Arthur" represents the highest achievement possible for Percivale; his refusal of the offer represents the tragic blindness of a knight who forsakes the world for a calling to which he was never summoned.

Percivale's limitations are made explicit by contrast with the successful quests of his own sister and Galahad; his spiritual strength is made explicit by contrast with the quests of Lancelot and Gawain. In Malory, Lancelot fulfills the role that Tennyson's Percivale holds; he is the most worthy of the questers who are denied the final vision; his sin prevents him from achieving his purpose and he becomes a contrast to the worthiness of the chosen trio of Galahad, Percivale, and Bors. Lancelot's partial glimpse of the vessel is a prelude to the complete vision achieved by the trio. Since the partial vision now belongs to Percivale in the poem, Tennyson reduces Lancelot's role to a long monologue delivered to the King, which elaborates his "remorseful pain," Lancelot's mental condition at the end of the previous idyll of *Elaine*.[24]

For his portrait of Lancelot Tennyson observes a small degree of fidelity to Malory; he overlooks the many adventures Lancelot has on his quest and he makes two episodes, his meeting with the hermit (III,

23 Clyde de L. Ryals, *From the Great Deep* (Athens, Ohio: Ohio University Press, 1967), p. 156.
24 Lancelot's role is abbreviated also because of Tennyson's denial of the traditional parentage of Galahad; this alteration makes Lancelot's role in the Grail story less important and removes the deep pathos that exists in Malory's account of the meeting of the father and the son during their quests.

xlviii) and his vision at the Castle of Carbonec (III, xcvi-xcvii), the basis of Lancelot's abbreviated account of his year-long search. Malory's long description of the hermit's examination of Lancelot and the knight's repentance becomes a simple statement about a past experience:

> Then I spake
> To one most holy saint, who wept and said,
> That save they could be pluck'd asunder, all
> My quest were but in vain; to whom I vow'd
> That I would work according as he will'd.

The scene at the Castle is also condensed; it must be less intense than Malory's account, since it lacks the dramatic preparation that Malory's longer presentation of Lancelot provided. In the poem Lancelot's partial glimpse of the Grail, based closely on a few selected details in the medieval version,[25] serves only to reveal the sin that is destroying the knight; his own narration of the incident lends pathos to the account and highlights his awareness of his human failing. Lancelot undertakes the quest so that the wholesome and the poisonous within him might be "pluck'd asunder"; he is doomed to defeat, since purity of soul is a condition, not a result, of a vision of the Grail. His partial glimpse, less satisfying than Percivale's incomplete vision, is both a reward for his repentance and an indication of his still sinful condition.

The lowest response to the Grail comes from Gawain, the least successful quester. In Malory, Gawain is more than an unsuccessful quester who resigns his mission very early; he is an earthbound knight whose vision is strictly and narrowly rooted in the material universe. The spiritual framework of the Grail story does not affect Gawain, who is placed firmly and blindly in the earthly realm of knightly adventures. Tennyson employs the unspiritual outlook of Malory's Gawain to develop further the depiction of Gawain he began in *Elaine;* Gawain's discourtesy, emphasized in the earlier idyll, now grows into frivolity and folly. Despite the fact that he swore his vow "louder than the rest," he forsakes the quest with ease and finds delight in "a silk pavilion in a field, / And merry maidens in it." Gawain the buffoon is also Gawain the religious skeptic in his address to Percivale:

> But as for thine, my good friend, Percivale,
> Thy holy nun and thou have driven men mad,
> Yea, made our mightiest madder than our least.
> But by mine eyes and by mine ears I swear,
> I will be deafer than the blue-eyed cat,
> And thrice as blind as any noonday owl,
> To holy virgins in their ecstacies,
> Henceforward.

25 The source is Malory, III, xcvi. Tennyson omits the concluding discussion of Lancelot's physical recovery during the following month at the Castle.

Arthur's response is a fitting summation of the Gawain created by the poet: "Deafer... Gawain, and blinder unto holy things / Hope not to make thyself by idle vows, / Being too blind to have desire to see." All the knights have varying degrees of success in their quests; each achieves according to his capability; Gawain stands at the lowest level, too blind to have even the desire to see.

The quartet of questers, Percivale, his sister, Galahad, and Lancelot, complemented by the negative frame of mind of Gawain, did not seem to satisfy the poet's conception of the Grail story. The prose draft of the idyll, contained in Harvard Notebook 38, reveals that the episode of Sir Bors was not part of the conception of the poem.[26] Though the inclusion of Bors does appear to be an afterthought, his presence has an important function in the series of contrasting quests. In Malory, Bors is spiritually lower than Galahad and Percivale so that he may return to Camelot and relate the adventures of the questers; since Tennyson has an expanded treatment of Percivale fulfill this function, Bors becomes unnecessary in Tennyson's original conception. The poet's later desire to incorporate him into the idyll reflects his intention to observe some fidelity to the chosen trio of Malory's successful questers; Bors's presence also evokes some of the pathos Malory achieves through the final meeting at court of Bors and Lancelot; most importantly, Bors completes the particular treatment of the Grail episode Tennyson is trying to create.

Galahad and Percivale's sister are summoned to the quest; Percivale and Lancelot act out of rashness and need; Bors is the only knight whose quest is prompted by selfless love:

> he well had been content
> Not to have seen, so Lancelot might have seen,
> The Holy Cup of healing; and, indeed,
> Being so clouded with his grief and love,
> Small heart was his after the Holy Quest:
> If God would send the vision, well: if not,
> The Quest and he were in the hands of heaven.

His quest leads to his imprisonment in a pagan land, an episode perhaps inspired by the harsh treatment Malory's trio receives upon their arrival in the still pagan city of Sarras. Bors's suffering is answered by the appearance of the Grail. The divine gift is bestowed upon the selfless knight. With true humility he returns to Camelot without the intention of forsaking Arthur's Order.

Bors is the ideal good knight. His selflessness makes him worthy of the vision of the Grail, and his humility prevents him from the personal presumption of expecting the vision. Arthur's belief that "if ever loyal man and true / Could see it, thou hast seen the Grail" is vindicated;

26 See Appendix 4.

loyalty and dedication to one's earthly commitment are answered. Bors's reaction to the gift is not Percivale's flight to the cloister, but pregnant silence and tears of humility.

Six varied responses to the Grail episode complete Tennyson's treatment of the quest. The final commentary must fall to the King, whose address to the knights sets the tone for the quest: "But one hath seen, and all the blind will see." Arthur's prophecy is correct; the quest does turn into "a sign to maim this Order which I made." His final address is the inevitable conclusion of the experience Percivale has recorded:

> And some among you held, that if the King
> Had seen the sight he would have sworn the vow:
> Not easily, seeing that the King must guard
> That which he rules, and is but as the hind
> To whom a space of land is given to plough,
> Who may not wander from the allotted field,
> Before his work be done.

The proper realm of man's activity is this earth; Arthur's Order, already in decay, is further plagued by the destructive influence of the Grail quest. The knights' inability to respond properly to the quest only accelerates the decay of the idealism momentarily made concrete in Camelot. The quest is valid for those few who are summoned to it. Even Arthur, disappointed as he is, can accept the necessity of the vocations of Galahad and Percivale's sister. For the rest of the knights, however, their vocation rests in Camelot; their highest hope lies in Arthur's final statement:

> Let visions of the night or of the day
> Come, as they will; and many a time they come,
> Until this earth he walks on seems not earth,
> This light that strikes his eyeball is not light,
> This air that smites his forehead is not air
> But vision—yea, his very hand and foot—
> In moments when he feels he cannot die,
> And knows himself no vision to himself,
> Nor the high God a vision, nor that One
> Who rose again: ye have seen what ye have seen.

For Arthur, as for Tennyson,[27] the spiritual exists behind the material; the soul does transcend the body, though the transcendence occurs within the earthly environment of man's physical world. The highest

---

27 The poet noted: "Yes, it is true that there are moments when the flesh is nothing to me, when I feel and know the flesh to be the vision, God and the Spiritual the only real and true. Depend upon it, the Spiritual *is* the real: it belongs to one more than the hand and the foot. You may tell me that my hand and my foot are only imaginary symbols of my existence, I could believe you; but you never, never can convince me that the *I* is not an eternal Reality, and that the Spiritual is not the true and real part of me" (*Memoir*, II, 90).

reality is a spiritual reality which exists behind but not apart from the physical world. The mysticism expressed in the King's speech is a mysticism which comes intuitively, unexpectedly, through man's proper fulfillment of his vocation in this life.

After a decade of anxiety and hesitation Tennyson completed his treatment of the one episode in the Arthurian legends that impeded the progress of his poem. Unable to accept the Grail as a symbol of divine grace, Tennyson accepted the plot of the quest as the basis of a study of human responses to the spiritual world. *The Holy Grail* is a study of the comparative validity of varied responses to this spiritual experience; ultimately, the idyll becomes a study of the folly of rash knights who forsake their "allotted field" for a distant vision. Even to Galahad, Malory's ideal spiritual knight, Tennyson denies some sympathy, since his role as ruler of the spiritual city robs Arthur's realm of one more worthy knight. Percivale, the centre of the poem, becomes the tragic hero, the knight whose high capability for effective rule in this world is unrealized because of his improper response to the Grail; with no support from Malory's account of the Grail quest Tennyson makes the idyll a tragedy, narrated most effectively by the hero who remains unaware of his tragedy. In the final line, "So spake the King: I knew not all he meant," Percivale reveals the personal blindness that prevents him from seeing the importance of his own "allotted field." He cannot understand the more natural mysticism of his King.

The quest for the Grail continues and accelerates the decay of the Round Table. The quest becomes the external force that harms a world already wounded by the adulterous behaviour of its Queen. By implying that the absence of the Grail (and, consequently, the seeming necessity of the quest) is dependent upon Guinevere's sin, Tennyson subtly links the external force of destruction with the sin at the centre of Arthur's realm. By employing Percivale as the centre of his treatment of the Grail and by connecting the story with the figure of Guinevere, Tennyson creates a version of the Grail quest to complement his earlier volume of idylls.

The completion of the Grail idyll permitted the poet to return to his general conception of an Arthurian poem and create a framework for the entire work. The conclusion to his poem already had a tentative form in the early *Morte d'Arthur*.[28] Consequently, the next movement in the series was the creation of a suitable beginning:

---

28 Despite the archaic style of the poem, which prompted him into serious doubt about incorporating it into the series, Tennyson admitted that this was "the natural close" to the poem (*Memoir*, II, 126). Consequently, he made the opening poem, like the *Morte d'Arthur*, "intentionally more archaic than the others" (quoted by Anne Thackeray Ritchie, "Alfred Tennyson," *Harper's New Monthly Magazine*, 68 [December 1883], 31). Tennyson commented: " 'The Coming and the Passing of Arthur' are simpler and more severe in style, as dealing with the awfulness of Birth and Death" (*Memoir*, I, 483).

He had made up his mind about the further episodes to be included, and had decided that, in spite of the stylistic difficulty, the old *Morte d'Arthur* should form the conclusion. The first new Idyll was to be a short preface describing Arthur's mysterious birth, his battles with Rome and with the heathen, his foundation of the Round Table and his marriage to Guinevere. He felt that he must hold back the Grail idyll until he could add two or three others to it, and was anxious lest the printed copies, which he had given to his friends, should pass into unauthorized hands.[29]

The "short preface," *The Coming of Arthur*, was Tennyson's version of the birth of Arthur.[30] Having reworked Malory's account of the Grail quest into his own treatment of the legend, he undertook to offer a similar reworking of the story of Arthur's birth. He employed Malory's account, but set it within a context which undercuts its credibility. The result was a deliberate confusion of the account by a series of conflicting reports.

In *Guinevere* Tennyson presented one version of Arthur's origin in the novice's report of her father's belief. That report now becomes one of a series, and Tennyson develops varying accounts, not to undercut the mystique of Arthur, but to offer alternative possibilities to the nature of his origin; he does not verify any one of them; he remains content merely to present them. The opening idyll calls into question the origins of Arthur, not to deny him his spiritual character, but rather to separate him from the Grail, which is purely and solely a divine object. Arthur may be an agent of the divine, yet, unlike the Grail, he is a human being; he is, as the novice reports, "well-nigh more than man," though he never sheds his manhood. In addition, his address to his wife in *Guinevere* made him appear as a god forgiving the sin of one of his creatures. Tennyson's present task is to create Arthur as a king whose special mission does not eclipse his recognizably human character. By refusing to offer one accepted version of Arthur's origin and by proposing a series of alternative reports, Tennyson distinguishes his hero from the Grail, an embodiment of the spiritual world; Arthur is an agent of the divine through his humanity.

In order to exhibit effectively the conflicting accounts, Tennyson returns again to Guinevere and makes Arthur's love for her the cause of a discussion of his regal identity. Malory's version of the betrothal of Arthur and Guinevere is simple and succinct; the King must marry and he chooses the beautiful daughter of Leodogran as his bride. Tennyson takes this brief moment in Malory and invents the story of Leodogran's loving concern that his daughter marry a king. Leodogran's anxiety is

29 Sir Charles Tennyson, p. 379.
30 In a copy of the trial-printing of the four new idylls (British Museum, Ashley 2104), the title of the opening idyll is "The Birth of Arthur." In the same copy the concluding idyll bears the title "The Death of Arthur," and *Pelleas and Ettarre* is entitled "Sir Pelleas."

precipitated by Arthur's request for Guinevere's hand, a request prompted by the young King's victory over the heathens who have been ravaging Leodogran's kingdom. Consequently, the idyll also becomes the earliest depiction of Arthur's power to accomplish his mission by routing the enemy: "And he drave / The heathen, and he slew the beast, and fell'd / The forest, and let in the sun, and made / Broad pathways for the hunter and the knight." The brief account of Arthur's victory finds its inspiration, not in Malory's account of Arthur's early battles, but in certain passages of the idylls of the 1859 volume. The bestial world of Doorm reflects the necessity of Arthur's ennobling Order; the same theme is developed again in *Lancelot and Elaine* when Elaine's father recounts their servant's sufferings at the hands of the heathen "till our good Arthur broke / The Pagan yet once more on Badon hill." Such situations are mirrored in the design of the mighty hall of Camelot:

> And four great zones of sculpture, set betwixt
> With many a mystic symbol, gird the hall;
> And in the lowest beasts are slaying men,
> And in the second men are slaying beasts,
> And on the third are warriors, perfect men,
> And on the fourth are men with growing wings,
> And over all one statue in the mould
> Of Arthur, made by Merlin, with a crown,
> And peak'd wings pointed to the Northern Star.

Leodogran's realm is the lowest zone: "Wherein the beast was ever more and more, / But man was less and less, till Arthur came." His kingdom, besieged briefly by Rience in Malory, is a wasteland waiting for the healing power of Arthur's presence.

When the three ambassadors, Ulfius, Brastias, and Bedivere,[31] report to Leodogran Arthur's wish to marry Guinevere, a request immediately granted in Malory, her perturbed father seeks to know Arthur's parentage. Bedivere offers the first and only full account of Arthur's birth; his report is loosely based on Malory's version:

> Sir, for ye know that in King Uther's time
> The prince and warrior Gorloïs, he that held
> Tintagil castle by the Cornish sea,
> Was wedded with a winsome wife, Ygerne:
> And daughters had she borne him,—one whereof
> Lot's wife, the Queen of Orkney, Bellicent,
> Hath ever like a loyal sister cleaved
> To Arthur,—but a son she had not borne.
> And Uther cast upon her eyes of love:
> But she, a stainless wife to Gorloïs,

31 The three knights do not appear together in Malory. Ulfius and Brastias are a pair of ambassadors in Malory's early chapters; Bedivere does not appear until the fifth chapter of the fifth book. Tennyson's inclusion of Bedivere is an attempt to relate more symmetrically the action of the idyll to the content of the *Morte d'Arthur*.

So loathed the bright dishonour of his love,
That Gorloïs and King Uther went to war:
And overthrown was Gorloïs and slain.
Then Uther in his wrath and heat besieged
Ygerne within Tintagil, where her men,
Seeing the mighty swarm about their walls,
Left her and fled, and Uther enter'd in,
And there was none to call to but himself.
So, compass'd by the power of the king,
Enforced she was to wed him in her tears,
And with a shameful swiftness: afterward,
Not many moons, King Uther died himself,
Moaning and wailing for an heir to rule
After him, lest the realm should go to wrack.
And that same night, the night of the new year,
By reason of the bitterness and grief
That vext his mother, all before his time
Was Arthur born, and all as soon as born
Deliver'd at a secret postern-gate
To Merlin, to be holden far apart
Until his hour should come.

There is already a certain degree of mystery, since Arthur is born on the same night that his father dies, though the death precedes the birth. Malory rooted his account in fuller detail; indeed, the difference between the medieval version and the idyll is the direction the poet is pursuing in his presentation of Arthur. Malory's King is conceived out of wedlock; through the agency and magic of Merlin, Uther, disguised as Gorloïs, sleeps with Ygerne and begets Arthur before Gorloïs is slain in battle; the marriage of Uther and Ygerne takes place shortly after Gorloïs' death. Tennyson removes any suggestion of illegitimacy; moreover, by making Arthur's birth almost simultaneous with Uther's death, both occurring on "the night of the new year," he casts a mysterious aura over Arthur in the most factual account of his origin in the idyll.

Bedivere's subsequent commentary is further removed from Malory. Merlin takes the young child to the household of Sir Anton[32] where Arthur is raised until the time arrives for him to assume the throne. The poet again adds mystery to Malory's account by omitting the concrete test of kingship, the episode of the sword that must be pulled from the stone, and substituting a short account of the controversy that occurred when Arthur came to the throne:

A hundred voices cried, "Away with him!
No king of ours! a son of Gorloïs he,
Or else the child of Anton, and no king,

32 Tennyson's substitution of Anton for Malory's character of Ector is inexplicable except as a matter of preference for the sound of the name. In George Ellis' *Specimens of Early English Romances* (London, 1805), I, 240, the foster parent is Antour.

Or else baseborn.'' Yet Merlin thro' his craft,
And while the people clamour'd for a king,
Had Arthur crown'd; but after, the great lords
Banded, and so brake out in open war.

The final detail, the outbreak of war, returns to Malory's narrative; the
added detail, the controversy at the coronation, rightly disturbs an
already suspicious Leodogran.

While Leodogran is debating "with himself / If Arther were the
child of shamefulness, / Or born the son of Gorloïs, after death, / Or
Uther's son, and born before his time," Bellicent, the wife of Lot of
Orkney and the daughter of Gorloïs and Ygerne, conveniently arrives at
Cameliard.[33] She is accompanied by her two sons, Gawain and Modred.[34] Bellicent's account of her childhood with Arthur does not present
another version of his origin; it modifies Bedivere's account by casting
the already mysterious birth into further ambiguity. She cannot comment on Arthur's heredity, except for the fact that his physical features,
unlike the dark features of her family, are "fair / Beyond the race of
Britons and of men." In her account Arthur simply appears:

I know not whether of himself he came,
Or brought by Merlin, who, they say, can walk
Unseen at pleasure—he was at my side,
And spake sweet words, and comforted my heart,
And dried my tears, being a child with me.

Bellicent reacts intuitively to Arthur's presence; she does not question
his origin; his kindness and love make her accept him openly without any
questioning. In an age of doubt her faith will not satisfy those who need
concrete proof for their beliefs and commitments. Her brief history of
her childhood is preceded by her version of Arthur's coronation, a
version that disregards the doubts and petty quarrels Bedivere mentioned and concentrates on the effect of Arthur on his knights:

But when he spake and cheer'd his Round Table
With large divine and comfortable words
Beyond my tongue to tell thee—I beheld
From eye to eye thro' all their Order flash
A momentary likeness of the king:
And ere it left their faces, thro' the cross
And those around it and the Crucified,
Down from the casement over Arthur, smote
Flame-colour, vert and azure, in three rays,
One falling upon each of three fair queens,

33 Lot's wife, named Morgawse in Malory, derives her name from Belisent, the name of
Lot's wife in Ellis's summary of *Merlin* (*Specimens*, I, 271).
34 In naming Lot's two sons as Gawain and Modred, Tennyson follows the chronicle
tradition of Geoffrey of Monmouth and Layamon; in Malory, Lot has four sons:
Gawain, Aggravayne, Gaherys, and Gareth, a grouping Tennyson noted in his character outline of the Arthurian legends (see Chapter I).

> Who stood in silence near his throne, the friends
> Of Arthur, gazing on him, tall, with bright
> Sweet faces, who will help him at his need.

Bellicent's account of the coronation, invented by the poet, recalls the effect of the Grail upon the knights: "But every knight beheld his fellow's face / As in a glory." Arthur's effect on his men is similar to the effect of the Grail; both alert the knights to their spirituality; the similarity in effect, however, emphasizes only the spirituality of Arthur. The Grail, inspiring as it is, calls only a select few to a cloistered spiritual union; Arthur as a man summons his knights to a commitment to the highest perfection of their humanity in this world.

The presence of the three Queens reflects Tennyson's desire to create a symmetrical pattern between the opening and closing idylls; the Queens will conduct Arthur on his final voyage. Similarly, the presence of the Lady of the Lake and her gift of the sword[35] echo Bedivere's journeys to cast the sword back into the lake.

Bellicent follows the account of her childhood and her presence at the coronation with a recitation of her visit to Bleys before his death, a visit wholly invented by Tennyson;[36] at this meeting Bleys tells her of the circumstances of Arthur's coming; his account is an elaboration of the report of the novice, though Bleys adds a messianic tone to the story. Again the emphasis falls, not on Arthur's origin, but on the reaction of a person to his presence. The third account, the most mystical of the three, describing Arthur's mysterious arrival by sea, a parallel to his later departure, focuses on Bleys's immediate reaction to the infant:

> "And this same child," he said,
> "Is he who reigns; nor could I part in peace
> Till this were told." And saying this the seer
> Went thro' the strait and dreadful pass of death,
> Not ever to be question'd any more
> Save on the further side.

Bleys is a prophet foretelling the kingly role destined for the child in a distinctly messianic context reminiscent of Simeon's prophecy about the infant Christ.

Bedivere's natural account of Arthur's birth has given way to Bellicient's intuitive acceptance of Arthur and Bleys's prophetic out-

---

35 Tennyson's account of Arthur's acquisition of the sword differs from Malory's version since he chose to omit the episode of the sword in the stone.

36 The episode may have been initially suggested by the following passage from Ellis: "The reader will remember that Nanters, king of Garlot, had married Blasine, uterine sister to Arthur, and had by her a son named Galachin. King Lot had married Belisent, the other daughter of Ygerna, and had had four sons, Wawain or Gawain, Gueheret, Gaheriet, and Agravain. Galachin, having observed that the progress of the enemy was chiefly owing to want of union among the Britons, one day inquired of his mother Blasine whether Arthur was indeed his uncle" (*Specimens*, I, 271-272).

burst. These statements, however, do not calm Leodogran, whose dream becomes the final testimony to Arthur's mysterious origin:

> Till with a wink his dream was changed, the haze
> Descended, and the solid earth became
> As nothing, and the king stood out in heaven,
> Crown'd. And Leodogran awoke, and sent
> Ulfius, and Brastias and Bedivere,
> Back to the court of Arthur answering yea.

The dream corroborates Bellicent's testimony; Leodogran has received sufficient evidence that he should give his daughter to Arthur in marriage.

The final section of the idyll returns to Malory's account of the early events of Arthur's reign, though Tennyson modifies it according to the themes of the earlier idylls. Thus, at Arthur's direction, Lancelot conducts Guinevere to Camelot, a detail that violates Malory, where Merlin conducts her, but remains faithful to Guinevere's recollection of the incident in *Guinevere*: "when Lancelot came, / Reputed the best knight and goodliest man, / Ambassador, to lead her to his lord / Arthur, and led her forth."[37] The marriage, briefly described, is performed by Dubric, a figure not found in Malory but already presented as the priest at Enid's wedding. The idyll ends with a brief reference to the Roman demand for tribute, Arthur's refusal, the subsequent battle, and Arthur's twelve great battles.[38]

The Coming of Arthur is a further demonstration of Tennyson's ability to employ Malory freely according to his own intentions. In *The Holy Grail* he created his version of the quest, which continually echoes the movement of Malory's account, though it bears no ultimate relationship; the same kind of source treatment is evident in the opening idyll. While employing, with alterations, Malory's straightforward account of Arthur's birth, Tennyson establishes a series of possible origins which surround Arthur with an aura of mystery and call into question his position in the natural order of life. The focus of the idyll is not Arthur's origin, but the form of others' acceptance of him. Bedivere's acceptance of the traditional story, Bellicent's intuitive response, Bleys's prophetic outburst, Leodogran's final acceptance through a dream, all these reactions throw the final emphasis on the acceptance of Arthur, not because

---

37 The detail looks back to Vivien's accusation to Merlin and, before that, to *Sir Launcelot and Queen Guinevere*.

38 The brief catalogue of activities which occupy the early years of Arthur's reign suggests that Tennyson now has no intention of incorporating the sequence with Lucius into his poem. In 1858 Tennyson was reading about the battle with the Romans in Malory (*Memoir*, I, 431). The ending of *The Coming of Arthur* leaves his poem, in relationship to Malory, at the opening of the "Tale of Gareth," a story he has already considered for his series (*Memoir*, I, 471). The twelve battles recall his earlier use of them in *Elaine*.

of his origin or lineage, but because of his nature as a king and as a man. In this manner Tennyson suggests that the presence of an ideal, the coming of a new order, automatically raises suspicions; natural skepticism forces people to doubt the origin and validity of an ideal upon its appearance.

Tennyson roots the presentation of Arthur in the idyll in concrete reality by studying him through the other characters. Despite the seeming centrality of Arthur, the poem does not enter his mind; we learn his possible origins and his nature only through the eyes and the faith of the characters. Tennyson uses the other characters in such a way that their attitudes testify to Arthur's existence as a human force in the world. In Bellicent's account of the coronation Arthur is transfigured in the colour of the stained-glass window, yet the knights' momentary likeness to their King is kinglike, not godlike. Such a moment emphasizes the mysterious power of Arthur's presence, but such moments are carefully rooted in concrete reality, here in his effect upon the knights. Tennyson draws continual attention to Arthur's practical intelligence; the idyll opens with a list of his accomplishments in Leodogran's realm; it closes with a brief enumeration of the battles of his early reign. Aware of the complexity of Arthur's nature, Tennyson must root him in the practical world so that the King does not become an inhuman or exclusively supernatural being. Such a dilemma is central to *Guinevere,* where the Queen moves from an awareness of her husband's seemingly inhuman nature to an acceptance that such a man is both "the highest and the most human too." In his presentation of Arthur Tennyson must exert special efforts that the portrait may always show that the King is "most human too."

Finally, lest Arthur's humanity be eclipsed by the emphasis on his idealistic vision, Tennyson adds a long monologue by the King on his desire for marriage:

> What happiness to reign a lonely king,
> Vext—O ye stars that shudder over me,
> O earth that soundest hollow under me,
> Vext with waste dreams? for saving I be join'd
> To her that is the fairest under heaven,
> I seem as nothing in the mighty world,
> And cannot will my will, nor work my work
> Wholly, nor make myself in mine own realm
> Victor and lord. But were I join'd with her,
> Then might we live together as one life,
> And reigning with one will in everything
> Have power on this dark land to lighten it,
> And power on this dead world to make it live.

Arthur reveals himself here as the lonely and human man that he is. Such a passage stands in direct contrast to much of the idyll, which concen-

trates on Arthur's idealistic vision. It is the human dimension that
separates Arthur from the solely supernatural nature of the Grail and
makes him a concrete individual striving to realize human perfection
within his "allotted field."

The Coming of Arthur is a deliberate attempt to create a framework
for the whole series. Satisfied that the *Morte d'Arthur* can be the
conclusion, Tennyson fills the opening idyll with verbal and thematic
parallels to it. The two idylls are closely linked by the reappearance of
Bedivere, the three Queens, and Excalibur. Most important to the
unifying pattern is the statement that Arthur makes at the beginning and
at the end of his career. At his marriage feast he proclaims: "Behold, for
these have sworn / To fight my wars, and worship me their king; / The
old order changeth, yielding place to new." Here the old order is the
order of Rome, "The slowly-fading mistress of the world"; the old order
is passing away and giving place to the new order of Arthur. Thirty-six
years earlier Tennyson had a dying Arthur tell Bedivere: "The old order
changeth, yielding place to new, / And God fulfills himself in many ways, /
Lest one good custom should corrupt the world." Here the dying order
is Arthur's Order; the repetition of the line in the conclusion to the entire
work will provide a moment of necessary optimism. In the incorporation
of the same line into *The Coming of Arthur* Tennyson reveals that the
framework for his projected Arthurian poem has been created. What
remains now is the necessity to embellish the intervening incidents and
to fill any thematic voids by new and appropriate idylls.

Pelleas and Ettarre, begun immediately after the completion of *The
Coming of Arthur,*[39] is the direct continuation and consequence of *The
Holy Grail;* it portrays the younger generation of knights who have come
to fill the void created by the Grail quest. By its structure and by its
relationship to its source *Pelleas and Ettarre* recalls the mode of composition of the 1859 idylls. For the first time since *Elaine* Tennyson has
chosen a story in which a woman could be the centre of attention. The
development noted in *Elaine,* whereby the woman becomes subordinate
to the man in thematic importance, is continued here; the idyll's centre is
Pelleas.[40] In addition, the idyll recalls the earlier volume in the continual
attempt to create a thematic connection between the female character
and Guinevere; Ettarre becomes the fourth woman to stand in relationship to the Queen. Lastly, the idyll, like *Vivien* and *Elaine,* takes a
specific incident in Malory and re-creates it according to its purpose in
the poem; unlike *Elaine,* however, *Pelleas and Ettarre,* containing so
much material added by the poet, makes no attempt to maintain fidelity

39   "By the end of February, 1869, he had finished *The Coming of Arthur,* and by the
      middle of May he was well under way with his next episode, that of *Pelleas and
      Ettarre*" (Sir Charles Tennyson, p. 381).
40   Pelleas' central position is also emphasized by the original title of the idyll, "Sir
      Pelleas" (see preceding footnote 30).

to Malory; the freedom Tennyson displayed in his treatment of the Grail story is again evident in his re-creation of the story of Pelleas and Ettarre.

Malory introduces the Pelleas incident (I, lxxix-lxxxii) as an episode on Gawain's journey after he has accompanied Uwain out of Camelot; the short incident, an example of a woman's pride in love, is also an example of Gawain's unstable behaviour. Gawain confronts Pelleas "making great mourn out of measure" for his unreciprocated love of Ettarde, a woman "so proud that she had scorn of him, and said, 'That she would never love him, though he would die for her.'" Aware of his seeming folly in permitting Ettarde's men to defeat and humiliate him, Pelleas contends that "love causeth many a good knight to suffer for to have his intent." In Malory the guilty party is Ettarde, whose pride scorns the worthy love of Pelleas.[41]

Gawain's agreement to assist Pelleas in his pursuit of his beloved leads to an open display of Ettarde's loose behaviour and Gawain's perfidy; instead of persuading Ettarde to love Pelleas, Gawain seduces her. After three days Pelleas comes to Ettarde's castle and discovers the couple asleep together. His initial reaction, "Alas! that ever a knight should be found so false," is followed by a desire to kill them, a desire never realized in action because of his refusal to "destroy the high order of knighthood." As a final gesture Pelleas leaves his sword across their throats. Upon waking Ettarde is shocked by the sword and decries Gawain's discourtesy:

"Alas!" she said to Sir Gawaine, "ye have betrayed me and sir Pelles also; for ye told me that ye had slain him, and now I know well it is not so, he is alive: and if sir Pelles had been as courteous to you as you have been to him ye had been a dead knight, but ye have deceived me and betrayed me falsely, that all ladies and damsels may beware by you and me." And therewith sir Gawaine made him ready, and went into the forest [I, lxxxi].

Nimue learns of Pelleas' plight and brings it about through magic that Ettarde falls madly in love with Pelleas, who now feels hatred for her. Ettarde dies for sorrow, and Nimue "rejoiced sir Pelles, and loved together during their lives" (I, lxxxii). Shortly thereafter Pelleas is made a knight at Arthur's court; Malory notes that "sir Pelles was a worshipful knight, and was one of the four that achieved the Sancgreal" (I, lxxxvii). Such a happy ending is possible in Malory's world, a world "where vice is punished and virtue rewarded by the 'right wys Iugement of God,' and where injured men redress the wrongs done to their honour with their own hands."[42]

41   Malory changed his French source which made Ettarde's scorn of Pelleas arise out of her consciousness of his low birth; by making Pelleas a lord "of many isles," Malory establishes Ettarde as inexcusably guilty in her pride.
42   F. Whitehead, "On Certain Episodes in the Fourth Book of Malory's *Morte Darthur*," *Medium Aevum*, 2 (1933), 206.

Whereas Malory's account of the Pelleas episode occurs shortly after the formation of the Round Table, Tennyson makes it part of the later ruin of the realm. Pelleas is now the centre of the story and the purpose of its insertion as an idyll; the episode becomes the sad delineation of the growth of a young knight in a decayed world. Gawain's perfidy and Ettarre's lust are the norm; they are not and cannot be punished. Pelleas' suffering will not be rewarded; the agent of his reward in Malory's account, Nimue, has already been completely damned as a character in *Vivien*.

For Tennyson, Pelleas is a young man of honesty, sincerity, and innocence. Whereas Malory's Pelleas has never met unhappiness in love, "never have I loved lady nor damsel till now, in an unhappy time" (I, lxxx), Tennyson makes him an inexperienced lover: "saving his own sisters he had known / Scarce any but the women of his isles, / Rough wives." His desire for love is the cry of an innocent but not reprehensible knight:

> O where? I love thee, tho' I know thee not.
> For fair thou art and pure as Guinevere,
> And I will make thee with my spear and sword
> As famous—O my queen, my Guinevere,
> For I will be thine Arthur when we meet.

His intention, to be as Arthur, is wholly laudable, but it becomes tragic in the present circumstances; in a blighted world he sees Guinevere as she should be, not as she is; he aspires to be an Arthur now that Arthur's vision is being openly mocked. Pelleas is a potential Arthur, but the potentiality is never realized; the world as personified in Ettarre's behaviour destroys the goodness of Pelleas.

Pelleas' admiration for and emulation of Arthur are developed in his first sight of Ettarre:

> And Pelleas gazing thought,
> "Is Guinevere herself so beautiful?"
> For large her violet eyes look'd, and her bloom
> A rosy dawn kindled in stainless heavens,
> And round her limbs, mature in womanhood,
> And slender was her hand and small her shape,
> And but for those large eyes, the haunts of scorn,
> She might have seem'd a toy to trifle with,
> And pass and care no more.

Arthur's first sight of his Queen led him to feel "the light of her eyes into his life / Smite on the sudden"; in that context there was no external description of Guinevere's beauty. Pelleas' first reaction to Ettarre is based solely on external form; Ettarre lacks the inner beauty that was present in Guinevere, though this absence remains undetected by her youthful admirer:

> But while he gazed
> The beauty of her flesh abash'd the boy,
> As tho' it were the beauty of her soul:
> For as the base man, judging of the good,
> Puts his own baseness in him by default
> Of will and nature, so did Pelleas lend
> All the young beauty of his own soul to hers,
> Believing her.

Clinging to the ideals espoused by Arthur, Pelleas is seduced by Ettarre's surface beauty; he fails to see her evil reality which stands in scorn of Arthur's vision.

Ettarre is a direct descendant of Tennyson's portraits of Vivien and Enid. From Vivien she derives animal imagery that underlines her sensuality. Whereas Vivien must exert great effort to seduce an elderly Merlin, Ettarre's simple deceit immediately controls the unsuspecting Pelleas. From Enid Ettarre receives great beauty; her physical beauty, however, is not a reflection of any inner goodness. Unlike Enid, she is a woman of selfish pride. She desires the title "Queen of Beauty," a title reserved for Guinevere; Enid, next to Guinevere in loveliness, receives the more honoured appellation, "Enid the Good." In the later stage of Camelot's decay beauty is an end in itself, a surface with no depth; goodness has no value. Like Guinevere, Ettarre is a woman of great beauty; unlike the Queen, she makes no pretence of being a good woman. After a brief display of seeming affection to inspire Pelleas to win the circlet, Ettarre refuses to wear a mask and shows herself as the lustful and proud woman she is.

Beneath Ettarre's pride stands a deep awareness of her own nature and the higher nature of the lover she rejects. In an original passage Tennyson offers Ettarre a moment of self-analysis:

> Why have I push'd him from me? this man loves,
> If love there be: yet him I loved not. Why?
> I deem'd him fool? yea, so? or that in him
> A something—was it nobler than myself?—
> Seem'd my reproach? He is not of my kind.
> He could not love me, did he know me well.
> Nay, let him go—and quickly.

In this instant of penetrating introspection Ettarre, a woman committed to a life of lust, admits the higher calling of her nature; she is aware of the love of Pelleas, its kind and its quality. Such a moment, however, is fleeting; her realm is the world of Vivien, the world of sensuality and selfishness.

Tennyson follows Malory's narrative structure with moderate care until the fatal union of Gawain and Ettarre, though he expands the details with descriptive embellishments. Whereas the tournament in which Pelleas wins the circlet and sword is unidentified in Malory,

Tennyson makes this "Tournament of Youth" a sad indication of the
condition of Arthur's Order. In *The Holy Grail* the knights held their
final jousts. Now, after the tragedy of that quest, a tournament is held in
which the King "withheld / His older and his mightier from the lists, /
That Pelleas might obtain his lady's love." The tournament itself is
honourable, though under the surface lurks the truth: "Had ye not held
your Lancelot in your bower, / My Queen, he had not won." The
pervasive presence of Guinevere's sin stands behind every incident in
the idyll, and what ultimately distinguishes Tennyson's treatment from
Malory's account, in addition to the embellishments, is the continual
association between Ettarre's behaviour and Guinevere's dishonour.

Gawain's appearance and his perfidy to Pelleas are borrowed directly from Malory, though Tennyson does make Gawain's oath more
solemn in an effort to increase his guilt. The poet casts aside the relationship of Gawain and Ettarre; unlike Malory, he does not describe even
briefly their amorous behaviour. During their three days together,
Tennyson follows Pelleas' wanderings. Even the sudden disclosure of
the false pair is noted only briefly:

> Then she, that felt the cold touch on her throat,
> Awaking knew the sword, and turn'd herself
> To Gawain: "Liar, for thou hast not slain
> This Pelleas! here he stood and might have slain
> Me and thyself." And he that tells the tale
> Says that her ever-veering fancy turn'd
> To Pelleas, as the one true knight on earth,
> And only lover; and thro' her love her life
> Wasted and pined, desiring him in vain.

The narrator consciously dismisses certain source material with the
intention of focusing, not on Ettarre's behaviour, but on the effects of
her behaviour on Pelleas' innocent youth.

Pelleas' sight of the falsity of Gawain and Ettarre destroys his
illusions. He realizes the truth about his own feelings: "I never loved
her, I but lusted for her." The Gawain-Ettarre union does not destroy
Pelleas; it brings him to disillusionment, which might not have been
destructive were it not for the diseased condition of Camelot. In his
anger he dreams "that Gawain fired / The hall of Merlin." The next
incident will lead him from disillusionment to despair when he learns
that Merlin's hall is being destroyed, not by Gawain, but by a sin at its
foundation.

In a further violation of Malory Tennyson reintroduces Percivale.
Pelleas wanders until he comes "Beside that tower where Percivale was
cowl'd." Percivale's appearance, linking the idyll even more closely
with its immediate predecessor, is bitterly ironic in the contrast between
Percivale's refusal to "be as Arthur in our land" and Pelleas' youthful

dream to "be thine Arthur when we meet." The encounter with Percivale is the final shattering blow to the youth; his disillusionment with Gawain and Ettarre must now be expanded to encompass the Queen herself: " 'Is the Queen false?' and Percivale was mute. / 'Have any of our Round Table held their vows?' " In the admission of Guinevere's adultery Percivale has removed Pelleas' final foundation for hope and idealism. The Queen is false; the vows have been broken. Percivale admits that if Arthur and his vision were not true, "Why then let men couple at once with wolves." Without Arthur's vision the world will reel back into its bestial and disordered state. Pelleas' disillusionment has poisoned his innocence; he cannot perceive and accept Percivale's belief in the truth of the King.

The final scenes of the idyll, invented by Tennyson, follow Pelleas' progressive mental deterioration. He overrides a hunchbacked cripple; for him Camelot is now only a "black nest of rats," and he wrongly believes that this symbol of Arthur's vision was built too high. With ironic symmetry Pelleas, the champion of the earlier tournament, now encounters Lancelot, the knight who was withheld from that tournament. Their combat is a sad commentary on the noble chivalry envisioned by Arthur for his realm; Pelleas lacks a sword and desires to be slain. Their encounter is a prelude to the conclusion of the idyll, the appearance of Guinevere. The Queen resumes her proper role as regal comforter:

> "O young knight,
> Hath the great heart of knighthood in thee fail'd
> So far thou canst not bide, unfrowardly,
> A fall from him?" Then, for he answer'd not,
> "Or hast thou other griefs? If I, the Queen,
> May help them, loose thy tongue, and let me know."

The role of comforter no longer suits Guinevere; Pelleas' understandable discourtesy is indicative of the respect and honour she can now expect to receive. In the midst of Pelleas' hissing Guinevere turns to Lancelot for sympathy, and each "foresaw the dolorous day to be." The idyll ends with the sudden reappearance of Modred, who senses that "The time is hard at hand."[43]

In adapting Malory's story Tennyson shows no sustained verbal or narrative fidelity. He makes Pelleas the centre of the story, removes Ettarre and Gawain to subordinate positions, and adds the appearance of Percivale and Lancelot. Most importantly, he portrays Ettarre in

---

43 With the exception of his arrival with his mother in *The Coming of Arthur*, Modred has only appeared in *Guinevere*, where he is portrayed as an agent of evil; his appearance here reflects Tennyson's intention of preparing for his appearance at the opening of the next idyll in the series.

comparison with Guinevere; Pelleas seeks a woman of Guinevere's supposed perfection; his growing realization of Ettarre's true nature is a growing realization of the true nature of the Queen. Guinevere, absent from Malory's version, is present throughout the idyll in the mind of Pelleas. Ettarre's insult to the Queen and Pelleas' final rude behaviour make Guinevere realize that she can no longer pretend to be the noble Queen of her husband's Order.

The importance of Guinevere emphasizes the connection between the idyll and the idylls of the 1859 volume. Ettarre is most closely related to Vivien in her lustful behaviour. At the same time Pelleas' admiration of the Queen recalls Geraint's early respect for Guinevere. Geraint's misunderstanding of Enid's goodness parallels Pelleas' misunderstanding of Ettarre's seeming goodness, though the two women are moral opposites. Such similarities do not hide the close resemblance between *Pelleas and Ettarre* and *Elaine*. In the latter idyll the simple and pure Elaine had her affections blighted and her life destroyed. Like Elaine, Pelleas is simple, honest, and noble; like her, he is totally innocent; his failure in love, however, does not lead to his death. His youthful innocence is turned to bitter hatred and indignation; confronted with the evil in Camelot, his idealism is turned to disillusionment, distraction, and, ultimately, to despair. Like Elaine, Pelleas suffers because of Guinevere's adultery; when he discovers that sin resides within the supposed purity of his Queen, his disillusionment becomes despair. His unsuspecting nobility of soul is attacked and overwhelmed by the reality of the decay in Camelot; his open-hearted confidence and unashamedly trusting nature are turned into bitter distrust of everyone and everything.

Pelleas stands as the embodiment of the confusion and despair that confront the idealistic man who looks upon the present condition of Arthur's society. Adultery runs rampant and no area of the kingdom is free of its taint. Before this idyll the adulterous disloyalty of the Queen has been silently poisoning the society and sowing the seed of the terror to come. In *Pelleas and Ettarre* the background for the ultimate ruin of Arthur's Order is portrayed. In the depiction of the disastrous effect of Camelot's present condition on one young knight, a condition diametrically opposed to Arthur's vision, the idyll becomes less a study of Pelleas' tragedy than a study of the society that precipitates such a tragedy. *Pelleas and Ettarre* is, as Tennyson noted, "almost the saddest of the Idylls"; here, indeed, is "the breaking of the storm."[44]

The fourth idyll of the volume, *The Passing of Arthur*, is not a new work but the incorporation of the earlier *Morte d'Arthur* into this larger poem by the addition of a suitable beginning and conclusion to the 272 lines composed nearly 36 years earlier. Satisfied with the quality of the

44 Eversley edition, V, 499.

earlier poem and its propriety within the scheme of his Arthurian work,[45] Tennyson adds an introduction to establish the necessary background to connect Arthur's passing as recorded in the *Morte d'Arthur* with his departure from Almesbury, described near the end of *Guinevere*.

In contrast to the *Morte d'Arthur*, where fidelity to Malory's text was the mode of poetic creation, the added introduction has no relationship to Malory. Both the final meeting of Arthur and his Queen and Guinevere's death as presented in *Guinevere* prevent fidelity to Malory's presentation of the meeting of a repentant Lancelot and a grieving Guinevere. Tennyson chooses to open the final idyll with Arthur's dream about Gawain:

> There came on Arthur sleeping, Gawain kill'd
> In Lancelot's war, the ghost of Gawain blown
> Along a wandering wind, and past his ear
> Went shrilling, "Hollow, hollow all delight!
> Hail, king! to-morrow thou shalt pass away.
> Farewell! there is an isle of rest for thee.
> And I am blown along a wandering wind,
> And hollow, hollow, hollow all delight."

In Malory's version of the dream Gawain appears to warn Arthur not to fight Mordred until Lancelot and his forces arrive. Though borrowing the concept of the dream from Malory, Tennyson remains faithful to his own portrait of Gawain; the dream, Gawain's final appearance in the *Idylls*, is a fitting climax to Tennyson's presentation of him.[46] Gawain represents the form of eternal reward that awaits a man of his moral instability and spiritual blindness; in *The Holy Grail* Arthur tells Gawain that men see "according to their sight"; in their confrontation with a final spiritual reality, men fare according to the vision that shaped their lives. In a further addition to the source, Bedivere interprets the dream with a final denunciation: "Light was Gawain in life, and light in death / Is Gawain, for the ghost is as the man."

Tennyson omits Modred's initial confrontation with Arthur at Dover and their subsequent meetings, which form the bulk of Malory's narrative before Arthur's departure from this earth. In Tennyson's poem there is only one major confrontation, at "the sunset bound of Lyonnesse"; in Malory this encounter is briefly dismissed:

never was there seen a more dolefuller battle in no Christian land: for there was but rushing and riding, foyning and striking, and many a grim word was there

45 The only alterations Tennyson made to the earlier poem are the deletion of the line "Sir Bedivere, the last of all his knights," the seventh line of the *Morte d'Arthur* now incorporated into the second line of *The Passing of Arthur*, and the small substitution of "So" for "And" in the first line, "So to the barge they came. There those three Queens / Put forth their hands, and took the King, and wept."

46 Gawain's appearances begin in *Elaine*, occur in each of the following idylls (according to the chronology of their composition), and end with this idyll. In the three idylls still to be written, Gawain will not be an active figure.

spoken either to other, and many a deadly stroke. But alway king Arthur rode
throughout the battle of sir Mordred many times, and did there right nobly as a
noble king should do; and at all times he never fainted. And sir Mordred that day
put him in devoir and in great peril, and thus they fought all the long day, and
never stinted till the noble knights were laid to the cold ground. And ever they
fought still till it was nigh night, and by that time was there a hundred thousand
laid dead upon the down [III, clxvii].

Arthur's forces are killed, except for Sir Lucan and Sir Bedivere. Before
his own departure, the King kills Mordred.

For Tennyson the final engagement of the forces is a horrid display
of physical and mental frenzy. With the termination of the temporal
realization of Arthur's vision, Arthur's own knights are reeling back into
their bestial states; their world now lacks direction and light. Without an
inspiring vision the kingdom returns to the chaos that prompted Leodogran to cry out to Arthur: "Arise, and help us thou! / For here between the
man and beast we die." Arthur's vision has become the subject of scorn,
ridicule, and abuse; a world without respect for this vision becomes a
world capable only of its self-destruction. Consequently, the final battle
is an impressionistic painting in which distinct figures lose their identity
in the chaos of which they are both the agents and the victims: "For
friend and foe were shadows in the mist, / And friend slew foe not
knowing whom he slew." The confusion of the battlefield is a confusion
created by Guinevere's sin, which always lies conspicuously at the
centre of Arthur's Order; thus the King rightly maintains: "Yet let us
hence, and find or feel a way / Thro' this blind haze, which ever since I
saw / One lying in the dust at Almesbury, / Hath folded in the passes of
the world." The "blind haze" from Almesbury, resulting in this final
confusion, prompts Arthur to question his own identity: "O Bedivere,
for on my heart hath fall'n / Confusion, till I know not what I am, / Nor
whence I am, nor whether I be King." As in *The Coming of Arthur,* the
immediate response to the problem of the King's identity comes from
Bedivere: "My King, / King everywhere! and so the dead have kings, /
There also will I worship thee as king." Arthur's kingship will be
vindicated by his vision even after his earthly passing; in this way Arthur
is the antithesis of Gawain's scepticism, both in this life and in eternity.

Arthur's final heroic act, "one last act of knighthood," is his slaying
of Modred. In this climactic encounter, borrowed from Malory, Arthur
destroys the agent of destruction who plotted the ruin of his house, the
serpent who exploited the sin of the Queen and exposed her failing to the
world of the court.

The brief introduction to the *Morte d'Arthur* does not explain the
manner in which Modred raised such an army against Arthur, nor does it
chronicle the King's activity between his departure from Almesbury and
his arrival in Lyonnesse. It does provide a suitable bridge between

Arthur's parting from his Queen and his subsequent parting from this world. The disorder of his realm was already evident in *Guinevere*. Blind confusion now reigns in Arthur's world; the "blind haze" from Almesbury has become "A deathwhite mist . . . over sand and sea."

The opening of *The Passing of Arthur* retains the slaying of Modred by the King and an altered form of the dream about Gawain; with these two exceptions the introduction shows no verbal or structural fidelity to Malory. Malory's brief account of the final encounter of the two armies becomes a detailed and vivid collage of confused soldiers battling without sight in a war that offers only death; Tennyson's presentation is less an expansion of Malory's version than a totally new battle, a verbal painting of frenzied confusion. Arthur's self-analysis on the battlefield and Bedivere's comforting words find no parallel in Malory. The introduction stands in striking contrast to the *Morte d'Arthur* in the treatment of its medieval source. The poet of the *Morte d'Arthur,* a faithful adherent to Malory who exerted scrupulous efforts to follow closely the narrative structure of his source, has become a poet who finds inspiration in Malory but who is guided ultimately by his earlier Arthurian poems and his unbridled sense of invention.

The closing twenty-four lines added to the *Morte d'Arthur* find no counterpart in Malory. After Arthur's disappearance on the barge, Malory follows Bedivere's wanderings; the following morning Bedivere meets a hermit, the Bishop of Canterbury, who shows him a new grave and explains that "this night, at midnight, here came a great number of ladies, which brought this dead corpse, and prayed me to bury him; and here they offered a hundred tapers, and gave me a hundred besants" (III, clxix). Malory retains the ambiguity of his source by adding a final personal statement:

> More of the death of king Arthur could I never find, but that ladies brought him unto the burials. And such one was buried here, that the hermit bare witness, that sometimes was bishop of Canterbury: but yet the hermit knew not of a certain that it was verily the body of king Arthur. For this tale sir Bedivere, knight of the round table, made it plainly to be written.
>
> Some men yet say, in many parts of England, that king Arthur is not dead; but, by the will of our Lord Jesu Christ, into another place: and men say, that he will come again, and he shall win the holy cross. I will not say that it shall be so; but rather I will say, that here in this world he changed his life. But many men say that there is written upon his tomb this verse:—*Hic jacet Arthurus rex quondam, rex futurus* [III, clxix-clxx].

Tennyson deletes the meeting with the hermit in order to leave Bedivere in his isolation. Bedivere's reference to the three dark Queens, a further connection with *The Coming of Arthur,* precedes the final sight:

> Then from the dawn it seem'd there came, but faint
> As from beyond the limit of the world,
> Like the last echo born of a great cry,

> Sounds, as if some fair city were one voice
> Around a king returning from his wars.

Arthur seems to have received the reward he deserves; his journey to earth was but a brief attempt to "Have power on this dark world to lighten it, / And power on this dead world to make it live." His attempt was in vain; Camelot has returned to the state of Leodogran's realm before Arthur's arrival. Arthur's presence and his vision stand as a testimony of the ideal to which men must aspire.

The Passing of Arthur, a combination of a long central section written in 1833-34 and based very closely on Malory and a new framework consisting of an introduction and a short conclusion only loosely related to Malory, is the fourth and final idyll of the new volume. Tennyson has written an idyll on the Grail quest, the episode that impeded progress on his Arthurian work. Now the pair of poems, *The Coming of Arthur* and *The Passing of Arthur,* offers him a satisfactory framework for the entire work. The three poems, accompanied by *Pelleas and Ettarre,* form the quartet of idylls published in December 1869 in the volume *The Holy Grail and Other Poems.*

The second quartet of idylls continues the thematic structure of the 1859 volume. Guinevere, the dominating presence of the earlier volume, makes fewer appearances, though she remains thematically present. Her sin stands behind the rash quest of the Grail; in the aftermath of the quest her dishonour drives an innocent young knight to despair. Though the idylls that frame the series focus intensely on the King, his origin— the subject of the opening idyll—is a topic for discussion only because of Leodogran's desire that his daughter find an appropriately regal husband. The *Idylls* now begins with a description of Guinevere: "Leodogran, the King of Cameliard, / Had one fair daughter, and none other child; / And she was fairest of all flesh on earth, / Guinevere, and in her his one delight."

At the same time the second quartet develops Tennyson's growing independence from Malory. *The Holy Grail* reworks some of the material of Malory's Grail story for a nineteenth-century audience; *Pelleas and Ettarre* takes an early incident in Malory, alters the centre of attention, and changes the ending so that the idyll becomes a concrete manifestation of the growing decay in Camelot. The opening idyll employs Malory's account of Arthur's birth in an altered form, but superimposes a series of conflicting accounts so that there remains no certainty about Arthur's origin. Only the central section of *The Passing of Arthur,* written under the title of *Morte d'Arthur* three decades earlier, observes a close fidelity to Malory's narrative. Tennyson's Arthurian world began as a re-creation of Malory; now it is becoming increasingly his own creation, inspired by, but not openly indebted to, Malory and his medieval world.

The presence of the four idylls within a volume of poems suggests that the Arthurian series is not yet complete. Despite the statement that the four idylls are ''printed in their present form for the convenience of those who possess the former volume,''[47] and despite the later publication of the series of eight idylls,[48] Tennyson regarded the four poems, not as the completion of his projected poem, but as additions. The volume was the poet's acknowledgement to his readers that he was continuing to move towards the completion of the Arthurian masterpiece that he had been planning since his childhood.

47 The page opposite the frontispiece of the 1869 edition has the following description:

These four ''Idylls of the King'' are printed in their present form for the convenience of those who possess the former volume.

The whole series should be read, and is to-day published, in the following order:—

THE COMING OF ARTHUR.

The Round Table.

GERAINT AND ENID.
MERLIN AND VIVIEN.
LANCELOT AND ELAINE.
THE HOLY GRAIL.
PELLEAS AND ETTARRE.
GUINEVERE.

THE PASSING OF ARTHUR.*

*This last, the earliest written of the poems, is here connected with the rest in accordance with an early project of the author's.

48 *The Holy Grail and Other Poems* first appeared in December 1869; the collected edition of the eight *Idylls of the King* first appeared in January 1870.

Chapter 4

1873: Autumn and Spring

The Last Tournament, Gareth and Lynette

> Knight after knight, as leaf after leaf, decaying and
> dropping off from all attempt to keep the promise of the
> Spring.[1]

The four idylls of 1869 indicated to the poet and to his readers the journey
that awaited him. Criticism of the volume was almost unanimously
favourable; only three contemporary reviews expressed negative reactions.[2] Indeed, the poet no longer feared the dictates of his reviewers;
even before the quartet was published he was reconsidering the possible
incorporation of the story of Sir Gareth into his poem.[3]

The next two idylls to be added to the series, *The Last Tournament*
and *Gareth and Lynette,* are the natural consequence of his earlier
creation, *Pelleas and Ettarre.* The latter poem, "the saddest of the
idylls," finds its antithesis in *Gareth and Lynette,* undoubtedly the
happiest of the idylls; with its springtime setting and its characters of
youthful innocence growing into noble manhood, the idyll suggests the
perfection that once belonged, however briefly, to Arthur's realm. *The
Last Tournament,* a sombre study of the autumn of the Round Table,

1   "The Meaning of Mr. Tennyson's 'King Arthur,' " *Contemporary Review,* 21 (May
    1873), 940. This unsigned review was written by the poet's friend James Knowles; a
    section of the review quotes directly, as it indicates, from his earlier article in
    Spectator, January 1, 1870, pp. 15-17, an article signed "J.T.K."
2   "Mr. Tennyson and the Round Table," *British Quarterly Review,* 51 (January 1870),
    200-214; "The Holy Grail and other Poems," *Quarterly Review,* 128 (January 1870),
    1-17; "The Laureate and His 'Arthuriad,' " *London Quarterly Review,* 34 (April 1870),
    154-186.
3   On October 7, 1869, Emily recorded in her journal: "He gave me his beginning of
    'Beaumains' ('Sir Gareth') to read, written (as was said jokingly) to 'describe a pattern
    youth for his boys' " (*Memoir,* II, 82-83).

continues the tragic movement of the Pelleas idyll by focusing intensely and despairingly on the decay of Camelot; the society that drove Pelleas to madness must now endure the product of that madness, the transformation of Pelleas into the Red Knight of the North.[4] In both idylls, Tennyson sought to complete his poem by incorporating Arthurian stories he had already studied as possible episodes for his own masterpiece.[5]

In *The Last Tournament*, which was already partially completed by November 1870,[6] Tennyson completes his depiction of Camelot after the Grail quest. The centre of the idyll is not a particular person or a pair of persons, but rather the present society as a whole. *Pelleas and Ettarre* studied Arthur's crumbling society by watching the effects of that society on one knight, Pelleas; *The Last Tournament* studies that society in its entirety, a society crumbling under its failure to recognize and respect the vision of its creator. As a result the idyll lacks any one person who coherently connects its episodes; like Camelot itself the poem respects no directing focus or centre.

Though Sir Charles Tennyson referred to the poet's beginning "to work at the Idyll on the story of Tristram, which he had determined to place just before *Guinevere*,"[7] and though Hallam Tennyson noted that "the bare outline of the story and of the vengeance of Mark is taken from Malory,"[8] *The Last Tournament* is, properly speaking, Tennyson's treatment of the final episode of the Tristram story. Tristram is not the centre of the poem, nor is the poem's titular event its centre. Camelot in decay is the subject of the poem; here is the final glimpse of the court before the journey to Almesbury, and, ultimately, to that "last dim battle in the west." The final depiction of Camelot utilizes an abbreviated version of the Tristram story as only one indication of the condition of the realm.[9]

---

4 Though the idyll never names the Red Knight by his former name of Pelleas, the Eversley edition makes this identification (V, 501). When Arthur meets the Red Knight, the narrator comments: "Arthur knew the voice; the face / Wellnigh was helmet-hidden, and the name / Went wandering somewhere darkling in his mind." The absence of Pelleas' name in the idyll suggests his complete transformation which makes him unworthy of his former title.

5 "He now began to turn over in his mind additional subjects which would fit into and complete his pattern, and which he could set about in earnest as soon as he settled down for the summer at Aldworth" (Sir Charles Tennyson, p. 388). He had already read the story of Gareth as early as February 1861 (*Memoir*, I, 471) and, more recently, October 1869 (see preceding footnote 3). As for the Tristram story, he had thought about such a poem in 1859 (*Materials*, II, 218).

6 *Memoir*, II, 100.

7 Sir Charles Tennyson, p. 394.

8 Eversley edition, V, 500.

9 By the time Tennyson turned to the Tristram story for his poem, two of his contemporaries had already written poems on the subject. In 1857 Swinburne published the first canto of *Queen Yseult*, an account of Tristram's parentage and early career. Arnold's *Tristram and Iseult*, the first modern treatment of the Tristram story in

Though *The Last Tournament* lacks a centre, the poem offers a guide to its world in the figure of Sir Dagonet, who appears at the beginning, at the middle, and at the end. The importance of Dagonet is evident in the short prose draft of the idyll found in Harvard Notebook 40.[10] In Malory, Dagonet, a relatively minor figure, appears only three times, each time in the Tristram section of the work. Sir Kay, the bully and the most foolish of Arthur's knights, sends Sir Dagonet, Arthur's fool, to challenge la Cote mal Taille to a joust (II, xliv). In his next appearance Dagonet is thrown into a well by Tristram; after this episode, Tristram attacks Dagonet and "got sir Dagonet by the head, and gave him such a fall, that he bruised him sore; so that he lay still" (II, lx). Dagonet again becomes the instrument of comedy when Dinadan plans a scheme whereby Mark believes Dagonet to be Lancelot and flees in terror from him (II, xcvii). Malory's Dagonet is Arthur's fool, though he is a fool only in the sense of clown or buffoon. He is the instrument of comedy for the other knights. His seemingly dim-witted nature allows him to be the butt of their jokes; moreover, his foolishness makes him a mirror-image of the equally foolish but naturally dim-witted Kay, who initiates Dagonet's first comical adventure.

Tennyson's Dagonet resembles Malory's figure in name only. Tennyson takes the medieval figure of the clown and re-creates it according to the figure of the wise fool most clearly exemplified by the Fool in *King Lear*. Dagonet's "foolish" nature gives him the licence to utter truths which would bring punishment on any other characters who might make similar statements; moreover, his perception makes his ironic statements a further method of delineating Camelot's tragedy.

In *King Lear*, the Fool, a professional jester, uses the language of the jester to point out the true folly that has overtaken his master:

> That lord, that counsel'd thee
> To give away thy land,
> Come place him here by me,—
> Do thou for him stand;
> The sweet and bitter fool
> Will presently appear;
> The one in motley here,
> The other found out there.[11]

Within such a statement are both irony and pity, irony directed at Lear's action whereby he became a fool and pity arising from his foolish

English, preceded Tennyson's poem by nineteen years. With its focus on Iseult of Brittany and with the death-scene aboard the ship, Arnold's poem has no connection with Tennyson's account.
10 See Appendix 4.
11 *The Plays of Shakespeare*, notes by Samuel Johnson and George Steevens (London, 1785); Vol. 9 contains *Troilus and Cressida, Cymbeline*, and *King Lear*. The edition owned by the poet, is mentioned in the *Memoir*, II, 427-429 and by Sir Charles Tennyson, p. 536. Tennyson's copy is now in the Tennyson Research Centre.

behaviour. By his own character the Fool sheds light on the comparative folly of the other characters; not only is Lear's foolishness thereby clarified, but the folly of Goneril and Regan, masked under the guise of reasonable behaviour, is equally criticized by the Fool's behaviour.[12] Unlike Lear's eldest daughters, the Fool will not eschew his proper obligation to his master, even though his master has abdicated the trappings of kingship.[13] Kent is led to conclude, "This is not altogether fool, my Lord," and the Fool wisely proclaims: "No, 'faith, lords and great men will not let me; if I had a monopoly out, they would have part on't; and ladies too, they will not let me have all the fool to myself: they'll be snatching."

Lear's wise Fool is the basis for Tennyson's creation of Dagonet. About *King Lear,* Tennyson commented:

> *King Lear* cannot possibly be acted, it is too titanic. At the beginning of the play Lear, in his old age, has grown half mad, choleric and despotic, and therefore cannot brook Cordelia's silence. This play shows a state of society where men's passions are savage and uncurbed. No play like this anywhere—not even the *Agamemnon*—is so terrifically human.[14]

The world of Shakespeare's tragedy is the world of Camelot that the poet wants to portray after the Pelleas idyll. Consequently, Tennyson takes the Fool from *King Lear* and makes him the foundation for his own treatment of Malory's Dagonet. Like Lear's Fool Dagonet displays unquestioning loyalty to his master, a loyalty shared in *King Lear* only by Cordelia and Kent and a loyalty unshared in *The Last Tournament.* Like his counterpart in Shakespeare's play Dagonet is committed to the habit of truth-telling; his utterances are mocking denunciations of the decayed morality of the knights of the Round Table.

Though Lear's Fool exists only in the company of his King, Tennyson makes Dagonet appear primarily with Tristram; only in the final lines of the poem, "in a death-dumb autumn-dripping gloom," do the Fool and his master face each other. In the confrontation of Tristram and Dagonet the Fool is the instrument that exposes Tristram's cynicism; rooted in the reality of the present condition of the court, his cynicism is denounced only through the seemingly foolish though basically idealis-

---

12   In Act One, Scene Four, the Fool is first mentioned as pining away because of Cordelia's forced departure for France. Throughout the scene there is a natural and expressed enmity between the Fool and Goneril. Near the end of the play, Regan admits: "Jesters do often prove prophets" (V, iii).

13   In abdicating the throne, Lear gives up "the sway, revenue, execution of the rest," but he wants to keep "the name and all th' additions of a king." Lear's folly in abdicating the responsibilities of the throne is expressed most succinctly by the Fool: "When thou clovest thy crown i' th' middle and gav'st away both parts, thou bor'st thine ass on thy back o'er the dirt. Thou hast little wit in thy bald crown when thou gav'st thy golden one away" (I, iv).

14   *Memoir,* II, 292. Hallam Tennyson noted: "My father often referred with pleasure to his creation of the half-humorous, half-pathetic fool Dagonet" (Eversley edition, V, 500).

tic beliefs of Dagonet. In the decayed world of Camelot the knights regard idealism as folly; the Fool is the only knight who can accept and honour Arthur's vision.

Tennyson's employment of the Tristram story reveals his familiarity with Malory's long narrative account and his own free adaptation and abbreviation of it.[15] Malory's *Tristram de Lyones,* one-third of his complete work, is primarily concerned with the development of the character of Tristram as a knight second only to Lancelot as the exemplar of all chivalric ideals. All events portrayed by Malory are devoted to his development. The opening section (II, i-xxxvii), only one-seventh of the complete *Tristram*, offers a fully detailed depiction of the relationship of Tristram and La Beale Isoud from the time of their first encounter, through Tristram's role as Mark's emissary for the King's marriage, through Mark's marriage, to Tristram's own unconsummated marriage to Isoud of Brittany. The remainder of Malory's *Tristram* follows closely the French Prose *Tristan* in chronicling the varied adventures of Tristram and the other knights of the Round Table; only intermittently is the relationship of Tristram and La Beale Isoud reintroduced or emphasized. Their love is already an accepted background to the later episodes; the love that dominated the opening chapters loses its central position, stands steadily in the background, and remains static throughout subsequent episodes. Malory's *Tristram* ends with Tristram's final defeat of Palomydes and his new role as Palomydes' godfather; on such a triumphant note Malory sets aside the character of Tristram and returns to him, much later, when Lancelot tells Bors of Tristram's death:

"for by sir Tristram I may have a warning: for when by means of the treaty sir Tristram brought again la beale Isonde unto king Marke, from Joyous Gard, look what fell on the end, how shamefully that false traitor (king Marke) slew that noble knight as he sat harping before his lady, la beale Isonde, with a sharp grounded glaive thrust him behind to the heart. It grieveth me," said sir Launcelot, "to speak of his death, for all the world may not find such a knight" [III, cxlvii].

Tennyson ignores the chronology of Malory's account and makes Tristram's first secret meeting with Isolt after his marriage the scene of his murder. The poet's habit of violating medieval chronology is further

15 Tennyson's knowledge of Malory's account is especially evident in two details pertaining to Mark. The rivalry between Tristram and Mark for the affection of Seguarides' wife instigates the hatred of Mark for Tristram: "But, as long as king Marke lived, he never after loved sir Tristram, though there was much fair speech between them, yet love was there none" (II, xiv). This episode stands behind Isolt's comment: "For, ere I mated with my shambling king, / Ye twain had fallen out about the bride / Of one—his name is out of me—the prize, / If prize she were—(what marvel—could she see)— / Thine, friend; and ever since my craven seeks / To wreck thee villainously." Mark's sudden appearance and the manner of his murder of Tristram are also borrowed directly from Malory (III, cxlvii).

indicated by the position of the idyll; Malory places Tristram's marriage and his many subsequent visits to Mark's wife before the Grail quest; Tennyson makes Tristram's adultery a sign of the pervasive decay throughout the realm after the quest.

In making the Tristram story indicate the ruin of Arthur's realm, Tennyson has necessarily changed the figure of Tristram. Malory follows the knight to the height of his chivalric glory; Tristram's stature makes him second only to Lancelot as an ideal knight, a position that Malory continually emphasizes. After the episode with Brewnor at the Castle Pluere the narrator comments: "then sir Tristram was called the strongest and the biggest knight of the world; for he was called bigger than sir Launcelot, but sir Launcelot was better breathed" (II, xxvi). Dynas the Seneschal makes a similar comparison: "Ye shall understand that sir Tristram is called peerless and matchless of any Christian knight; and of his might and his hardiness, we know no where so good a knight, but if it be sir Launcelot du Lake" (II, xxxii). At the same time that Tristram assumes this high position of knighthood, he also becomes comparable to Lancelot in his adulterous love of a queen. Malory wants the relationship of Tristram and Isoud judged in the same light as the adultery of Lancelot and Guinevere. By retaining the few cross-references in his source to the two pairs of lovers and by adding a few brief comments,[16] Malory carefully controls his narration so that Tristram's love of Isoud is seen as similar in quality to Lancelot's love of his Queen, though it must remain subordinate in thematic importance. The ultimate distinction between Tristram and Lancelot lies in the centrality of Lancelot to the world of Camelot and the relative unimportance of Tristram to Arthur's Order.

Tennyson's Tristram can never achieve the stature of his medieval counterpart; *The Last Tournament* is the autumn of the Round Table. Tristram is a cynical realist dedicated to the practice of free love; his cynicism, rooted in the discrepancy between the knights' vows and their present conduct, never becomes bitter. Unlike Pelleas, who becomes the product of his society, Tristram is the ideal representative of such a world, the personification of the ideals that his world now upholds.

16 Malory makes the comparison of the two pairs of lovers more explicit by his elevation of Tristram in the continual contrasts to Lancelot and by his whitening of the character of Isoud. For the latter, he eliminates the bed-trick for the first night in Mark's marriage and thereby alters the motivation for the attempted murder of Brangwayne; no suggestion of treachery on Isoud's part remains. Though many comments comparing Lancelot and Tristram are found in the French prose versions, an example of one explicit comparison not recorded in French versions is Malory's statement: "all kings, lords, and knights, said, 'Of clear knighthood and pure strength, of bounty and courtesy, sir Launcelot and sir Tristram bare the prize above all knights that ever were in king Arthur's days' " (II, clviii). A good study of Malory's *Tristram* in the light of its source is Thomas C. Rumble, " 'The Tale of Tristram': Development by Analogy," *Malory's Originality*, pp. 118-183.

Tristram never becomes tragic because he is only dimly aware of the possible heights man may reach; he himself is the beast to which man has returned; Tristram is more pitiable than detestable.

In his three confrontations in the poem, first with Lancelot, then with Dagonet, and finally with Isolt, Tristram's nature becomes evident as the world in which he lives simultaneously asserts its nature. In his brief exchange with Lancelot Tristram likens himself to Arthur's greatest knight: "Right arm of Arthur in the battlefield, / Great brother, thou nor I have made the world; / Be happy in thy fair Queen as I in mine."[17] The comparison, valid in Malory, is only partially valid in the poem. Whereas Malory continually likens Tristram to Lancelot in regard to their knightly prowess and their adulterous entanglements, Tennyson maintains these points of comparison at the same time that he introduces a contrast in their attitudes to Arthur's vision. In the idyll Lancelot is a chastened and remorseful knight, painfully conscious of the sin he has committed and the effects of the sin on a once-glorious realm; he cannot regard the stately galleries with their white-robed women at the Tournament; he cannot intervene in the Tournament to uphold the laws that are being broken; he would be a hypocrite to set himself as the enforcer of Arthur's laws. Lancelot stands powerless in his awareness of the horrid reality about him. Tristram, on the other hand, accepts the reality of the Tournament with cynical delight. Both Lancelot and Tristram see the world as it is; Lancelot's horror stands in contrast to Tristram's delight.

In Tristram's encounter with Dagonet, the hypocrisy of Arthur's realm is even more evident. Dagonet the fool perceives the true folly of Tristram's cynicism, though Tristram cannot see the wisdom beneath Dagonet's superficial folly. Dagonet condemns Tristram's behaviour: "For when thou playest that air with Queen Isolt, / Thou makest broken music with thy bride, / Her daintier namesake down in Brittany— / And so thou breakest Arthur's music too." Tristram does have a seemingly honest vindication of his action: "Fool, I came late, the heathen wars were o'er, / The life had flown, we sware but by the shell— / I am but a fool to reason with a fool." When Tristram arrived at Camelot, Arthur's idealism was already an object of derision. The vows that were to unite the knights under their king seemed hollow and meaningless because their substance was not being respected; contrary to his own cynical outlook, Tristram's reaction to the vows does not deny their importance but shows the difficulty for any individual when the vows remain unobserved.[18] Unlike Pelleas, who was driven to madness by his realization

---

17   All quotations in this chapter from the *Idylls* are from the Imperial Library edition of 1873. Although *The Last Tournament* was first published in the *Contemporary Review* of December 1871, there are only a few minor word changes which distinguish the 1871 text from the text of the 1873 edition.

18   In *Perception and Design in Tennyson's Idylls of the King* (Athens, Ohio: Ohio

of Camelot's sinful society, Tristram accepts the present plight of the
court and enjoys the depravity.

Dagonet's world, the true vision that Arthur represents, becomes
folly in the eyes of the other knights, who mock "his one true knight— /
Sole follower of the vows." The mock-knight has become the one true
knight; the idealism of Camelot is being upheld only by a wise and
unappreciated fool. In the honesty of his perception, Dagonet sees the
true condition of the realm:

> and when the land
> Was freed, and the Queen false, ye set yourself
> To babble about him, all to show your wit—
> And whether he were King by courtesy,
> Or King by right—and so went harping down
> The black king's highway, got so far, and grew
> So witty that ye play'd at ducks and drakes
> With Arthur's vows on the great lake of fire.

The music of Camelot has become a sound which only the Fool and
Arthur and the angels hear. To mortals entrapped in the world of the
flesh and blind to the spiritual world beyond the merely earthly realm,
dancing to such a sound can seem only utter folly.

At the end of his encounter with Tristram the Fool offers his own
description of Arthur:

> Ay, ay, my brother fool, the king of fools!
> Conceits himself as God that he can make
> Figs out of thistles, silk from bristles, milk
> From burning spurge, honey from hornet-combs,
> And men from beasts—Long live the king of fools!

The description has been verified already, both by the conversion of
Edyrn and by the conversion of the Fool:

> Swine? I have wallow'd, I have wash'd—the world
> Is flesh and shadow—I have had my day.
> The dirty nurse, Experience, in her kind
> Hath foul'd me—an I wallow'd, then I wash'd—
> I have had my day and my philosophies—
> And thank the Lord I am King Arthur's fool.

To Tristram, confronted by the reality of this world and unable to see
beyond appearances, the Fool is but a fool, and his words are foolish and
meaningless talk. Though Tristram does reject the faith of the Fool, his
rejection indicates his failure to recognize its possible validity. Tristram's immoral behaviour becomes both an indictment of the society

University Press, 1969), John R. Reed expresses the same idea: "The vows were
never true nor false, but always merely the high ideal, assuming validity through being
enacted. Tristram's very discarding of the vows proves them to have been all that
Arthur meant them to be. The fact is not in the vows, but in those who fail to maintain
them" (p. 119).

whose sinfulness blinds him to any experience beyond the momentary pleasures of the senses and an indictment of Guinevere's sin which stands still at the centre of this society.

In his encounter with Isolt Tristram reveals himself as a man of lust; no longer Malory's loving worshipper of his beloved, he is the aggressive and unloving animal in pursuit of his female prey. Love has become lust in an autumnal world of "yellowing woods." The horror of his behaviour with Isolt does have an earthly precedent:

> Ah then, false hunter and false harper, thou
> Who brakest thro' the scruple of my bond,
> Calling me thy white hind, and saying to me
> That Guinevere had sinn'd against the highest,
> And I—misyoked with such a want of man—
> That I could hardly sin against the lowest.

Tristram and Isolt are aware of the quality of their relationship; they invoke Guinevere to excuse themselves: "Crown'd warrant had we for the crowning sin / That made us happy."

Tristram's treatment of Isolt is indicative of his bestiality; he makes light of his marriage to Isolt of Brittany, maintaining that "the name was ruler of the dark";[19] in a further attempt to blacken his character Tennyson omits the important detail from Malory that the marriage remained unconsummated through Tristram's own choice. Tennyson's knight could never display such restraint. Tristram treats Mark's wife with a flirtatious frivolity and a physical excitement reminiscent of Ettarre's more sophisticated treatment of Pelleas; though relegated to the role of a sensual but inactive recipient of Tristram's lust, Isolt does display an acute awareness of Tristram's exclusively sensual interest:

> For when had Lancelot utter'd aught so gross
> Ev'n to the swineherd's malkin in the mast?
> The greater man, the greater courtesy.
> Far other was the Tristram, Arthur's knight![20]
> But thou, thro' ever tarrying thy wild beasts—
> Save that to touch a harp, tilt with a lance
> Becomes thee well—art grown wild beast thyself.

And she is conscious of her own need of the vows Tristram mocks:

> The man of men, our King—My God, the power
> Was once in vows when men believed the King!
> They lied not then, who sware, and thro' their vows

---

19 Though the detail of the similar names is obvious, no medieval author offers it as Tristram's sole excuse for his marriage. In *Queen Yseult* Swinburne employs this idea, borrowed from the romance of *Sir Tristrem*, which noted: "The maiden more he sought, / For sche Ysonde hight" (III, xxxiv). In the medieval romance, however, the detail is only a further inducement for Tristram to fall in love with the second woman.

20 This line, added in the 1873 edition, emphasizes explicitly the difference between the Tristram who was once committed to Arthur's Order and the later Tristram now speaking to Isolt.

> The King prevailing made his realm:—I say,
> Swear to me thou wilt love me ev'n when old,
> Gray-hair'd, and past desire, and in despair.

In her desire for a vow of security Isolt implies that within man there is a real need for the stability Arthur's Order offers; stability cannot exist in a world of free love.

Isolt's need for a vow prompts Tristram to narrate his version of the history of Arthur's realm:

> For once—ev'n to the height—I honour'd him.
> "Man, is he man at all?" methought, when first
> I rode from our rough Lyonnesse, and beheld
> That victor of the Pagan throned in hall—
> His hair, a sun that ray'd from off a brow
> Like hillsnow high in heaven, the steel-blue eyes,
> The golden beard that clothed his lips with light—
> Moreover, that weird legend of his birth,
> With Merlin's mystic babble about his end
> Amazed me; then, his foot was on a stool
> Shaped as a dragon; he seem'd to me no man,
> But Michael trampling Satan; so I sware,
> Being amaz'd: but this went by—The vows!
> O ay—the wholesome madness of an hour—
> They served their use, their time; for every knight
> Believed himself a greater than himself,
> And every follower eyed him as a God;
> Till he, being lifted up beyond himself,
> Did mightier deeds than elsewise he had done,
> And so the realm was made.

Contrary to his statement to Dagonet, Tristram did see Camelot in its glory when the validity of the vows was indicated by their observance; his account of the kingdom's creation is the account of a practical realist, a man who must stand "amaz'd" at events which betoken more than their concrete appearances indicate. Tristram's practicality becomes cynicism only when Guinevere's dishonour begins to undermine the integrity of Arthur's Order:

> but then their vows—
> First mainly thro' that sullying of our Queen—
> Began to gall the knighthood, asking whence
> Had Arthur right to bind them to himself?
> Dropt down from heaven? wash'd up from out the deep?
> They fail'd to trace him thro' the flesh and blood
> Of our old kings: when then? a doubtful lord
> To bind them by inviolable vows,
> Which flesh and blood perforce would violate:
> For feel this arm of mine—the tide within
> Red with free chase and heather-scented air,
> Pulsing full man; can Arthur make me pure
> As any maiden child? lock up my tongue

From uttering freely what I freely hear?
Bind me to one? The wide world laughs at it.

Blinded by flesh and blood, Tristram cannot conceive of Arthur's true
nature; he shares the skepticism of his fellow knights. The sin of the
Queen, rooted in the world of the flesh, has greater meaning for Tristram
than the spiritual vision Arthur espouses. Consequently, Tristram's
cynicism makes him a "worldling of the world."

Grounded in a cynicism rooted in fleshly reality, Tristram is a
pitiable indictment of his society. Isolt's reservation about his behaviour, "But thou . . . art grown wild beast thyself," is not answered
because it cannot be answered, though she does succumb to his costly
gift and his fleshly enticement. As he "bow'd to kiss the jewell'd
throat," Mark "clove him thro' the brain."

Tennyson has employed the Tristram story in order to offer one
exemplum of the present deterioration of Camelot. Tristram, Malory's
glorious knight, has become a cynical creature of the flesh, unaware of
any higher calling. Malory's Isoud, the ideal beloved, always thoughtful,
honest, and totally devoted to her lover, remains a secondary figure,
important only as the object of Tristram's lust. Tennyson's Isolt does
become jealous in her reaction to Tristram's reference to her old age
when she will be "past desire." Her fear properly reflects the insecurity
of her love that must exist in a world dedicated only to the passions.

Tennyson gives Mark a relatively unimportant, indeed non-
existent, role until his sudden and brief appearance; Mark is the butcher-
ing instrument of Tristram's death. Mark's "way" is not a form of life
without order; in his murderous action Mark is a principled man, though
his principles are those of Old Testament personal vengeance. Unenlightened by Arthur's spiritual vision, he acts according to his own law.
Tristram is enlightened by Arthur's vision, though he ignores the vows
he once swore; the consequence is his deliberate failure to follow the
King's enlightenment, a failure which, he realizes, makes him worse
than he would have been if, like Mark, he remained always unenlightened: "The vow that binds too strictly snaps itself— / My knighthood taught me this—ay, being snapt— / We run more counter to the
soul thereof / Than had we never sworn." The ultimate irony is that
Tristram's attitude to the vows leaves him with an order in society that
will allow Mark's personal vengeance.

Finally, the passion of Tristram and Isolt, openly condemned by the
poet, finds its sanction in the behaviour of the Queen and her lover.
Vivien has already found justification for her seductive poses in Guinevere's sin; Ettarre refuses to accept Guinevere's criticism of her treatment of Pelleas, since the Queen can no longer be a sincere advocate of
true love. Now the openly sensual behaviour of Tristram finds warrant
in the Queen's sin, and Isolt's qualms about their adulterous union are

somewhat calmed by her inability to find a proper example set by Guinevere, the Queen Paramount.

Tennyson's treatment of Malory's story of Tristram shows his total disregard of the chronology of Malory's narrative, his freedom with Malory's characters, and his adaptation of the story so that it becomes a moral exemplum of Arthur's degraded realm. In addition, the idyll is more than an abbreviated version of the Tristram legend; it embodies much more than the condensed depiction of Tristram's lust for Isolt. The Tournament of Youth, the early focus of the preceding idyll, is followed by the Tournament of the Dead Innocence, a sorry description of the fate of innocence in this setting. The Tournament, not based on any single tournament in Malory, exists as a final depiction of the death of an ideal; it is a complete mockery of the principles and standards Arthur has established in his kingdom.

The Tournament of the Dead Innocence is a tragedy from its inception. It is established in order to present the ruby necklace of an innocent babe who died in Guinevere's care; Guinevere's sin comes to poison the life of the realm, and, in this episode, the Queen cannot protect the life of a baby.[21] The jewels which Guinevere cannot bear to behold are the prize. The Tournament is interrupted, even before its beginning, by the sudden appearance of a maimed churl. Brutally mistreated by the Red Knight of the North, the churl was attacked when he called upon the name of Arthur; the name that had bound the knights to their King has now become the cause of slaughter. Arthur's question, ''Man was it who marr'd Heaven's image in thee thus?'' has a double meaning in its application both to the churl and to the Order. An "evil beast" has wrought this villainy, though the beast has spoken the truth:

> Tell thou the King and all his liars, that I
> Have founded my Round Table in the North,
> And whatsoever his own knights have sworn
> My knights have sworn the counter to it—and say
> My tower is full of harlots, like his court,
> But mine are worthier, seeing they profess
> To be none other than themselves—and say
> My knights are all adulterers like his own,
> But mine are truer, seeing they profess
> To be none other; and say his hour is come,

21 As Kathleen Tillotson first noted (*Mid-Victorian Studies* [London: Athlone Press, 1965], p. 84, n. 1), the episode of the child is taken in part from Sharon Turner's *History of the Anglo-Saxons*, II, 139-140, in the account of Nestling, a foundling discovered by King Alfred: ''One day as he was hunting in a wood, he heard a cry of an infant in a tree, and ordered his huntsmen to examine the place. They ascended the branches, and found at top, in an eagle's nest, a beautiful child, dressed in purple, with golden bracelets, the marks of nobility, on his arms. The King had him brought down and baptized, and well educated; from the accident, he named the foundling Nestigum.'' The significance of the story for Tennyson, the death of the child, has no foundation in the legend about King Alfred.

> The heathen are upon him, his long lance
> Broken, and his Excalibur a straw.

The heathens Arthur had cleansed from his realm have returned to destroy it; more importantly, the heathens are not foreigners; their leader is a former knight of the Round Table, a disillusioned product of the ideal society Arthur established.

As a consequence of this new attack Arthur must abdicate his role at the Tournament and lead his younger knights against this "Satan in the North." His decision to allow Lancelot to arbitrate the field emphasizes both the high position Lancelot should merit and the tragic absence of any knight who still espouses Arthur's principles. The idyll chronicles the "flat confusion and brute violences" that are destroying the realm.

Tristram's three encounters in the poem depict his movement back into the beast; Arthur's adventures in the North reveal the same backward movement in his knights. The North is a world similar to Doorm's kingdom and to Leodogran's kingdom before Arthur's arrival: "A roar of riot, as from men secure / Amid their marshes, ruffians at their ease / Among their harlot-brides, and evil song." Arthur does not fight the Red Knight but allows his drunken condition to be his destruction. Pelleas' death does not end the strife; a slaughter follows "Till all the rafters rang with woman-yells, / And all the pavement stream'd with massacre." Lancelot remains powerless to stop the breaking of the rules of the Tournament; in a similar way Arthur, able to speak but unable to be heard, remains powerless to stop the carnage his "younger knights, new-made," are inflicting. Before his own eyes Arthur is forced to behold his knights "reel back into the beast."

The Tournament and the simultaneous foray by Arthur and his younger knights against the Red Knight of the North are incidents with no foundation in Malory. To these invented episodes Tennyson added his narrative condensation of Tristram's affair with Isolt. The product is a seemingly unstructured idyll that reflects the lack of order in Camelot. Only the Fool, a mock-knight, adheres to Arthur's idealism. When Arthur returns to Camelot, "All in a death-dumb autumn-dripping gloom," the Fool is present to greet him; he alone can sincerely express his personal commitment and loyalty; no longer the jester of a healthy court, the Fool can only sob: "I shall never make thee smile again."

The Tournament, created in honour of a death, becomes a graphic and horrifying depiction of the present condition of Camelot. The depiction is complemented by the activities of Arthur's forces in the North and by the lust of Tristram in the West. The slaughter in the North, caused by the defiant violence of the Red Knight, owes its existence to the adultery that precipitated Pelleas' despair and madness; Tristram's behaviour seems to find justification in the Queen's behaviour. Guinevere remains the prominent cause of the destruction of Camelot. In this idyll she is only momentarily present, but her disloyalty pervades the poem. As Arthur leaves for the North, the poet offers a brief glimpse of the Queen:

> In her high bower the Queen,
> Working a tapestry, lifted up her head,
> Watch'd her lord pass, and knew not that she sigh'd.
> Then ran across her memory the strange rhyme
> Of bygone Merlin, "Where is he who knows?
> From the great deep to the great deep he goes."

At the end of *Pelleas and Ettarre* Guinevere "foresaw the dolorous day to be"; that day is at hand and Arthur's departure brings an involuntary sigh of regret and remorse from his sinful Queen.

The Last Tournament completes Tennyson's depiction of the destruction of Arthur's Order. Tristram's cynicism seems valid in a world where no one follows the King's spiritual ideals; Lancelot cannot speak, Guinevere departs for her bower, Arthur's voice cannot be heard. Tristram's philosophy seems the only natural and tenable outlook in this world. The idealism of Arthur has been assigned to the mouth of a Fool who remains its only spokesman.

Pelleas and Ettarre, the "saddest of the idylls," has led to *The Last Tournament*, the most ironic of the idylls. The disillusionment of Pelleas has been replaced by the cynicism of Tristram and by the powerlessness of Lancelot and Arthur. The glorious vision that was the foundation of Arthur's Order has been abused, rejected, and destroyed; Arthur's own knights become the beasts his Order sought to eliminate. The final spokesman for the order is a wise fool named Dagonet, based on the similar figure of Lear's Fool; Dagonet, the unheeded voice of wisdom, seems to this present world of Camelot only the shallow and foolish clown he was in Malory's world.

Like *The Last Tournament, Gareth and Lynette* draws inspiration from *Pelleas and Ettarre*. Whereas *The Last Tournament* completes the autumnal deterioration of Camelot, *Gareth and Lynette* stands in direct opposition to the setting, the characters, and the themes of the Pelleas idyll. With the demise of Camelot's glory, Pelleas' youthful innocence develops into disillusionment and madness; with the glory of Arthur's Order in its prime, Gareth's youthful innocence develops into nobility and practical idealism. *Gareth and Lynette* is an extended study of the glory of Arthur's realm, a study of the momentary realization of the Order. For Tristram that moment of glory was "the wholesome madness of an hour"; after Tristram's cynical description of the "madness," Tennyson returns to re-create and finish his portrayal of the springtime joy of Gareth and Camelot.

The composition of *Gareth and Lynette* frames the composition of
The Last Tournament.[22] The early prose draft of the idyll in Harvard
Notebook 40 reveals Tennyson's original plan of composition; he would
return to the familiar practice of establishing a comparison between a
female figure and Guinevere; the adulterous Bellicent would see herself
as similar to Guinevere in her behaviour; consequently, the idyll would
begin when the shame of the Queen's adultery was already evident in the
realm.[23] Such an opening would retain the blemished character of
Gareth's mother from Malory; it would make the idyll too similar to
Geraint and Enid in its dependence upon the growing rumour of Guinevere's dishonourable behaviour. Such a plan would deprive the completed series of any idyll which features the full glory of the Order.
Lastly, by remaining faithful to Malory's portrait of Gareth's mother,
the poet would cast doubt on the credibility of her earlier account of
Arthur's coronation and her own reverence for him.

The presence of the episode of Sir Dagonet in the prose draft of
Gareth and Lynette suggests Tennyson's simultaneous interest in the
Gareth episode and the Tristram story. His subsequent creation of *The
Last Tournament* depicts the final corruption of the realm; with the
completion of his study of Camelot's deterioration Tennyson returns to
the Gareth project with the intention of creating an antithesis to the
Pelleas idyll. He deletes the reprehensible aspect of Bellicent's charac-
ter and eliminates any reference to Guinevere; as a result, the world of
Gareth becomes, as it is in Malory, a world of perfection where Arthur's
vision has been realized.

Gareth and Lynette falls naturally into two distinct parts. First, the
poet offers an original depiction of Gareth's boyhood based on themes
established in earlier idylls. Then he follows Gareth's adventures on
behalf of Lynette with a fidelity to Malory similar to the technique of
adaptation and condensation evident in his handling of the *Mabinogion*
account of Geraint's life.

In the opening section of the idyll Gareth is seen in a family setting.
Bellicent, a loving but overprotective mother, is anxious that her
youngest son not leave home; her other sons, Gawain and Modred, have
already departed for Camelot.[24] Gareth yearns to follow his King, to be

22 The opening of the idyll was already written by October 1869 (see preceding footnote
    3); *The Last Tournament* was partially written by November 1870 (*Memoir*, II, 100)
    and completed by May 1871 (*Memoir*, II, 104). *Gareth and Lynette* was published at
    the end of 1872, together with *The Last Tournament*, in a volume entitled *Gareth and
    Lynette Etc.*
23 See Appendix 4.
24 In Malory, as in Tennyson's early prose outline of characters (see chapter 1), Gareth
    has three older brothers: Gawain, Gaherys, and Aggravayne. Tennyson's omission of
    two of them reflects his desire for simplicity through reduction; the emphasis on
    Modred as Gareth's brother is a further attempt to deny a blood relationship between
    Arthur and Modred.

"A knight of Arthur, working out his will, / To cleanse the world."
Despite his mother's plea that he remember her lonely condition with a
senile husband as her only companion,[25] Gareth has one ambition:
"follow the Christ, the King, / Live pure, speak true, right wrong, follow
the King— / Else, wherefore born?" The idealism that created the
Round Table finds its restatement in the faith and the innocence of
Gareth.

In her continuing attempt to prevent Gareth's departure Bellicent
reminds him of those who doubt the King's identity: "Sweet son, for
there be many who deem him not, / Or will not deem him, wholly proven
King." At the same time she must confess her own acceptance of
Arthur: "Albeit in mine own heart I knew him King." Her argument
loses its force since she voices both her acceptance of Arthur and the
kingdom's incomplete acceptance; she hopes that Gareth will wait until
Arthur proves his kingship by his actions; Bellicent needs concrete
evidence for the faith she already espouses. Her reasoning fails to alter
Gareth's intention; without the addition of such evidence, Gareth can
express his faith in Arthur and answer the call to the King's vision.

In Malory the *Tale of Gareth* is a "Fair Unknown" romance, the
story of a young man whose unrevealed nobility manifests itself in a
series of knightly adventures.[26] When Gareth arrives at court, he deliberately casts aside the riches with which his mother has decked him and
obtains three promises from Arthur; the first promise, granted immediately, provides him with "meat and drink sufficiently for these
twelvemonths" (I, cxviii). At the end of that period he receives his two
remaining promises: to become a knight and to be granted Lynette's
commission. As he rides away to save Lynette's sister, Kay and Lancelot follow; the former engages him in combat and is defeated; the latter
fights with him to a final draw. In this manner Gareth proves his valour to
Lancelot, his idol, and he can reveal to him his true lineage. Subsequent
encounters continue to show his strength; after a total of six combats
Gareth meets and defeats the Red Knight of the Red Lands who has been
besieging Castle Perilous for two years. After this seemingly climactic
episode a new series of adventures precedes Gareth's final union in
marriage with Lyones.[27]

25 In Malory, Lot is killed by Pellinore; Tennyson invents the portrait of Lot's senility to
    increase the possible validity of Bellicent's desire that Gareth remain at home.
26 A full discussion of the genre is found in E. Brugger, " 'Der Schöne Feigling' in der
    arthurischen Literatur," *Zeitschrift für romanische Philologie*, 61 (1941), 1-44; 63
    (1943), 123-173, 275-328; 65 (1945), 121-192, 289-433. R. H. Wilson, "The 'Fair Un-
    known' in Malory," *PMLA*, 58 (1943), 1-21, studies Malory's account of Gareth in
    relation to romances with a similar theme. For a discussion of the form of Malory's
    Tale of Gareth with references to Tennyson's treatment of the story, see Larry D.
    Benson, "Sir Thomas Malory's *Le Morte Darthur*," *Critical Approaches to Six
    Major English Works*, edited by R. M. Lumiansky and Herschel Baker (Philadelphia:
    University of Pennsylvania Press, 1968), pp. 81-131.
27 The "new series of adventures," equal in length to the series of encounters which

Malory's *Tale of Gareth* is a depiction of Arthur's Order as a working reality; for Tennyson the Tale portrays a world of innocence and perfection which Arthur envisioned but which no idyll has as yet studied. The Round Table has been established; the vows are being honoured; the story of Gareth holds a similar position in both Tennyson and Malory. The medieval Gareth arrives at Camelot on the feast of Pentecost; Tennyson's knight sets out from home "past the time of Easterday."[28] *Gareth and Lynette* is the spring of the Round Table, a world of realized ideals, a world where a dream has become reality.

Secondly, Malory's *Tale of Gareth* is a study in the revelation of identity; the plot becomes an appropriate continuation of the theme established in the opening idyll. In *The Coming of Arthur* Arthur's right to kingship is called into question; the final emphasis falls, not on his lineage, but on his nature as a king, his accomplishments and his effectiveness in the regal position. The new idyll studies the same theme, the problem of acceptance. Lynette's slow acceptance of Gareth as her knight begins only as he defeats his opponents; she cannot see his nobility until his deeds indicate it. She resembles Bellicent, who hesitates to commit her son to the Order until Arthur's accomplishments verify his kingship to the world. Gareth's acceptance of Arthur is a lesson which many, including Guinevere, will learn in the course of the tragedy of Camelot. Gareth accepts the King for the significance of his vision.

Gareth's first glimpse of Camelot is Tennyson's attempt to paint Arthur's dream at the moment of its realization. Already under the malign influence of Ettarre, Pelleas does not comment on the concrete world of Camelot when he arrives at the court; his only comment, "Black nest of rats... ye build too high," occurs on his subsequent return to the hall. Tristram also ignores the physical world of Camelot; his reflections upon his arrival at court refer to Arthur. The only extended description of Camelot is uttered by Percivale when he remembers the glory that was Camelot:

> For all the sacred mount of Camelot,
> And all the dim rich city, roof by roof,
> Tower after tower, spire beyond spire,
> By grove, and garden-lawn, and rushing brook,
> Climbs to the mighty hall that Merlin built.

Now, however, the poet allows a young man to see Camelot as Arthur created it; the description will be evidence that the highest idealism can have a reality, that Arthur did not "build too high."

precedes the final combat with the Red Knight of the Red Lands, was not employed by Tennyson since he substituted Lynette for Lyones as Gareth's beloved.

28 In Harvard Notebook 40 Gareth sets out for Camelot when "the King was holding the feast of Pentecost at King-Keredon in Wales" (3r). In the poetic draft of the idyll in the same Notebook, when Gareth sets out, "it was nigh the time of Pentecost" (12r).

Tennyson defined the world of Camelot:

Of course Camelot for instance, a city of shadowy palaces, is everywhere symbolic of the gradual growth of human beliefs and institutions, and of the spiritual development of man. Yet there is no single fact or incident in the "Idylls," however seemingly mystical, which cannot be explained as without any mystery or allegory whatever.[29]

Gareth's approach to Camelot becomes the poet's concrete delineation of this conception. Gareth's companions show only fear and misunderstanding when they see the city: "Lord, there is no such city anywhere, / But all a vision." For Gareth's companions a vision is an unreal and therefore not valid world. Camelot, however, is a vision in that it embodies the spiritual world in concrete reality; Camelot is one man's dream of man's highest capability. In contrast to his friends' skepticism Gareth sees the city as a reality that is a vision; he sees and accepts the physical and the spiritual reality of the world that confronts him. His questioning of Merlin is an attempt to calm his companions:

> but these, my men,
> (Your city moved so weirdly in the mist)
> Doubt if the King be King at all, or come
> From fairyland; and whether this be built
> By magic, and by fairy Kings and Queens;
> Or whether there be any city at all,
> Or all a vision: and this music now
> Hath scared them both, but tell thou these the truth.

In Merlin's response is a full understanding of Arthur; here is Merlin's realization, which Guinevere will later share, that Arthur is "the highest and most human too," that the most complete reality is ultimately spiritual:

> And as thou sayest it is enchanted, son,
> For there is nothing in it as it seems
> Saving the King; tho' some there be that hold
> The King a shadow, and the city real:
> Yet take thou heed of him, for, so thou pass
> Beneath this archway, then wilt thou become
> A thrall to his enchantments, for the King
> Will bind thee by such vows, as is a shame
> A man should not be bound by, yet the which
> No man can keep; but, so thou dread to swear,
> Pass not beneath this gateway, but abide
> Without, among the cattle of the field.
> For an ye heard a music, like enow
> They are building still, seeing the city is built
> To music, therefore never built at all,
> And therefore built for ever.

Arthur's world is the full realization of man's capability; outside Camelot man remains "among the cattle of the field"; inside this world

29 *Memoir*, II, 127.

man aspires to his highest calling. Camelot, rooted in reality, is built to the spiritual music of Arthur's vision; it cannot cease growing; it is the paradox of true humanity, its physical and simultaneously spiritual dimension.

The extended description of Camelot reaches its climax in Gareth's sight of the King:

> The splendour of the presence of the King
> Throned, and delivering doom...
>   but in all the listening eyes
> Of those tall knights, that ranged about the throne,
> Clear honour shining like the dewy star
> Of dawn, and faith in their great King, with pure
> Affection, and the light of victory,
> And glory gain'd, and evermore to gain.

The passage recalls Tristram's first sight of Arthur:

> That victor of the Pagan throned in hall—
> His hair, a sun that ray'd from off a brow
> Like hillsnow high in heaven, the steel-blue eyes,
> The golden beard that clothed his lips with lights—
>   ... for every knight
> Believed himself a greater than himself,
> And every follower eyed him as a God;
> Till he, being lifted beyond himself,
> Did mightier deeds than elsewise he had done,
> And so the realm was made.

These two reactions are similar; the only difference is the later development of the two knights. In Gareth's time the court's appearance is indicative of its true glory; by the time Tristram wins the necklace appearance is divorced from reality. The consequence of the change is the ultimate achievements of the two knights.

Before setting in motion the relationship of Gareth and Lynette, Tennyson introduces three original episodes which emphasize Arthur's right to be King and vindicate the faith in him Gareth expressed to Bellicent. The world Merlin described to the three strangers is now seen in its confrontation with practical problems. In the first episode a widow, robbed by Uther, seeks justice at the hands of the King; more than generous in his recompense, Arthur instructs the court: "No boon is here, / But justice, so thy say be proven true. / Accursed, who from the wrongs his father did / Would shape himself a right!" In the second episode another widow, bereft of her husband by the King in the Barons' War, seeks assistance from Arthur, even though she aligned herself with those who deemed the King "basely born." Despite Kay's objections Arthur extends his justice: "Thou that art her kin, / Go likewise; lay him low and slay him not, / But bring him here, that I may judge the right." The King's judgments reflect his new form of justice; indeed, "The kings of old had doom'd thee to the flames," but Arthur espouses justice complemented by compassion and love, principles enunciated by "that deathless King." In contrast to Arthur's justice is "Mark's way," a justice based on personal vengeance and retribution. With appropriate irony, the third visitor to the court is Mark's messenger. Tennyson portrays Mark as a man of unmitigated villainy: "a man of plots, / Craft, poisonous counsels, wayside ambushings." Arthur's hatred of Mark is not personal animosity, but instinctive renunciation of a brand of justice that is the negation of his own principles. The King's refusal to admit Mark reiterates the stipulation that men like Mark have no home in this new world; Mark must remain "among the cattle of the field." The three episodes portray the new justice operating in Camelot and demonstrate the code of behaviour Gareth must exercise in his adventures. Lancelot's later statement to Gareth becomes a fitting proclamation of Gareth's achievement of Arthur's ideal: "And thou hast wreak'd his justice on his foes."

After the long introduction to Gareth's story Tennyson turns to Malory's narrative. He joins his introduction to the medieval account by making Bellicent force a promise from her son:

> Prince, thou shalt go disguised to Arthur's hall,
> And hire thyself to serve for meats and drinks
> Among the scullions and the kitchen-knaves,
> And those that hand the dish across the bar.
> Nor shalt thou tell thy name to anyone.
> And thou shalt serve a twelvemonth and a day.

Gareth's personal choice of a disguised identity in Malory has become the consequence of Bellicent's demand in the poem. Tennyson closely follows Malory's narrative structure until the defeat of the Red Knight of the Red Lands. Gareth appears before Arthur's throne:

Right so came into the hall two men, well beseen and richly, and upon their shoulders there leaned the goodliest young man, and the fairest that ever they saw [I, cxviii].	Last, Gareth leaning both hands heavily Down on the shoulders of the twain, his men.

He seeks the opportunity to work among Arthur's kitchen-knaves for a year and a day.[30] Kay's immediate scorn only reveals his blindness to true nobility:

I dare well undertake that he is a villain born, and never will make	This fellow hath broken from some Abbey, where,

30 In Tennyson, Gareth asks his request for one year. Because of the introduction of this demand from Bellicent, Tennyson does not need to retain the device of the three promises exacted from Arthur by Gareth.

man; for and he had been come of a
gentleman, he would have asked of
you horse and harness, but such as
he is he hath asked. And sithence he
hath no name, I shall give him a
name, that shall be Beaumains; that
is to say fair hands, and into the
kitchen I shall bring him, and there
he shall have fat brewis every day,
that he shall be as fat by the
twelvemonth's end as a pork hog...
pain of my life he was brought up and
fostered in some abbey; and
howsomever it was they failed of
meat and drink, and so hither he is
come for sustenance [I, cxviii-cxix].

God wot, he had not beef and brewis
   enow,
However that might chance! but an
   he work,
Like any pigeon will I cram his crop,
And sleeker shall he shine than any
   hog...
Tut, an the lad were noble, he had
   ask'd
For horse and armour: fair and fine,
   forsooth!
Sir Fine-face, Sir Fair-hands? but see
   thou to it
That thine own fineness, Lancelot,
   some fine day
Undo thee not—and leave my man to
   me.

Whereas Malory includes Gawain with Arthur and Lancelot in their
perceptive appreciation of Gareth, Tennyson must eliminate Gawain
from the grouping, since his presentation of Gawain cannot sustain any
complimentary traits.

In Tennyson, Bellicent's remorse about her demand of Gareth
prompts her to nullify his promise; as his servitude ends, his desire for
knighthood expresses itself immediately. In contrast to Malory, where
Lancelot knights Gareth after the beginning of his adventures, Tennyson
places the knighting earlier in the plot in order to emphasize the close
relationship between Arthur and Lancelot. Gareth's desire for knighthood in secrecy prompts Arthur's partial refusal: "Make thee my knight
in secret? yea, but he, / Our noblest brother, and our truest man, / And
one with me in all, he needs must know." With this exception, Gareth's
request is granted.

Lynette's plea for assistance from the King is slightly altered by the
poet in order to enhance Lancelot's stature; whereas Malory's peti-
tioner demands "for to have sir Launcelot du Lake to do battle with him,
or sir Tristram, or sir Lamoracke de Gallis, or sir Gawaine" (I, cxxx),
Tennyson makes Lynette ask only for Lancelot. Her reaction to Gareth
is similar in both accounts, though the poetic version reveals Tennyson's customary expansion of detail:

"Fie on thee," said the damsel;
"shall I have none but one that is
your kitchen page." Then was she
wrath, and took her horse and
departed [I, cxx].

"Fie on thee, King! I ask'd for thy
   chief knight,
And thou hast given me but a
   kitchen-knave."
Then ere a man in hall could stay her,
   turn'd,
Fled down the lane of access to the
   King,

> Took horse, descended the slope
> street, and past
> The weird white gate, and paused
> without, beside
> The field of tourney, murmuring
> "kitchen-knave."

Following a practice exemplified so clearly in the *Morte d'Arthur* and later in *Geraint and Enid* and *Lancelot and Elaine,* Tennyson feels free to add any descriptive embellishments which make his subject-matter more vivid. Similarly, he describes in detail, without any correspondence in his source, the physical setting.[31]

The correspondence between Malory and Tennyson continues in Kay's malicious pursuit of Gareth. Fidelity accompanied by expansion is the poet's method. Malory's Kay comments: "I will ride after my boy of the kitchen, for to wit whether he will know me for his better" (I, cxxi). Tennyson's Kay has much more abuse to utter before he concludes: "I will after my loud knave, and learn / Whether he know me for his master yet." In both accounts Kay's departure is openly denounced by Lancelot, though Malory includes Gawain with Lancelot in the vocal condemnation. Kay's meeting with Gareth reveals a continuing similarity of treatment:

right so came sir Kaye and said, "What, sir Beaumains, know ye not me?" Then he turned his horse, and knew that it was sir Kaye, which had done him all the despite as ye have heard afore. "Ye?" said sir Beaumains, "I know you for an ungentle knight of the court, and therefore beware of me." Therewith sir Kaye put his spear in the rest, and ran upon him, and with his sword in his hand; and so he put away the spear with his sword, and with a foin thrust him through the side, that sir Kaye fell down as though he had been dead [I, cxxi].	for there was Kay. "Knowest thou not me? thy master? I am Kay. We lack thee by the hearth." And Gareth to him, "Master no more! too well I know thee, ay— The most ungentle knight in Arthur's hall." "Have at thee then," said Kay: they shock'd, and Kay Fell shoulder-slipt.[32]

Though Malory follows Kay's defeat with the combat of Lancelot and Gareth, Tennyson divides Gareth's encounter with Lancelot into two

31 A small change is evident here. In Tennyson, Gareth receives a warhorse and a spear and shield from Arthur; in Malory, Gareth receives a horse and armour from his dwarf, a character omitted by Tennyson; Malory's Gareth leaves the court without spear or shield.

32 Since Tennyson reduces the number of Gareth's combats, he also reduces the details here so that this episode, minor in contrast to the later combats, does not diminish the importance of the three central encounters.

episodes: the knighting, which occurred before his departure from the court, and their combat, reserved for a later and more significant position after Gareth's three major encounters.

Closer adherence to the source occurs when the plot focuses on the relationship of Gareth and Lynette:

When he had overtaken the damsel, anon she said, "What doest thou here? thou stinkest all of the kitchen, thy clothes be all bawdy of the grease and tallow, that thou hast gotten in king Arthur's kitchen. Weenest thou," said she, "that I allow thee for yonder knight that thou hast slain? nay, truly, for thou slewest him unhappily and cowardly; therefore, return again bawdy kitchen page. I know thee well; for sir Kaye named thee Beaumains: what are thou but a lusk and a turner of broaches, and washer of dishes."—"Damsel," said sir Beaumains, "say to me what ye list, I will not go from you whatsoever ye say; for I have undertaken of king Arthur for to achieve your adventure, and I shall finish it to the end, or I shall die therefore."—"Fie on thee, kitchen knave, wilt thou finish mine adventure? thou shalt anon be met withal, that thou wouldest not, for all the broth that ever thou suppest, once look him in the face."—"I shall assay," said Beaumains [I, cxxii].

Perforce she stay'd, and overtaken spoke.
    "What doest thou, scullion, in my fellowship?
Deem'st thou that I accept thee aught the more
Or love the better, that by some device
Full cowardly, or by mere unhappiness,
Thou hast overthrown and slain thy master—thou!—
Dish-washer and broach-turner, loon!—to me
Thou smellest all of kitchen as before."
    "Damsel," Sir Gareth answer'd gently, "say
Whate'er ye will, but whatsoe'er ye say,
I leave not till I finish this fair quest,
Or die therefore."
    "Ay, wilt thou finish it?
Sweet lord, how like a noble knight he talks!
The listening rogue hath caught the manner of it.
But, knave, anon thou shalt be met with, knave,
And then by such a one that thou for all
The kitchen brewis that was ever supt
Shall not once dare to look him in the face!"
    "I shall assay," said Gareth with a smile
That madden'd her.[33]

33 Tennyson's dependence upon Malory's text is further indicated by the poem's original reading of these lines; in the Widener MS of the poem, the lines facing page 82 read: "Dishwasher, & broachturner, lu(sk) & loon." The presence of "lusk" until the final proof is yet another indication of the close fidelity. For a discussion of the Widener MS, see Edgar F. Shannon, Jr., "The Proofs of 'Gareth and Lynette' in the Widener Collection," *Papers of the Bibliographical Society of America*, 41 (1947), 321-340.

In the similarity of the accounts, Tennyson's reliance on Malory's text reveals his desire for a structural fidelity which includes some degree of verbal fidelity.

In Malory's following episode a man tells Gareth of his master's plight: six thieves are trying to kill him. Without hesitation, Gareth rushes to the man's assistance; he kills three of the attackers; the other three flee, but Gareth overtakes them and kills them. Gareth feels compelled to reject an offer of hospitality because of his prior commitment to Lynette's sister; because night approaches, Lynette accepts the hospitality.

Tennyson takes this short episode and expands its content and its significance. No longer is Gareth unthinking in his determination to assist the knight; he seeks Lynette's permission before setting out. The poet changes the setting so that the attack occurs in a colourful mere where the knights are "blackshadow'd nigh the mere, / And mid-thigh-deep in bulrushes and reed." Lastly, the knight, nameless and characterless in Malory, becomes a "stalwart Baron, Arthur's friend." His attackers hate him because he is "cleanser of this wood." Like Gareth he is attempting to follow Arthur's example and cleanse the world. The Baron recognizes Gareth's nobility because of his deed:

> Friend, whether thou be kitchen-knave, or not,
> Or whether it be the maiden's fantasy,
> And whether she be mad, or else the King,
> Or both or neither, or thyself be mad,
> I ask not: but thou strikest a strong stroke,
> For strong thou art and goodly therewithal,
> And saver of my life.

He appreciates and accepts the nobility Lynette still ignores. The brief episode of the rescue becomes a further example of the theme of acceptance and the seeming necessity of proving one's ability through action.

The episode heralds a marked departure from Malory's narrative in its depiction of Lynette's behaviour to Gareth. Her reply is haughty: "I fly no more: I allow thee for an hour. / Lion and stoat have isled together, knave, / In time of flood," yet the reply reflects a slight softening; Tennyson's heroine does not remain as adamant as her medieval counterpart in her condescension to Gareth. The poet's substitution of Lynette as Gareth's beloved necessitates the gradual softening of her dislike, a softening that continues to mark her attitude towards Gareth.[34]

The remainder of the idyll is a condensation of the combats in Malory's account. The Red Knight of the Red Lands, the besieger of Castle Perilous, is the seventh knight Gareth meets in Malory; Tennyson condenses the seven encounters into four distinct but closely related

---

34 Tennyson creates the series of songs after each of the three encounters as a further indication of the growth in their affection.

episodes. Taking inspiration from the detail that four of Malory's seven combatants are brothers, he gives his four knights a similar relationship. Furthermore, by allegorizing the presentation of the four, he makes Gareth's struggles the "war of Time against the soul of man." Each represents a specific stage of man's life. The allegory, having no basis in Malory, does not overwhelm the concrete description of each combatant; the descriptions remain dependent upon Malory. Each encounter has its foundation in the allegorical scheme, with appropriate pictorial embellishments borrowed from Malory.

The knight who guards the first bridge, Sir Morning-Star, represents the many trials and temptations of youth; his appearance is a selective combination of four knights in Malory's account. From Sir Persuante of Inde, Gareth's sixth opponent, Morning-Star inherits his blue outfit; from the Red Knight of the Red Lands, he inherits the description of a pavilion; from the Green Knight, Gareth's fourth foe, he receives the horn and the consequent appearance of the damsels;[35] from the Black Knight, the first brother Gareth defeats, Tennyson borrows a dialogue about Gareth's lineage which he gives to Morning-Star:

"... I shall put him down upon his feet, and his horse and his armour he shall leave with me; for it were shame for me to do him any more harm... now yield thy lady from thee lightly; for it beseemeth not a kitchen knave to ride with such a lady."—"Thou liest," said sir Beaumains: "I am a gentleman born, and of more high lineage than thou art" [I, cxxiv].

"For this were shame to do him
  further wrong
Than set him on his feet, and take his
  horse
And arms, and so return him to the
  King.
Come, therefore, leave thy lady
  lightly, knave.
Avoid: for it beseemth not a knave
To ride with such a lady."
  "Dog, thou liest.
I spring from loftier lineage than
  thine own."

After Morning-Star's defeat, Gareth is willing to spare his life only if Lynette desires such an act of mercy; Gareth acts in this manner after his defeat of the Green Knight in Malory. The order of events is identical in both accounts: Lynette refuses to extend mercy to the defeated knight; Gareth immediately prepares to kill his victim; his preparation is arrested by Lynette's intervention. Gareth sends Morning-Star to Arthur, though the Green Knight must go to Camelot only at a future date of Gareth's choice.

Gareth's encounter with the second knight, Noon-Sun, a representation of the middle years of life, is a similar combination of details. His red attire recalls the red attire of both the fifth and the final combat-

35 In Malory there are two damsels; Tennyson gives Morning-Star a trio of female attendants.

ants in Malory. The manner of their encounter derives from Malory's description of Gareth's first adventure with a nameless knight on a bridge; though Gareth "smote the other upon the helm, that his head was stunned, and therewith he fell down into the water, and there was drowned," Lynette contemptuously calls out: "thou weenest thou hast done doughtily, and that is not so; for the first knight's horse stumbled, and there he was drowned in the water, and never it was by thy force and might" (I, cxxiii). Though Tennyson makes Gareth equal to his second opponent, he employs Lynette's abusive lie as the basis for their anti-climactic combat: "The hoof of his horse slipt in the stream, the stream / Descended, and the Sun was wash'd away."

The third knight, Evening-Star, the representative of old age, is an original creation. His description, "only wrapt in harden'd skins / That fit him like his own," finds no correspondence in Malory; the original portrayal, along with the figure of the grizzled damsel who arms him, is the result of his allegorical role; in Evening Star the allegory dictates an old knight for whom Malory's combatants cannot function as models. Gareth's long and arduous encounter with him, reminiscent of the long encounters with Persuante and with the Red Knight of the Red Lands, is brought to a conclusion by Lynette's heartening cry: "Shame me not, shame me not. I have prophesied— / Strike, thou art worthy of the Table Round— / His arms are old, he trusts the harden'd skin— / Strike— strike—the wind will never change again." In this final moment there is an echo of a similar situation in Malory, where Lynette brings Gareth's encounter with the Red Knight to an end with her exclamation: "O, sir Beaumains, where is thy courage become. Alas! my lady, my sister, beholdeth thee, and she sobbeth and weepeth, so that it maketh my heart heavy" (I, cxxxiv). Though the content of these entreaties is different, their crucial timing and their effect are identical; both exclamations inspire Gareth to bring his combat to an immediate and successful termination.

After the third encounter Tennyson allows the affection between Gareth and Lynette to manifest itself openly. With true humility, Lynette apologizes for her earlier behaviour. Gareth assures her that her only failing was her mistrust of the King. Trust is the basis of the power and the efficacy of Arthur's Order; trust in him and his wisdom makes the vows a valid code of behaviour. Lynette's failing is her lack of trust, not in Gareth her champion, but, more importantly, in the King whose vision creates the Order that now includes Gareth.

The following scene, the interlude in the cavern, is borrowed directly from Malory. In the medieval account the dwarf conducts the couple to a hermitage where Lyones has left "wine in two flagons of silver, they are of two gallons; and also two casts of bread, with fat venison baked, and dainty fowls; and a cup of gold" (I, cxxxi); in

Tennyson's account the hermitage contains "bread and baken meats and good red wine / Of Southland, which the Lady Lyonors / Had sent her coming champion." Tennyson's hermitage, however, serves the important function of offering Gareth instructions about his challengers:

"Sir Knave, my knight, a hermit once was here,
Whose holy hand hath fashion'd on the rock
The war of Time against the soul of man.
And yon four fools have suck'd their allegory
From these damp walls, and taken but the form.
Know ye not these?" and Gareth lookt and read—
In letters like to those the vexillary
Hath left crag-carven o'er the streaming Gelt—
"Phosphorus," then "Meridies"—"Hesperus"—
"Nox"—"Mors," beneath five figures armed men,
Slab after slab, their faces forward all,
And running down the Soul, a Shape that fled
With broken wings, torn raiment and loose hair,
For help and shelter to the hermit's cave.

Lest the allegory dominate the tale, Tennyson reintroduces Lancelot, who, with shield covered, overcomes Gareth in combat. Their encounter is partially based on their earlier encounter in Malory, though neither party is victorious in Malory. Lancelot's sudden appearance destroys the slight degree of pride discernible in Gareth's boast: "There rides no knight, not Lancelot, his great self, / Hath force to quell me." Lancelot's humility, "Thrown have I been, nor once, but many a time," is a lesson for Gareth. In addition, Lancelot's presence precipitates Lynette's dilemma, whether she should advocate Lancelot's battle with the fourth knight and thereby protect her now beloved Gareth, or whether she should advocate Gareth's encounter lest he miss "the full flower of this accomplishment." Her quandary is resolved by a further manifestation of Lancelot's nobility, his offer to lend Gareth his horse and arms so that the young knight may be "Lancelot-like," the highest compliment an aspiring knight can now receive.

The conclusion of the idyll bears little resemblance to Malory. The fourth brother is dressed in black, not because of borrowing from Malory's Black Knight, but because of his allegorical role as Nox or Mors. As in Malory's depiction of the final combat with the Red Knight of the Red Lands, Gareth blows a horn, but the horn no longer summons men to arm the knight, since Death stands alone. As in Malory, Lyonors appears at a window; since her role as Gareth's beloved has been usurped by Lynette, her appearance is relatively unimportant. Unlike Malory's final combat the encounter is deliberately anti-climactic; having already defeated the struggles in this life, Gareth easily overcomes Death, who proves to be a mere boy, horrid only because of his frightening, though false, appearance.

The final details of the idyll are the result of Tennyson's handling of Malory's plot. The Red Knight of the Red Lands is besieging Lyones because he loves a woman whose brothers, she maintains, were slain by Lancelot or Gawain; in the springtime of Tennyson's Arthurian world, Lancelot cannot bear any suspicion of deceit or imperfection; consequently, the young combatant becomes the instrument of his older brothers' hatred of "the King, and Lancelot, the King's friend." Similarly, the idyll must end with Gareth's marriage to Lynette, the natural outcome of their steadily growing affection. Though "he that told the tale in older times / Says that Sir Gareth wedded Lyonors," Tennyson has the security of his re-creation to proclaim his altered ending. His reference to Malory's conclusion reflects his awareness of his dependence upon a close fidelity to his source not practised since the composition of *Geraint and Enid* and *Lancelot and Elaine*. In other idylls of greater originality, such as *Pelleas and Ettarre*, he feels no need to point out his divergence from Malory. When his fidelity remains so close and so detailed, he proclaims explicitly this moment where he rejects a crucial element of Malory's account.

Gareth and Lynette is Tennyson's only complete depiction of the glorious realization of Arthur's dream. Begun as a consequence of the Pelleas idyll, the poem is the exact antithesis of the world Pelleas confronts. The autumnal world of decaying ideals and unheeded vows is here a springtime of realized ideals and honoured vows. Arthur's vision is a living reality; Guinevere has not sinned. Indeed, Guinevere makes no appearance in the idyll; her name is not even mentioned. The women of Camelot have no taint of imperfection: "And out of bower and casement shyly glanced / Eyes of pure women, wholesome stars of love; / And all about a healthful people stept / As in the presence of a gracious king."

The title characters of the idyll stand in direct relationship to the title characters of earlier idylls. Like Pelleas, Gareth looks forward to his fulfillment as a knight of the Round Table; like Pelleas, he is inexperienced in love: "and as for love, God wot, I love not yet, / But love I shall, God willing." Unlike Pelleas, however, he will realize his highest ambitions, since the spring of Camelot will be conducive to their fulfillment; the perfection of the court, indicated by the observance of the vows, has an ennobling effect on Gareth which it will fail to achieve in any other knight. Gareth is also related to Geraint, a knight of similar youth and innocence; the absence of Guinevere's sin allows Gareth to remain a perfect knight, untarnished even by a rumour that will ignite Geraint's jealousy. Gareth is the epitome of the immense potential that is realized in a world where the King receives the faith and the trust of all his subjects.

Unlike the heroines of other idylls Lynette is not fashioned in relationship to Guinevere. The idyll studies Lynette's gradual awareness and acceptance of Gareth as his true identity manifests itself in his actions. Instead of standing in direct relationship to the beauty or the possible goodness or the fallen nature of the Queen, Lynette stands in contrast to Enid, the heroine of the following idyll. Enid's unselfish love for Geraint and her devotion to him are qualities Lynette must obtain; at the end of *Gareth and Lynette* she does achieve a loving union with Gareth which equals the union that exists between Geraint and Enid both before the emergence of the rumour and after Geraint's long trial of his wife's affection.

In addition to creating two new characters, *Gareth and Lynette* allows Tennyson to expand his treatment of three main figures of his Arthurian world. First of all, the idyll exhibits the true nobility of Lancelot before he succumbs to the sin that will ruin the Order. The idyll focuses on Lancelot and his importance both to Arthur and to Gareth, in order to demonstrate his centrality to the Order. Arthur describes him as "noblest" and "truest," two adjectives which Gareth will also employ to describe him. The close relationship developed between Gareth and Lancelot in the medieval account becomes an impetus to Tennyson to emphasize that relationship and to strengthen the relationship between Arthur and Lancelot. To enhance Lancelot's stature Tennyson makes him, not only Gareth's idol, but also his teacher: "Lancelot on him urged / All the devisings of their chivalry / When one might meet a mightier than himself." *Gareth and Lynette* depicts the perfection of Arthur's Order before its inner deterioration begins and the perfection of Lancelot before his personal debasement begins.

Tennyson introduces Merlin and Mark into the Gareth story in order to broaden their participation in his Arthurian world. Merlin is the wise seer who offers a true understanding of Arthur's vision; his words to Gareth heighten the later tragedy of his submission to Vivien's wiles. To give Mark a further presence before his appearance at the end of *The Last Tournament,* Tennyson introduces his messenger in order to explain, through Arthur's own words, Mark's irredeemable nature. Mark's form of justice, evident in his murder of Tristram, is the bestial behaviour Arthur's Order must eradicate; Mark is the kind of king Arthur must destroy so that the ideals of Camelot may assert themselves in this world.

Lastly, *Gareth and Lynette* offers the only fully developed study of Camelot as Arthur envisioned it; it dramatizes the power of such a world by the effect of its ennobling vision on one young knight. The idyll occupies a crucial position at the outset of the series; only through it can we fully appreciate the tragic loss the world experiences in its rejection of Arthur and his vision.

In the treatment of its source *Gareth and Lynette* occupies a unique position in the completed series. Unlike its immediate predecessor in time of composition, *The Last Tournament*, a highly original treatment of a portion of the Tristram story, *Gareth and Lynette* is a precarious combination of close fidelity and complete originality. The opening section finds no justification in Malory; the portrayal of Bellicent violates Malory's depiction of Gareth's mother. The major section of the poem, Gareth's adventures on behalf of Lynette, remains faithful to the tone, the narrative structure, and often the details of Malory's text. Tennyson adds only an allegorical treatment of Gareth's challengers. Though verbal fidelity is less marked than it was in the *Morte d'Arthur*, the poet's strict adherence to sections of his source does align the idyll with the earlier poem. *Gareth and Lynette* exhibits both Tennyson's deliberate originality with regard to his source and his conscious dependence upon it.

Tennyson's treatment of Malory in *Gareth and Lynette* sheds further light on his comment to Knowles:

"Gareth" is not finished yet. I left him off once altogether, finding him more difficult to deal with than anything excepting perhaps "Aylmer's Field." If I were at liberty, which I think I am not, to print the names of the speakers "Gareth" "Linette" over the short snip-snap of their talk, and so avoid the perpetual "said" and its varieties, the work would be much easier. I have made out the plan however, and perhaps some day it will be completed; and it will be then to consider whether or no it should go into the *Contemporary* or elsewhere.[36]

Tennyson abandoned the idyll once in order to write *The Last Tournament*. When he returned to its composition, he realized his problem of beginning with an account of Bellicent's adultery; by erasing any imperfection in her character and by removing Guinevere from the story, he exercised his originality; he created an introduction, not found in Malory, to a depiction of Camelot in its glory which is found in Malory. At the same time, as his comment to Knowles suggests, his difficulty with the dialogue of the story, a difficulty which resides in the structure of his source, is reflected in his deliberate dependence upon Malory. Close fidelity to Malory only augmented the difficulty of trying to create a treatment of the story which might overcome the structure of the incidents with the "short snip-snap of their talk." Yet his difficulty with the conversation seemed to force him to remain excessively dependent upon Malory for the plot progression of the story. The consequence of this difficulty is an idyll that contains both his earlier method of close dependence upon a source and his later method of complete independence of that source.

The publication of *Gareth and Lynette* and *The Last Tournament* in the same volume in 1872 is a prelude to their incorporation into the

36 *Memoir*, II, 113-114.

Library edition of his poetry already being published.[37] The concluding volumes of this edition contain the whole series of the *Idylls of the King* and offer Tennyson a further opportunity to augment and amend earlier idylls in a continuing effort to achieve a satisfying unity to his poem. Because of the revisions of the *Idylls,* the final two volumes, though advertised for publication in September 1872, did not appear until January 1873. The additions and revisions incorporated into the edition reflect themes which have been developing through the creation of the individual idylls and the special areas of attention which the poet has been developing in *Gareth and Lynette* and in *The Last Tournament.*[38]

The major additions are found in the opening and closing idylls. In *The Coming of Arthur* the poet continues his delineation of the glory of Camelot, described in its full realization in *Gareth and Lynette,* with the addition of the knights' eulogy on the establishment of Arthur's Order.[39] An anticipation of the exuberant faith Gareth will espouse, the song reflects the strength and the righteous ambition of an obedient and trusting knighthood: "The King will follow Christ, and we the King / In whom high God hath breathed a secret thing."

The widow's reference to the Barons' War in *Gareth and Lynette* becomes more significant with the opening idyll's added description, in abbreviated form, of Arthur's victory over the Barons. Tennyson's account, based on Malory, contains a catalogue of Barons who have corresponding counterparts in Malory's longer treatment of the War. Arthur's call, "Ho! they yield!" recalls Merlin's advice to Arthur in the same scene in Malory: "Ye have never done: have ye not done enough? Of three-score thousand ye have left on live but fifteen thousand: it is time for to say, ho!" (I, xv). The poetic version omits this criticism of the King and contents itself with a brief and cursory enumeration of the Barons defeated by Arthur.

The presentation of the Barons' War allows Tennyson to introduce Lancelot into the opening idyll:

> He laugh'd upon his warrior whom he loved
> And honour'd most. "Thou dost not doubt me King,
> So well thine arm hath wrought for me to-day."

37 The opening pages of the 1872 edition of the two idylls reads: "Of these two Idylls, *Gareth and Lynette* follows *The Coming of Arthur,* and *The Last Tournament* immediately precedes *Guinevere.* The concluding volumes of the Library edition will contain the whole series in its proper shape and order."

38 In this discussion I am deliberately disregarding two forms of revision: the replacement of a few adjectives and adverbs by more descriptive words and the substitution of "ye" for "you," "thy" for "your," and "ay" for "yes" in the 1859 quartet of *Idylls.* The latter form of revision is an attempt to align these four idylls more closely with the somewhat more archaic phrasing of the opening and closing idylls.

39 Written in November 1872 (*Memoir,* II, 117), the knights' song was described by the poet: "It seems to me all right for the knights going forth to break the heathen. It is early times yet, and many years are to elapse before the more settled time of 'Gareth.' I must say that to me the song rings like a grand music" (*Memoir,* II, 117).

> "Sir and my liege," he cried, "the fire of God
> Descends upon thee in the battle-field:
> I know thee for my King!" Whereat the two,
> For each had warded either in the fight,
> Sware on the field of death a deathless love.
> And Arthur said, "Man's word is God in man:
> Let chance what will, I trust thee to the death."

In this scene, which has no basis in Malory,[40] Tennyson emphasizes, as he did in the Gareth idyll, Lancelot's centrality in the Order and his close relationship to the King. The ending of *Lancelot and Elaine*, Lancelot's long soliloquy, is the beginning of Tennyson's creation of this noblest of knights; in *Pelleas and Ettarre* Tennyson introduces a confrontation between Pelleas and Lancelot; in both *Gareth and Lynette* and *The Last Tournament* Lancelot holds a prominent position unmerited according to his presence in the corresponding episodes in Malory, but justified by Tennyson's intention of developing Lancelot's role in the poem.

Lancelot's initial encounter with Arthur on the battlefield becomes the inspiration for the other major addition to the idyll:

> Far shone the fields of May thro' open door,
> The sacred altar blossom'd white with May,
> The Sun of May descended on their King,
> They gazed on all earth's beauty in their Queen,
> Roll'd incense, and there past along the hymns
> A voice as of the waters, while the two
> Sware at the shrine of Christ a deathless love:
> And Arthur said, "Behold, thy doom is mine.
> Let chance what will, I love thee to the death!"

Arthur offers complete and unending love to his Queen in a deliberate echo of his earlier bestowal of unending trust in his greatest knight. Lancelot and Guinevere stand with Arthur at the centre of the Order; their disloyalty to the King is a betrayal of the love and the trust extended to them. The crucial importance of this sinful pair to the creation and destruction of Camelot becomes the conclusion to Arthur's reflective soliloquy now added to *The Passing of Arthur:*

> I found Him in the shining of the stars,
> I mark'd Him in the flowering of His fields,
> But in His ways with men I find Him not.
> I waged His wars, and now I pass and die.
> O me! for why is all around us here
> As if some lesser god had made the world,
> But had not force to shape it as he would,
> Till the High God behold it from beyond,
> And enter it, and make it beautiful?
> Or else as if the world were wholly fair,
> But that these eyes of men are dense and dim,

40   In Malory, Lancelot enters long after the Round Table has been established.

And have not power to see it as it is:
Perchance, because we see not to the close;—
For I, being simple, thought to work His will,
And have but stricken with the sword in vain;
And all whereon I lean'd in wife and friend
Is traitor to my peace, and all my realm
Reels back into the beast, and is no more.
My God, thou hast forgotten me in my death:
Nay—God my Christ—I pass but shall not die.

Added to strengthen the humanity of the King, the soliloquy is the utterance of a man who sees himself, not as a divine force, but as the humble instrument of the divinity. The soliloquy is also the final commentary on the tragedy that befell Camelot; the support Arthur found in Guinevere and Lancelot ultimately betrays the dream that was momentarily realized.[41]

The two remaining additions in the 1873 edition also reflect new structural principles that are slowly developing in the creation of the *Idylls.* Merlin, whose role had been restricted almost completely to his role in *Merlin and Vivien,* is introduced into *Gareth and Lynette* to strengthen his role in the complete series; now he is described before the moment of his downfall:

He walk'd with dreams and darkness, and he found
A doom that ever poised itself to fall,
An ever-moaning battle in the mist,
World-war of dying flesh against the life,
Death in all life and lying in all love,
The meanest having power upon the highest,
And the high purpose broken by the worm.

Similar in tone to Arthur's soliloquy, the passage restates the theme, the "war of Time against the soul of man," or, as the epilogue will term it, "Sense at war with Soul." The addition indicates Tennyson's realization that Merlin's personal tragedy occurs too suddenly; this small explanation of his melancholy foreshadows the later and longer addition to *Merlin and Vivien* which will depict in greater detail the growing decay in the realm.[42] The reference to "the high purpose broken by the

41 The only other noteworthy addition to the closing idyll is the repetition of the already repeated phrase, "From the great deep to the great deep he goes," in the new passage: "But when that moan had past for evermore, / The stillness of the dead world's winter dawn / Amazed him, and he groan'd, 'The King is gone.' / And therewithal came on him the weird rhyme, / 'From the great deep to the great deep he goes.'"

42 The Library edition also altered one important line in the idyll. Before this edition, Vivien encounters the King "when Arthur, walking all alone, / Vext at a rumour rife about the Queen." Now the encounter occurs "when Arthur, walking all alone, / Vext at a rumour issued from herself." The change prohibits any criticism of Arthur for negligence in regard to his wife's behaviour by omitting any suggestion of his knowledge of the adultery at this time; it also enhances the evil stature of Vivien which will receive further development in subsequent additions to the series.

worm'' looks ahead to Pelleas' song about ''a worm within the rose,'' the other major addition to the 1873 edition.

Minor revisions in the edition are further attempts, necessitated by the two new idylls, to maintain narrative clarity and consistency. Thus in *Lancelot and Elaine* the reference to Lamorack, ''And Lamorack, a good knight, but therewithal / Sir Modred's brother, of a crafty house,'' is deleted in favour of a reference to Gareth, ''And Gareth, a good knight, but therewithal / Sir Modred's brother, and the child of Lot.'' The poet's rejection of his original opening of the Gareth idyll makes Lamorack a superfluous character in this Arthurian world. In another revision Tennyson changes Merlin's description of Guinevere's first glimpse of Lancelot, ''To fetch her, and she took him for the King,'' to read, ''To fetch her, and she watch'd him from her walls. / A rumour runs, she took him for the King.'' Since the earlier version may offer a possible excuse for Guinevere's behaviour, Tennyson alters Merlin's report so that the original fact becomes only a rumour.

Lastly, *Geraint and Enid* is now divided into two sections, a definite step towards the final creation of a poem in twelve books. Not until 1886 is each section given its own title.

The epilogue, ''To the Queen,'' also added in 1873,[43] is a tribute to the poet's affection and respect for Queen Victoria and a commentary on his poem. The description of the poem as ''New-old'' looks back to Tennyson's fear, expressed forty years earlier in *The Epic*, that men may be blinded to themes of contemporary relevance when such material is presented through the poetic re-creation of old stories; his humble plea, ''Perhaps some modern touches here and there / Redeemed it from the charge of nothingness,'' finds a restatement, ''accept this old imperfect tale, / New-old.'' The poet's description of his creation is a deliberate attempt to justify his treatment of the legends:

> shadowing Sense at war with Soul
> Rather than that gray king, whose name, a ghost,
> Streams like a cloud, man-shaped, from mountain peak,
> And cleaves to cairn and cromlech still; or him
> Of Geoffrey's book, or him of Malleor's, one
> Touch'd by the adulterous finger of a time

43 Emily's journal entry of December 25, 1872 recorded that the poet had just completed the epilogue (*Memoir*, II, 119). The immediate purpose of the epilogue was an answer to ''that Canadian bit of the *Times*. Villainous'' (*Memoir*, II, 117): ''A leading London journal had written advocating that Canada should sever her connection with Great Britain, as she was 'too costly': hence these lines'' (Eversley edition, V, 511). Tennyson's conception of the British Empire was not dissimilar to his ideal of the Order of the Round Table: ''One of the deepest desires of his life was to help the realisation of the ideal of an Empire by the most intimate union of every part of our British Empire. He believed that every different member so united would, with a heightening of individuality to each member, give such strength and greatness and stability to the whole as would make our Empire a faithful and fearless leader in all that is good throughout all the world'' (*Memoir*, II, 223).

That hover'd between war and wantonness,
And crownings and dethronements.

Tennyson's poem reshapes the medieval accounts of Arthur's career into a vehicle for his own statement of an idealistic philosophy of significance to his generation. "The general decay of faith / Right through the world" finds a remedy and a hope in the ennobling vision of Arthur. Malory's "gray king" has become the "Soul," a human embodiment of the highest calling of man.[44]

The contemporary relevance of the *Idylls* becomes explicit:

> take withal
> Thy poet's blessing, and his trust that Heaven
> Will blow the tempest in the distance back
> From thine and ours: for some are scared, who mark,
> Or wisely or unwisely, signs of storm,
> Waverings of every vane with every wind,
> And wordy trucklings to the transient hour,
> And fierce or careless looseners of the faith,
> And Softness breeding scorn of simple life,
> Or Cowardice, the child of lust for gold,
> Or Labour, with a groan and not a voice,
> Or Art with poisonous honey stol'n from France,
> And that which knows, but careful for itself,
> And that which knows not, ruling that which knows
> To its own harm: the goal of this great world
> Lies beyond sight.

The immorality and dishonour of the decaying Camelot become a warning and an indictment of the growing decadence of Victorian England. Tennyson's dissatisfaction with the moral temper of his age does not send him to the Arthurian world as an escape; on the contrary, his re-creation of the legends is an attempt to reform his generation by showing the effects of base sensuality, selfish materialism, and spiritual blindness on the inhabitants of Camelot. In later years he described even more explicitly the moral purpose of his poem:

You must not be surprised at anything that comes to pass in the next fifty years All ages are ages of transition, but this is an awful moment of transition. It seems to me as if there were much less of the old reverence and chivalrous feeling in the world than there used to be. I am old and I may be wrong, for this generation has assuredly some spirit of chivalry. We see it in acts of heroism by land and sea, in fights against the slave trade, in our Arctic voyages, in philanthropy, etc. The truth is that the wave advances and recedes. I tried in my "Idylls" to teach men these things, and the need of the Ideal. But I feel sometimes as if my life had been a very useless life.[45]

44 In "Tennyson's 'Allegory in the Distance,' " *PMLA*, 68 (1953), 418-424, S. C. Burche offers some reasoned thoughts on the precise form of the allegory in the poem.
45 *Memoir*, II, 337.

If Victorian society heeds the lesson of the poem, it will avoid Camelot's fate:

> yet—if our slowly-grown
> And crown'd Republic's crowning common-sense,
> That saved her many times, not fail—their fears
> Are morning shadows huger than the shapes
> That cast them, not those gloomier which forego
> The darkness of that battle in the West,
> Where all of high and holy dies away.

If society continues on its path of social decadence, the tragic plight of Victorian England also becomes only the prelude, "the prelude of the final act of the tragedy which culminates in the temporary triumph of evil, the confusion of moral order, closing in the great 'Battle of the West.' "[46]

The 1873 edition incorporated two new idylls into the series: *Gareth and Lynette,* along with the additions to the opening idyll, reflects the creation of Arthur's Order and its springtime realization; *The Last Tournament* continues to depict the autumnal decay of *Pelleas and Ettarre.* The epilogue enunciates the social relevance of the *Idylls.* The series, however, was not complete. Tennyson looked upon the edition, not as a final achievement, but as an important assessment of the present condition of his accomplishment. As the edition was being published, he was already creating a new idyll and an expanded introduction to *Merlin and Vivien* in his relentless task of achieving a complete depiction of his Arthurian world. In 1873 Tennyson still remained unaware of the fact that his subject-matter had one important parallel to his version of Camelot; like his Camelot, the Arthurian legends are "never built at all, / And therefore built for ever." The power of Arthur's vision would prevent Tennyson from ever creating a satisfactory complete work.

46   Ibid., II, 131.

Chapter 5

Towards a Completion

Balin and Balan

So Balin bare the crown, and all the knights
Approved him, and the Queen, and all the world
Made music, and he felt his being move
In music with his Order, and the King.[1]

After the publication of the Library edition of the *Idylls of the King*
Tennyson's Arthurian poem remained incomplete. Hallam Tennyson
commented: "With the publication of 'Gareth and Lynette' in 1872 my
father thought that he had completed the cycle of the 'Idylls'; but later he
felt that some further introduction to 'Merlin and Vivien' was necessary,
and so wrote 'Balin and Balan.' "[2] Internal evidence, however, suggests
the poet's continuing dissatisfaction with the series. The short description of Merlin's melancholy added to *Merlin and Vivien* and Arthur's
denunciation of King Mark in *Gareth and Lynette* foreshadowed the
long introduction to *Merlin and Vivien*[3] and the new idyll of *Balin and
Balan*.[4] At the conclusion of *Geraint and Enid* Geraint's suspicions
about the Queen's adultery were pacified: "And though Geraint could
never take again / That comfort from their converse which he took /
Before the Queen's fair name was breathed upon, / He rested well

1 All quotations from *Balin and Balan* are from the 1885 edition of *Tiresias and Other
   Poems* (London: Macmillan).
2 *Memoir*, II, 121.
3 The new introduction was added in 1874 in the ten-volume edition of Tennyson's
   Works (London: Henry S. King).
4 Sir Charles Tennyson dates the composition of the idyll "during the latter part of 1872
   and the succeeding months" (p. 402). *Balin and Balan* was first published in 1885 in
   Tiresias and Other Poems; it was subtitled, "An introduction to 'Merlin and Vivien.' " In the following year it was incorporated into the series in the New Miniature
   edition of Tennyson's *Works* (London: Macmillan).

content that all was well.'' The transition from this calm atmosphere to the world of Vivien where ''a storm was coming'' presented no adequate preparation for the decay throughout the realm at the time of Merlin's seduction. Tennyson himself remarked that *Merlin and Vivien* entered the series ''far too soon as it stands.''[5] Consequently, *Balin and Balan* and the new introduction to *Merlin and Vivien*, two episodes which must be studied together because of their simultaneous creation and their interdependence,[6] offered a proper introduction to Mark and Vivien, the first explicit depiction of the adulterous relationship of Lancelot and his Queen, and the first portrait of a knight who experiences difficulty and failure in his attempt to follow Arthur's ideal.

Balin and Balan is Tennyson's final employment of Malory. Eschewing the close fidelity observed in some of the earlier idylls, this last addition to the series is nonetheless not an original creation, since it depends upon Malory for its inspiration, many of its incidents, and its general structure. Malory's story of Balin, condensed, tightened, and abbreviated, is refashioned according to Tennyson's own Arthurian world so that the completed idyll is an intregal member of the series. Tennyson practises originality, not by creating his own episode, but by observing token adherence to the structure of his source while reworking every episode and re-creating every character.

Malory's *Balin, or The Knight of the Two Swords,* a fully developed adventure in itself, occurs during Arthur's attempt to establish his realm. Balin, a young knight imprisoned for six months because of his slaying of Arthur's cousin, achieves renown and honour when he draws out a magic sword from its scabbard. His subsequent refusal to return the sword to the damsel who brought it leads to her lament: ''ye shall slay with the sword the best friend that ye have, and the man that ye most love in this world; and the sword shall be your destruction'' (I, xxvii). The remainder of the adventure chronicles Balin's fatal destiny.

Balin incurs Arthur's disfavour again when he slays the Lady of the Lake to avenge the murder of his mother. Though his major goal becomes the recovery of Arthur's favour, he discovers that his presence precipitates tragedy. Envious of Balin's success in winning the sword, Launceor attacks him; Balin's victory prompts Launceor's lady to commit suicide.[7] Balin now captures Rience, Arthur's foremost enemy; this moment of personal glory precedes Balin's mission to conduct a moaning knight to Camelot so that Arthur can learn the cause of the lament. As he leads the knight to the King, an invisible knight named

---

5 Alfred Domett, *The Diary of Alfred Domett, 1872-1885,* edited by E. A. Horsman (London: Oxford University Press, 1953), p. 79.
6 The prose drafts of the idyll (see Appendix 4) show the close relationship between the idyll and the new introduction to *Merlin and Vivien.*
7 At this juncture in Malory's narrative Mark makes his first appearance; he buries the two lovers.

Garlon kills Balin's companion. Balin assumes the dead knight's quest
and accompanies his damsel; when another knight joins them, he is also
slain by Garlon. The end of their journey is the castle of King Pellam,
where Balin slays Pellam's brother Garlon. Garlon's death leads directly
to Pellam's vow to kill Balin, Balin's seizure of the holy spear, and the
dolorous stroke inflicted upon Pellam.

   After eight days of wandering Balin meets Garnish, a knight awaiting his lady. Balin happens to discover the lady lying with another
knight; the discovery causes Garnish to kill the lady, her lover, and
himself. Finally, Balin reaches a large cross which warns any lone rider
to depart; when a horn blows, he feels himself summoned to disobey the
written warning. He arrives at a castle where an ancient custom demands that he joust with the knight on the island. Balin heeds a suggestion about the poor quality of his armour and exchanges his shield. The
knight of the island is Balin's own brother Balan, who fails to recognize
him with his new shield. In their combat both die. A lady comes from the
tower and answers Balan's dying request that they be laid to rest together.

   Malory's Balin is an obstinate and rash knight whose personal
heroism leads only to misfortune. Malory's source, the French prose
Romance of Merlin, centres on Balin as a tragic victim of fortune; Malory
removes many of the references to fortune and centres the tragedy
within Balin's character.[8] His tragedy is his failure to learn from past
experience; he follows his impetuousness even though it continually
brings him to ruin; he is the victim of his own rashness: "Balin has the
opportunity at every step to 'torne agayne,' and fails to do so through the
same rash heedlessness with which in the very beginning he had refused
to return the damsel's sword, despite her repeated warning that 'and ye
woll nat leve that swerde hit shall be youre destruccion.'"[9] Situated
before Guinevere's arrival at Camelot and the creation of the knights'
oath, the story of Balin depicts the recklessness and the selfishness
Arthur's Order must eradicate. Balin's behaviour operates within a
world void of principles; the oath will present a consistent standard by
which all actions may be judged. The universality of the standard contrasts with Balin's self-centred nature; at this time Balin can judge his
behaviour only in the light of his own isolated experience: "God
knoweth I did none other but as I would you did to me" (I,xlii).

   Tennyson makes Malory's presentation of an unestablished realm
the barometer of the early decay of the established realm, the one stage

8   For a study of Malory's relationship to his source, see Laura A. Hibbard, "Malory's
    'Book of Balin,'" *Medieval Studies in Memory of Gertrude Schoepperle Loomis*,
    edited by Roger S. Loomis (New York: Columbia University Press, 1927), pp. 175-
    195.
9   Thomas C. Rumble, "Malory's 'Balin' and the Question of Unity in the *Morte
    Darthur*," *Speculum*, 41 (1966), 83.

in the history of Camelot that his poem has not depicted. He shortens the structure of his plot by reducing it to a study of Balin in his confrontation with Garlon and Pellam and his fatal encounter with his brother. The condensation is an attempt, not to tighten a long episodic narrative, but to focus attention on these two episodes and use them as the basis for developing a new conception of the characters of the story.

Balin and Balan resembles *The Last Tournament* in its narrative movement. Like *The Last Tournament* it has a five-part structure; it opens in and near Camelot and alternates this locale with the setting of Pellam's castle. In addition, the world of Pellam serves the same function as Pelleas' Round Table of the North; it is a deliberate creation of an Order in opposition to Arthur's Order. Camelot in decay is the subject of *The Last Tournament;* Camelot in early decay is the subject of *Balin and Balan*; both idylls are panoramic studies of the many inhabitants of their world. No other idyll has the large cast of *Balin and Balan*: Arthur, Guinevere, Lancelot, Merlin, Vivien, Vivien's squire, Balin, Balan, Pellam, Garlon, Mark. Moreover, none of these characters plays a major role. Dagonet is the guide to the world of *The Last Tournament;* in a similar fashion Balin is the guide to the world of his idyll, though he does have a greater presence in the plot. Balin cannot achieve personal stability. Trapped by his rash behaviour, he often fails to perceive clearly. He follows a path to destruction which becomes a series of reactions, sometimes perceptive, sometimes invalid, to the many characters of the idyll. Dagonet's reactions to other characters are a proper guide to the foulness of Camelot's society; Balin's reactions are not a proper guide since he cannot believe in his own perceptions. Only with the depiction of the early confusion and decay in Arthur's kingdom is Tennyson ready to turn to the more overtly evil world of *Merlin and Vivien*.

In both Malory and Tennyson, Balin expresses man's struggle for a higher life; there is a strong tension between Balin's personal aspirations and the environment in which he seeks to achieve his goals; the resulting conflict produces a growth in his awareness of the responsibilities and commitments of life in society. Yet this similarity in Balin's conflict belies the fact that Tennyson's account has no final correspondence to Malory. An understanding of the differences between the two versions of the story becomes an understanding of Tennyson's creation.

Tennyson uses Malory's appellation of Balin as ''le Savage'' as the basis for his depiction.[10] In the poem Balin is a knight whose violent moods prompt Arthur to name him ''the Savage.'' His behaviour is evidence that he has not reached the higher calling of his being; he remains in the bestial world where he carries an appropriate shield: ''this

10   In Malory, Balin tells Garnish : ''My name is Balin le Savage'' (I, xli). No explanation of the history of the epithet is given.

rough beast upon my shield, / Langued gules, and tooth'd with grinning savagery." His struggle is his attempt to curb his tendency towards passionately excessive action; he needs standards outside of himself to provide a proper code of conduct: "now would strictlier set himself / To learn what Arthur meant by courtesy, / Manhood, and knighthood." Balin's ultimate failure reflects his misunderstanding of himself and his choice of an inappropriate model for his self-improvement.

Balin never realizes the higher calling of man. Arthur tells him: "As children learn, be thou / Wiser for falling!" Yet Balin cannot understand the command. In the preceding idyll Edyrn rose from his bestiality to become a respected knight of the Round Table. Balin never fully accepts the possibility of his own ascension to a higher level. Trapped by a vivid consciousness of his violent moods, Balin sees Arthur's Order as an ideal outside of himself to which he must aspire; he does not understand that Arthur's standard is a command to all men to realize their potential as fully developed human beings. Arthur advises him to "walk with me, and move / To music with thine Order and the King," but Balin never understands that Arthur's Order is, indeed, "thine Order," the Order of each man. Arthur's statement to Balin is a command that Balin realize the potential within himself; the Order reflects the highest calling of each man. Arthur's vision of an ideal Order is a vision of each man's realization of himself. The Order becomes a reflection, not only of Arthur, but of each knight.

The consequence of Balin's continual self-doubts is his conviction of the inaccessibility of Arthur's vision:

> Too high this mount of Camelot for me:
> These high-set courtesies are not for me.
> Shall I not rather prove the worse for these?
> Fierier and stormier from restraining, break
> Into some madness ev'n before the Queen?

His struggle for self-improvement leads to his death; he tries in vain to master his passions without realizing that the form of his struggle is inherently wrong: "yet he strove / To learn the graces of their Table, fought / Hard with himself, and seem'd at length in peace."[11] Balin is defeating rather than improving himself through deliberate self-denial. He tries to deny his lower tendencies rather than convert them to their proper function; the lower are "a means to the higher":

To Tyndall he once said, "No evolutionist is able to explain the mind of Man or how any possible physiological change of tissue can produce conscious thought." Yet he was inclined to think that the theory of Evolution caused the world to regard more clearly the "Life of Nature as a lower stage in the manifestation of a principle which is more fully manifested in the spiritual life of

---

11 By using the word "with" rather than "within" to describe Balin's inner struggle, Tennyson suggests the unnaturalness of self-denial.

man, with the idea that in this process of Evolution the lower is to be regarded as a means to the higher."[12]

Balin's attempt to deny and ultimately to negate his passions proves unsuccessful; his "violences" return to destroy him. Aware of the power of his passions, Balin elects to deny their existence rather than accept them and master their excess. Self-control is a natural and necessary state in self-improvement, whereas self-denial can only lead to destruction.[13]

Balin's failure to realize his higher calling is a reflection of the evil of self-denial and a reflection of the decay now spreading throughout the realm. In *Gareth and Lynette* Tennyson studies Gareth's growth to full manhood through his association with his idol and friend, Lancelot; moreover, he emphasizes Gareth's proper choice of Lancelot as an idol by stressing the close relationship between Lancelot and Arthur. In *Balin and Balan* a young knight also chooses Lancelot as his idol; the world of Camelot, however, has grown into decay and Lancelot can no longer assume his proper role. Snared in the guilt of adultery, Lancelot cannot offer Balin the guidance he freely extended to Gareth.

Unaware of Lancelot's sin, Balin wrongly assumes that the glory of Lancelot's knighthood comes from his worship of the Queen:

> But this worship of the Queen,
> That honour too wherein she holds him—this,
> This was the sunshine that hath given the man
> A growth, a name that branches o'er the rest,
> And strength against all odds, and what the King
> So prizes—overprizes—gentleness.

In *Gareth and Lynette* Lancelot's glory comes from his obedience to the King; now his glory seems to come from the "sunshine" of the Queen. Balin's decision to "bear some token of his Queen" is the final step in his commitment to a false goodness. Like Pelleas, Balin is a source of mockery in his belief in "the fairest and the best / Of Ladies living." Unlike Edyrn he does not have an Enid in whom he can trust; unlike Enid, Guinevere cannot become the source of a knight's regeneration.

In his presentation of Balin struggling to move beyond his bestiality, Tennyson develops his brother Balan as a figure of calm reason and wise guidance. In Malory, Balan serves a passive function. While the two brothers are together, Balin commits no act which fortune can turn into sorrow. Any aid Balan offers his brother comes in battle. Their deaths reflect and accent the overwhelming presence of evil fortune governing Balin's life. Balan, the man most beloved by Balin, concludes the catalogue of broken and distorted loves Balin encounters. Tennyson

12 *Memoir*, I, 323.
13 Compare Ida's advice in *Oenone:* "Self-reverence, self-knowledge, and self-control, / These three alone lead life to sovereign power."

introduces Balan as Balin's "better" and makes him directly responsible for preventing his brother from injuring himself. Balan is the perceptive voice of reasonable behaviour: "Let not thy moods prevail, when I am gone / Who used to lay them! hold them outer fiends, / Who leap at thee to tear thee; shake them aside, / Dreams ruling when wit sleeps!"

In the final combat Balin's violent rejection of his shield, the symbol of Camelot's Order, is the direct cause of his own death and the death of his brother. When Balin openly rejects Camelot's world, Balan, as the voice of reason and self-control, can no longer exist. Balin's outburst foreshadows his slaughterous movement back into the beast: "let the wolves' black maws ensepulchre / Their brother beast, whose anger was his lord."

In Malory, Balan dies shortly before Balin. In Tennyson the deaths occur simultaneously. Balin and Balan are halves of a coherent whole. Balan's belief that his brother's moods are "outer fiends" suggests his role as a concrete embodiment of that inner awareness Balin cannot achieve. The manipulation of their deaths by the poet underlines the inextricable nature of their relationship. In their deaths Balin sees his failure: "My madness all thy life has been thy doom, / Thy curse, and darken'd all thy day; and now / The night has come. I scarce can see thee now." Clasped together in death, they realize that they were born and are to die sealed by a common fate. Balin and Balan appear as the conflicting qualities of the passions and the higher reason of man; they never resolve the conflict. The unity of their life and death suggests the representation of one man.[14]

Tennyson's creation of a decaying Camelot as a world no longer conducive to a knight's growth into full manhood is complemented by his creation of the world of Pellam's court. Like Balin, Pellam represents the evil of self-denial; whereas Balin's self-doubts about his personal worthiness make him practise self-denial rather than self-control, Pellam vows his superiority to Arthur's Order by choosing a path of religious asceticism based solely on self-denial. Pellam comes to deny his humanity in a quest for ascetic perfection. His excessive behaviour is equally destructive of his potential as a complete human being.

In Malory, Pellam is a relatively minor character. The brother of Garlon, he vows to kill Balin to avenge his brother's murder. In their fatal combat, Balin kills Pellam with the "dolorous stroke."[15] Pellam's

14 Tennyson suggests this representation by altering Malory's relationship of the two brothers so that they become twins: "We two were born together."
15 Tennyson's prose account of the idyll, *The Dolorous Stroke*, a bridge between Malory and the final version of the poem, is reprinted in *Memoir*, II, 134-141, and Eversley edition, V, 425-432; it shows the shift in meaning created by Tennyson in his treatment of the story. For Malory the "dolorous stroke" is Balin's blow against Pellam; for Tennyson the stroke is the final slaughter of the two brothers. The change emphasizes Tennyson's ultimate concern, which is not Pellam, but the destruction of Balin and Balan.

special significance rests in his lineage; descended from Joseph of Arimathea, he possesses the spear that entered the side of Christ:

for in that place was part of the blood of our Lord Jesus Christ, that Joseph, of Arimathy, brought into this land, and there himself lay in that rich bed. And that was the same spear that Longius smote our Lord to the heart; and king Pellam was nigh of Joseph's kin, and that was the most worshipful man that lived in those days: and great pity it was of his hurt, for the stroke turned him to great dole, tray, and teen [I, xli].

In addition to his illustrious lineage, Pellam has an equally impressive progeny; his son Pelles is the father of Elaine, the mother of Galahad.[16]

Tennyson re-creates Pellam without any significant attention to his presentation in Malory. Pellam becomes two different rulers: the "Christless foe" who stands with Lot against Arthur's Order[17] and the converted ruler who espouses an asceticism which contradicts the Order. He represents two extremes, which stand in opposition to Arthur's vision of man's commitment to his "allotted field." In his youth Pellam stands with Urien and Arthur's enemies; his conversion to Christianity is a passionate, violent, and destructive reaction: "but seeing that thy realm / Hath prosper'd in the name of Christ, the King / Took, as in rival heat, to holy things." Pellam becomes another Percivale, who forsakes the world for the shelter and isolation of the cloister; he denies the earthly in order to achieve personal sanctification apart from the world, a sanctification to which he is not summoned. Once Arthur's "Christless foe," he becomes an enemy to Arthur's intention of establishing his realm through the transformation of this earth.

Tennyson blackens Pellam by making Malory's factual details about his lineage a product of Pellam's fertile but dishonest imagination:

> And finds himself descended from the Saint
> Arimathaean Joseph; him who first
> Brought the great faith to Britain over seas;
> He boasts his life as purer than thine own;
> Eats scarce enow to keep his pulse abeat;
> Hath push'd aside his faithful wife, nor lets
> Or dame or damsel enter at his gates

16 In Malory, Galahad comments about his sword: "And with that sword he slew his brother Balan, and that was great pity, for he was a good knight, and either slew other through a notorious stroke that sir Balan gave unto my grandfather, king Pelles (III, xxxiii). The substitution of Pelles for Pellam, reflecting Malory's failure to give his work a final revision, has led to subsequent confusion, evident in Tennyson's employment of Pelles in his prose account, *The Dolorous Stroke,* and in his correct use of Pellam in the poem. In Malory, Pellam is the father of Pelles; Galahad's incorrect use creates Tennyson's confusion. In Southey's edition of Malory, the stroke is "dolorous," not "notorious" (XII, v).

17 Lot, Arthur's enemy, dies in Malory's account of the story of Balin; Tennyson introduces Pellam as united with Lot against Arthur. The reference brings further unity to the series through the earlier references to Lot as the husband of Bellicent in *The Coming of Arthur* and *Gareth and Lynette.*

> Lest he should be polluted. This gray King
> Show'd us a shrine wherein were wonders—yea—
> Rich arks with priceless bones of martyrdom,
> Thorns of the crown and shivers of the cross,
> And therewithal (for thus he told us) brought
> By holy Joseph hither, that same spear
> Wherewith the Roman pierced the side of Christ.

Malory's holy spear "that Longius smote our Lord to the heart" becomes an object of deceit, "The longest lance his eyes had ever seen / Point-painted red."

Arthur and his Order have a new enemy, not a heathen king, but a converted ascetic who establishes his court as a direct contrast to Camelot. Gareth sees the physical structure of Camelot:

> Far off they saw the silver-misty morn
> Rolling her smoke about the Royal mount,
> That rose between the forest and the field.
> At times the summit of the high city flash'd;
> At times the spires and turrets half-way down
> Prick'd through the mist; at times the great gate shone
> Only, that open'd on the field below:
> Anon, the whole fair city had disappear'd.

In contrast is Balin's sight of Pellam's hall:

> lichen-bearded, grayly draped
> With streaming grass, appear'd, low-built but strong;
> The ruinous donjon as a knoll of moss,
> The battlement overtopt with ivytods,
> A home of bats, in every tower an owl.

For Balin Camelot is festal joy:

> The Lost one Found was greeted as in Heaven
> With joy that blazed itself in woodland wealth
> Of leaf, and gayest garlandage of flowers,
> Along the walls and down the board; they sat,
> And cup clash'd cup.

Pellam imposes abstinence upon his court; he "Eats scarce enow to keep his pulse abeat." Lastly, Arthur, who married Guinevere that they might "live together as one life," stands in contrast to the converted Pellam who "Hath push'd aside his faithful wife."

Pellam's court is not intentionally evil, nor is Pellam a wholly blind man. His court is closed to Vivien. Yet his abdication of responsibility for the temporal affairs of his realm blinds him to the evil of his son Garlon, in whose hands he leaves his worldly affairs. Through the new power abdicated by his father, Garlon, an agent and friend of Vivien, becomes a direct antagonist to Arthur and his realm.[18]

18 In Malory Garlon and Pellam are brothers; lest their relationship diminish the importance of the more central pair of brothers, Tennyson changes their relationship, first to

In addition to transforming Malory's figures of Balin, Balan, Pellam, and Garlon in order to depict the destructive effects of self-denial, Tennyson superimposes upon his abbreviated version of Malory's plot the evil machinations of Vivien and the adultery of Lancelot and Guinevere. Though Malory's story of Balin occurs before Guinevere's appearance in Camelot, Tennyson makes her adultery stand behind the entire plot. Designed as an introduction to *Merlin and Vivien*, the idyll deliberately withholds Vivien's entrance until after the garden scene between Lancelot and the Queen in which their relationship is openly revealed.[19] When Balin happens to overhear a conversation between the Queen and her knight, he rejects the implications of their statements; he cannot believe in the possibility of their adultery; he imagines that his violent nature is returning to plague him:

> Queen? subject? but I see not what I see.
> Damsel and lover? hear not what I hear.
> My father hath begotten me in his wrath.
> I suffer from the things before me, know,
> Learn nothing; am not worthy to be knight;
> A churl, a clown![20]

Balin's self-questioning becomes a rejection of the Queen only after Vivien confronts him and weaves her deceit:

> Ay, thou rememberest well—one summer dawn—
> By the great tower—Caerleon upon Usk—
> Nay, truly we were hidden: this fair lord,
> The flower of all their vestal knighthood, knelt
> In amorous homage—knelt—what else?—O ay
> Knelt, and drew down from out his night-black hair
> And mumbled that white hand whose ring'd caress
> Had wander'd from her own King's golden head,
> And lost itself in darkness, till she cried—

nephew-uncle in a prose draft (see Appendix 4), finally to son-father in the completed poem.

19   The importance of the garden scene, the first appearance of the lovers together in the whole series, is further emphasized by its absence in *The Dolorous Stroke*. In that prose synopsis, Vivien tells the same lie to Balin; taking inspiration from her falsehood, Tennyson adds the garden scene to give her lie credibility in Balin's mind.

20   This important passage has caused unnecessary problems for critics. Though Buckley comments, "But when he comes inadvertently upon a clandestine tryst of Lancelot and Guinevere, he cannot but feel that his old madness has returned" (p. 179) and Reed echoes this point of view, "When he overhears the compromising conversation of Lancelot and Guinevere, he supposes that it is his own imagination imputing evil in what is really innocent speech" (p. 131), other critics misinterpret the passage. In *King Arthur's Laureate* (New York: New York University Press, 1971), J. Phillip Eggers comments: "Balin trusts his impressions in all things. For example, he overhears Guinevere and Lancelot in their garden meeting. He is instantly sure of their adultery—when even the reader cannot be" (p. 179). In *Tennyson's Doppelgänger—Balin and Balan* (Lincoln, England: Keyworth and Fry, 1971), J. M. Gray describes this passage: "He interprets as intrigue their curious behaviour while they believe themselves unobserved" (p. 14).

> I thought the great tower would crash down on both—
> "Rise, my sweet King, and kiss me on the lips,
> Thou art my King."

Vivien's lie destroys Balin's faith in his idol and in his Queen; Vivien even dares to suggest that he prey upon the couple whom he was striving to emulate: "See now, I set thee high on vantage ground, / From whence to watch the time, and eagle-like / Stoop at thy will on Lancelot and the Queen." Vivien's behaviour would have no effect upon Balin if his glimpse of the adulterous pair had not offered credibility to her account. Vivien succeeds in returning Balin to his bestiality, where his "weird yell, / Unearthlier than all shriek of bird or beast, / Thrill'd thro' the woods."

The drafts of the idyll in the Harvard Notebooks reveal Tennyson's difficulty in finding the proper entrance for Vivien into the poem.[21] The first prose draft in Notebook 37 occurs before the story of Balin, since Garlon is now withholding the tribute; here Vivien's introduction would occur in Mark's court, a scene ultimately placed in the new introduction to *Merlin and Vivien*. The later poetic account in Notebook 33 is a possible bridge between *Balin and Balan* and *Merlin and Vivien*, since Vivien arrives at Camelot as a messenger of the death of the two brothers. Tennyson's final decision to make her an agent of Mark and to establish their relationship in the new introduction to *Merlin and Vivien* is a further step in his consolidation of all the evil figures in the poem. Vivien, who seeks her escort Garlon, becomes the agent of Mark, who, in *The Coming of Arthur*, is established as the symbol of the lawlessness Arthur's vision cannot tolerate.

At the same time Vivien enters *Balin and Balan* only after the depiction of the adultery. A woman of complete evil from the world of Mark, she can operate within Arthur's realm only when sin exists there. Guinevere's disgrace allows Vivien to spread her evil in Camelot.

The close relationship between *Balin and Balan* and the new introduction to *Merlin and Vivien* did not lead Tennyson to publish them together. The new introduction developed the relationship of Mark and Vivien and depicted Guinevere's love for Lancelot. The later publication of *Balin and Balan* reflected Tennyson's desire to assess the need for any further introduction to *Merlin and Vivien*. His final decision to publish the idyll in 1885 and to incorporate it into the series in the following year indicated his realization that some further introduction is needed, not so much to *Merlin and Vivien*, but to the entire series as it begins to depict the deterioration of the Order.

The position of *Balin and Balan* within the series is the key to its meaning. The springtime glory of *Gareth and Lynette* leads to the

21 See Appendix 4.

somewhat blemished perfection of the realm in *Geraint and Enid*. In the latter idyll the adultery remains only a rumour; Geraint and Enid do reach mutual perfection in their marriage. *Merlin and Vivien*, on the other hand, opens with the realm in decay; Merlin cannot deny Vivien's accusations about Guinevere's behaviour and the added introduction reveals that the adultery is already a known fact in Lyonnesse. Between *Geraint and Enid* and *Merlin and Vivien* must come an idyll to show the slowly accelerating decay in Camelot. Consequently, using the seemingly chaotic structure of *The Last Tournament* with its presentation of the ruined realm as his model, Tennyson creates a study of that realm as the ruin takes its initial form; he transforms the story of Balin, Malory's tale of unreasonable behaviour before the establishment of the oath, into a study of the destructive power of self-denial. Balin chooses self-denial as the seemingly proper road to self-improvement; he becomes another Pelleas, a knight driven mad by his awakening to the awful truth of Camelot's moral condition. Malory's Pellam becomes a heathen king whose conversion to Christianity is a flight into self-denying asceticism; he is another Percivale, retreating from the affairs of this world for the sterility of ascetic isolation.

These two distinct studies of self-denial take place within a world where evil is an increasingly active force. The Order that must guide Balin's efforts proves to be tarnished and he flounders in a world of hypocrisy and deceit. Vivien makes her first appearance as the agent of Mark; she succeeds in destroying Balin's faith in the Order only because Guinevere's behaviour is now visible in Camelot. The sin that stands at the heart of Arthur's Order is a licence for the appearance of evil.

Balin and Balan is the first idyll in the series to lack a happy ending, yet unlike the final idylls, the poem does not have a tragic ending. Balin and Balan die in their final combat, but they die under the illusion that "Pure as our own true Mother is our Queen." Their deaths resemble Elaine's pathetic death in her refusal to face the reality of the adultery. Only later will the sin become so widespread and its effects so disastrous that the complete ruin of the realm will force all its inhabitants to see the condition of the Order and will compel the sinners to accept the consequences of their actions.

Balin and Balan exhibits Tennyson's most sophisticated employment of Malory. The originality of *Guinevere* rests in the poet's creation of the entire incident; *The Last Tournament,* the opening section of *Gareth and Lynette,* and *Merlin and Vivien* exhibit, to a lesser degree, a similar form of originality. Other idylls achieve their originality by embellishing the source, by adding new incidents, and by altering characters and motivations in order to conform to Tennyson's Arthurian world. *Balin and Balan* achieves originality by transforming Malory's story from within the plot; the idyll seems similar to Malory's account because of its duplication of a few episodes and its employment of the same characters. Tennyson condenses Malory's account and superimposes upon it the figure of Vivien and the presence of the adultery; the completed idyll, though based on Malory, finds its ultimate source in Tennyson's Arthurian world. Tennyson invents no character in the idyll, but no character bears any direct relationship to his medieval counterpart; each character is a unique creation by the poet. Even though the ending seems similar to Malory's conclusion, the adultery, aided by Vivien's deceit, is now the cause of the deaths. In spite of the apparent similarity between Malory and Tennyson, the latter achieves originality in this idyll by re-creating in and through his medieval source.

In 1886 the ten idylls became twelve with the nominal division of the Geraint idyll into *The Marriage of Geraint* and *Geraint and Enid* and the incorporation of *Balin and Balan* into the series.[22] Even the new edition of the poem did not end Tennyson's interest in the Arthurian world. The final years of his life found him still fascinated with the story of Camelot.

Though unrelated to the *Idylls, Merlin and the Gleam* has a special position in a study of Tennyson's Arthurian poetry. Despite his dislike of any critical concern with his biography,[23] Tennyson wrote the poem "for those who cared to know about his literary history."[24] Because of his lifelong commitment to the Arthurian legends, he chose a character from that world, Merlin, as the appropriate figure for his "literary history." Merlin's pursuit of Nimue, unrelated to the story of her seduction of the aged seer that stands behind *Merlin and Vivien*,[25] represented the poet's pursuit of his literary vocation:

Of "Merlin and the Gleam," written in August, 1889, he says: "In the story of 'Merlin and Nimue' I have read that Nimue means the Gleam,—which signifies in my poem the higher poetic imagination. Verse IV is the early imagination, Verse V alludes to the Pastorals."[26]

22 The New Miniature Edition of *The Poetical Works of Alfred Lord Tennyson*, twelve volumes (London: Macmillan, 1886-1891).
23 Hallam Tennyson commented: "He himself disliked the notion of a long, formal biography" (*Memoir*, I, xii). In "Notes on Characteristics of Tennyson," Jowett wrote: "He would have wished that, like Shakespeare, his life might be unknown to posterity" (*Tennyson and His Friends*, p. 186).
24 *Memoir*, I, xii. Hallam Tennyson commented: "He thought that 'Merlin and the Gleam' would probably be enough of biography for those friends who urged him to write about himself" (*Memoir*, I, xv).
25 The absence of any reference in *Merlin and the Gleam* to the name "Nimue" may be a reflection of the poet's desire to emphasize the poem's complete separation from the account of the seduction that stands behind the presentation of Merlin and his seductress in the *Idylls*.
26 *Memoir*, II, 366. For a detailed reading of the poem, see *Memoir*, I, xii-xv. In "Tennyson's Merlin," *SP*, 44 (1947), 549-566, G. S. Haight finds William F. Skene's *The Four Ancient Books of Wales* to be the source for the identification of Nimue as the poetic imagination; he also points out Wordsworth's identification of "gleam" as "the fitful nature of inspiration" in *Elegiac Stanzas Suggested by a Picture of Peele Castle in a Storm:* "and add the gleam, / The light that never was, on sea or land, / The consecration, and the Poet's dream." Tennyson's fondness for this poem is noted in

The *Idylls of the King* has a prominent position within the poem:

> Then, with a melody
> Stronger and statelier,
> Led me at length
> To the city and palace
> Of Arthur the King;
> Touch'd at the golden
> Cross of the churches,
> Flash'd on the Tournament,
> Flicker'd and bicker'd
> From helmet to helmet,
> And last on the forehead
> Of Arthur the blameless
> Rested the Gleam.

Tennyson unites King Arthur with Arthur Henry Hallam:

> Clouds and darkness
> Closed upon Camelot;
> Arthur had vanish'd
> I knew not whither,
> The King who loved me,
> And cannot die.

The poem recalls the same union of the legendary King and Hallam suggested in the presentation of Arthur in the early *Morte d'Arthur*. *Merlin and the Gleam* becomes a further testimony to Tennyson's love of the Arthurian legends; though the poem has no source, Tennyson chose an Arthurian figure rich in associations as his inspiration.

At that time Tennyson was also contemplating a new treatment of the Tristram story: "he thought of weaving into a great stage drama the legend of 'Tristram of Lyonnesse,' as he had been obliged to cut it down to suit his treatment of the 'Idylls of the King.' "[27] His treatment of the Tristram story in *The Last Tournament* was brief and succinct; he studied only the final moments in the relationship of Tristram and Mark's wife as one element in his depiction of Arthur's decayed realm. The "great stage drama" would offer Tennyson the opportunity to devote himself to the Tristram story as a complete subject in itself. The project, however, remained an unrealized undertaking; revisions to the *Idylls* still occupied his attention.

In 1890 Tennyson incorporated one small addition into *Guinevere*.[28] In its original form the idyll presented the final meeting of Lancelot and Guinevere:

Memoir, I, 151. In "Tennyson and the Sinful Queen—A Corrected Impression," *Notes and Queries*, new series, 5 (December 1958), 507-511, John Killham reiterates MacCallum's assertion that Tennyson's identification of Nimue with the "gleam" resulted from his reading of John Veitch's poem "Merlin," published in April 1889.

27   *Memoir*, II, 372-373.
28   The addition first appeared in the one-volume edition of *The Poetical Works of Alfred, Lord Tennyson* (London: Macmillan, 1890).

> And then they were agreed upon a night
> (When the good King should not be there) to meet
> And part for ever. Passion-pale they met
> And greeted.

Tennyson revised the passage:

> And then they were agreed upon a night
> (When the good King should not be there) to meet
> And part for ever. Vivien, lurking, heard.
> She told Sir Modred. Passion-pale they met
> And greeted.

By this addition Modred becomes the source of the disclosure of the meeting, but Vivien becomes the efficient cause of the disclosure;[29] her "lurking" behaviour allows her to overhear the information later relayed to Modred. Still a villain, Modred becomes the agent of Vivien. Consequently, Tennyson further tightens the relationship of the evil characters in his Arthurian world. The new introduction to *Merlin and Vivien* made Vivien an agent of Mark; her presence in *Balin and Balan* occurred after her meeting with Mark and before her appearance in Camelot, the two events recorded in the new introduction.[30] With the establishment of the relationship of Modred and Vivien, Mark comes to stand behind the entire poem as the motivating force of evil working ceaselessly for the destruction of Arthur's Order.

The final addition to the *Idylls* was a one-line description of Arthur:

On the other hand, having this vision of Arthur, my father thought that perhaps he had not made the real humanity of the King sufficiently clear in his epilogue; so he inserted in 1891, as his last correction, "Ideal manhood closed in real man," before the lines:

> Rather than that gray king, whose name, a ghost,
> Streams like a cloud, man-shaped, from mountain peak,
> And cleaves to cairn and cromlech still.[31]

Tennyson realized that the stern warning about contemporary social decadence in the epilogue cast the humanity of his hero into the background. The final correction brought his Arthurian masterpiece to a close with a testimony to that humanity.

29 Tennyson united Modred and Vivien in the disclosure scene in his early scenario of the Arthurian legends (see Chapter 1).
30 The introduction employs the flashback technique to recount Vivien's presence at Mark's court before the events of *Balin and Balan*. Such a time-scheme is further evidence of the interdependence of the introduction and the Balin idyll.
31 *Memoir*, II, 129. The line first appeared in volume eight (1899) of the twelve-volume edition of *The Life and Works of Alfred, Lord Tennyson*, edited by Hallam, Lord Tennyson (London: Macmillan, 1898-1899).

Chapter 6

The Realm of Tennyson's King

How can I in my little life, in my small measure, and
in my limited sphere reflect this highest Ideal?[1]

The six decades that span Tennyson's fascination with the Arthurian
legends reveal that the centre of his Arthurian interest was always the
figure of the King. From his earliest forays into the world of Camelot, the
lines entitled "Avalon" in the Cambridge Notebooks and the early
Morte d'Arthur, until his final addition to the completed poem, "Ideal
manhood closed in real man," Tennyson made his re-creation of the
Arthurian world an attempt to present a panoramic study of the King and
the realm that was the embodiment of his vision. Guinevere was the
poet's avenue into the legends, but Arthur was always the reason for the
employment of the material. Tennyson reshaped events so that the evil
growing in the realm emanated from the Queen's dishonour; similarly,
he structured the poem so that the human and the spiritual statures of the
King manifested themselves concurrently. The chronological development of the *Idylls of the King* revealed Tennyson's continuing concern
with a proper presentation of Arthur, a presentation complicated and
handicapped by the more complete presentation of Guinevere.

In *Vivien* the action centres on the title character and her seduction
of Merlin; Arthur is an unseen and not yet important presence. In *Enid,*
however, Arthur does make a significant appearance; visibly moved by
Edyrn's conversion, he exclaims:

> Full seldom does a man repent, or use
> Both grace and will to pick the vicious quitch
> Of blood and custom wholly out of him,
> And make all clean, and plant himself afresh.
> Edyrn has done it, weeding all his heart
> As I will weed this land before I go.

1 *Memoir,* II, 129.

149

Edyrn becomes an inspiration to a humble and idealistic young monarch; moreover, in his opening statement to Geraint, Arthur admits his own early misjudgment:

> Prince, when of late you pray'd me for my leave
> To move to your own land, and there defend
> Your marches, I was prick'd with some reproof,
> As one that let foul wrong stagnate and be,
> By having look'd too much thro' alien eyes,
> And wrought too long with delegated hands,
> Not used mine own.

In *Guinevere* Arthur appears as a godlike being criticizing his wife for the failure of their earthly mission; if his account of the ruin of Camelot makes him seem proud and inhuman, Guinevere's comment negates such a verdict: "Now I see thee what thou art, / Thou art the highest and most human too." *Elaine*, the final idyll of the 1859 quartet, completes the portrayal of Guinevere's relationship with Arthur by depicting its earlier stage; here Guinevere calls him "the faultless King, / That passionless perfection" and concludes that "he is all fault who hath no fault at all."[2]

In the second quartet of idylls, Tennyson brings Arthur into the foreground. In *The Holy Grail* Arthur is the true mystic whose understanding of the spiritual realm does not blind him to the importance of this world; alone of all his knights, he realizes that the proper road to the Ideal must pass through the real world. In *The Coming of Arthur* Tennyson continues his portrait of a mystic monarch by presenting a series of conflicting accounts of Arthur's origin; Bellicent's description of the coronation makes Arthur stand out among his knights as a Christ-like agent of the divine will. Yet lest this aspect of his character overshadow his humanity, the idyll also depicts the King as a strong warrior routing the heathen and as a lonely man desiring marital union with Guinevere. In *The Passing of Arthur* Tennyson adds a presentation of a dying King who is moved to self-doubt by the failings of the world: "for on my heart hath fall'n / Confusion, till I know not what I am, / Nor whence I am, nor whether I be king."

The 1869 volume does present a detailed portrait of Arthur, yet the dominant impression remains of an ideal monarch trying to realize his spiritual vision in this world, a superhuman being whose spiritual stature overshadows his humanity. Tennyson himself is conscious of this direc-

2 In "The Blameless King? The Conceptual Flaw in Tennyson's Arthur," *Ball State University Forum*, 10 (1969), Lois Lewin uses this passage as evidence of Arthur's "failure as a man, as a husband" and concludes that "Arthur's failure is the saint-like failure of those who expect too much of mankind" (p. 41). Guinevere's statement is the verdict of an unenlightened queen; to read her outburst to Lancelot as a valid commentary on Arthur is to accept this statement as a conclusion, whereas her attitude will change significantly in the course of the poem.

tion in his presentation of the King; in a letter to Drummond Rawnsley which accompanied a copy of the volume, he wrote: "In return for your gift I send you my new volume. Arthur is mystic & no mere British Prince as I dare say you will find out."[3]

The remaining idylls offered Tennyson the opportunity to develop more fully the humanity of his King.[4] In *The Last Tournament* Arthur goes to war against the Red Knight of the North; the behaviour of his forces makes their successful excursion a tragedy: "in the heart of Arthur pain was lord." In *Gareth and Lynette* Arthur's ability to be King, questioned in *The Coming of Arthur*, manifests itself clearly in his three judgments on practical matters.[5] In *Balin and Balan* Tennyson incorporates a glimpse of Arthur as a youthful warrior, not through the words of another knight,[6] but through the King's personal confrontation with the title figures when "The light-wing'd spirit of his youth return'd / On Arthur's heart." Such episodes offer a fuller depiction of Arthur as a human being, yet the King ultimately exists as the ideal man; the incidents that develop the human side of his character never diminish his presence as an agent of the divine, as the superhuman being sent to show the necessity and the value of man's acceptance of his spiritual nature. "Ideal manhood closed in real man" is an appropriate description of Tennyson's Arthur, though its accuracy is questionable; though the purpose of the poem is to teach "the need of the Ideal," Arthur's "Ideal manhood" tends to overshadow the "real man."

The study of Tennyson's growing independence from his medieval sources in his re-creation of the Arthurian world also reveals his growing dependence upon Guinevere as the controlling force in the structural development of this world. In her own idyll, *Guinevere*, the Queen emerges as a full and complete human character; Arthur sinks into the background. Subsequent idylls find Tennyson attempting to develop Arthur's human presence. Yet the poem seems burdened by his first presentation of Arthur, the ideal monarch working God's will on this earth. The poet has to develop the King's humanity because he began his portrait of Arthur with a depiction of Arthur's idealism in its Christ-like expression to a repentant Queen. Arthur's unbending and relentless

3 The letter, contained in the Harvard Tennyson Loose Papers MS Eng. 952.2.11, is undated, but the envelope is postmarked December 1869.
4 In "Tennyson's Paradoxical King," *Victorian Poetry*, 1 (1963), 258-271, Stanley Solomon pays careful attention to the balance between the ideal and the real in the King in order to refute those critics who prefer to study Arthur as a failed human being. The article, however, tends to imply that Camelot's tragedy is partially the tragedy of Arthur, "the 'blameless King', who is paradoxically to blame for the destruction of his own kingdom" (p. 259).
5 Other additions to the 1873 Library edition served a similar function, especially the one-line addition to Arthur's speech to Guinevere (see Chapter 2, footnote 30) and his long reflective soliloquy at the beginning of the closing idyll (see Chapter 4).
6 In *Elaine*, Lancelot described Arthur's prowess in battle at great length.

commitment to the Ideal stands in contrast to the graphic depiction of Guinevere's agonized humanity. Later idylls only reveal Tennyson's valiant efforts to show Arthur's own humanity.

Tennyson began his Arthurian creation with the woman who sees too late, with a human Queen who commands our respect and sympathy. Guinevere becomes an example to the reader of the failure of humanity "to love the highest when we see it." The poet began his presentation of Camelot with a vivid delineation of reality in the form of Arthur's Queen, and he never managed to create an equally vivid delineation of the ideal within the reality of Arthur. The failure to offer a satisfying portrait of Arthur's humanity reflects the fact that Tennyson's presentation of reality in Camelot begins and ends with Guinevere. Here the poet found his key into the Arthurian world, though he also found a deceptive path which prevented him from creating the full humanity of the ideal. Guinevere's leap of faith, her sudden insight into the true nature of her husband and her proper relationship to him, this is the leap of faith Tennyson wants his audience to make. In a world where Arthurs seem to disappear, the poet wants his audience to see Guinevere as a warning of man's need to love the Ideal. And Guinevere as a vivid exemplar of the humanity of this world prevents the poet from investing his ideal King with an equally sympathetic humanity.

Though Tennyson's King betrays none of the human blemishes of Malory's monarch, he is not a duplication of the more perfect Arthur of the earlier chroniclers. Tennyson moved beyond the Arthur of Joseph of Exeter and Alberic and created a new King, an ideal monarch who is the embodiment of the divine will. Arthur's mission is a commitment to the divine command to realize his highest calling in this world through an attempt to make humanity more aware of its full capability. Arthur is the highest human being, Christ-like in his perfection, human in his inability to realize a permanent manifestation of his vision in this world.

In his unique creation of Arthur, Tennyson made the *Idylls of the King* a religious poem. Arthur's life is a testimony to his faith; his vision and its momentary incarnation in Camelot are a testimony to man's capability. The decay of Camelot is not the tragedy of Arthur nor the tragedy of his vision;[7] it is the tragedy of a society which remains blind to the full implications of its own human nature. And Guinevere stands at the centre of this world, the lesson to mankind of its own blindness, for

---

7   Recent criticism has tended to see the tragedy of Camelot as Arthur's personal tragedy. Ryals finds that Arthur "stands, finally, in moral terms, as both the hero and the villain of the *Idylls of the King*" (p. 90). Such a misreading of the poem leads to growing critical concern with Arthur's personal failings, an area which violates Tennyson's own statement that his King is "blameless" or, as the epilogue states, "Ideal manhood closed in real man." In "Tennyson's *Idylls of the King* as Tragic Drama," *Victorian Poetry*, 4 (1966), Henry Kozicki develops Ryals' theory: "Tennyson does not develop Arthur as an agent causally related to a decaying society, yet Arthur must bear the sins and pollutions of it" (p. 18).

she is aware only when it is too late of man's highest calling. The passions of this earthly experience delude and destroy man if man refuses to see beyond this experience. The movement of Camelot back into the beast is a negation of Arthur's principles and a vindication of their necessity.

The realm of Tennyson's King is the realm of the spirit:

> Guided by the voice within, the Ideal Soul looks out into the Infinite for the highest Ideal; and finds it nowhere realized so mightily as in the Word who "wrought With human hands the creed of creeds." But for Arthur, as for everyone who believes in the Word however interpreted, arises the question, "How can I in my little life, in my small measure, and in my limited sphere reflect this highest Ideal?" From the answer to this question come the strength of life, its beauty, and above all its helpfulness to the world.[8]

Yet the realm of the spirit is the realm of this world, or, as the poet remarked, "Depend upon it, the Spiritual *is* the Real."[9] Arthur's attempt to create a realization of the Ideal in a fallible world is his glory; the attempt to create a perfect Order is doomed to failure, but the attempt is the achievement. Like all men Arthur is confined to this world, yet the confinement does not restrict his understanding of man's spirituality. Like Arthur men must penetrate to an appreciation and an acceptance of their own capability. The tragedy of Tennyson's Camelot is the tragedy of a society which, confronted with the Ideal, turns aside and blinds itself to the spiritual depth of man.

In later years, Tennyson commented about the *Idylls of the King:* "They have taken my hobby, and ridden it too hard, and have explained some things too allegorically, although there is an allegorical or perhaps rather a parabolic drift in the poem."[10] The "drift," as he noted, is "the dream of man coming into practical life and ruined by one sin."[11] Yet Tennyson's preference for the term "parabolic" suggests a final method of approaching the completed series. Tennyson's distrust of the term "allegory" reflects his continual opposition to literary classifications which restrict poetic meaning: "I hate to be tied down to say, '*This* means *that*,' because the thought within the image is much more than any one interpretation."[12] Allegory tends to limit the interpretation of a

---

8 *Memoir*, II, 129.
9 Ibid., II, 90. The poet also commented: "Matter is a greater mystery than mind. What such a thing as a spirit is apart from God and man I have never been able to conceive. Spirit seems to me to be the reality of the world" (*Memoir*, II, 424).
10 Ibid., II, 126-127.
11 "The general drift of the 'Idylls' is clear enough. 'The whole,' he said, 'is the dream of man coming into practical life and ruined by one sin. Birth is a mystery and death is a mystery, and in the midst lies the tableland of life, and its struggles and performances. It is not the history of one man or of one generation but of a whole cycle of generations'" (*Memoir*, II, 127).
12 *Memoir*, II, 127. "Most explanations and analyses, although eagerly asked for by some readers, appeared to my father somewhat to dwarf and limit the life and scope of the great Arthurian tragedy" (*Memoir*, II, 134).

poem; it demands a close correspondence between the literal events and their allegorical significance. By denying a deliberate allegorical intention in the poem, Tennyson hoped to silence the wrong interpretations of the *Idylls* and to allow new readers to approach the poem without preconceived prejudices. Tennyson's preference for "parabolic" is related to his concept of the "drift" of the *Idylls*.[13] A parable does not demand the close connection between each event in the story and its moral significance; consequently, each idyll is a study of the growth or decay of Camelot and each idyll becomes, at the same time, part of the complete depiction of "the thought within the image."[14]

In the completed series Tennyson has accomplished his early ambition: "if I meant to make any mark at all, it must be by shortness, for the men before me had been so diffuse, and most of the big things except 'King Arthur' had been done."[15] The idyll structure allowed him to create short poems, which together create an epic study of King Arthur.[16] His earliest plan, to use the Arthurian legends for a study of "the great religions of the world,"[17] was never realized; a later plan, to "write twelve 'Idylls,' one for each knight of the Round Table,"[18] bears a close

13 Tennyson showed no distinction in his employment of the words "allegory" and "parable" in his poetry. Both words occur twice in the *Idylls*. "The four fools have suck'd their allegory" from the walls in *Gareth and Lynette;* Gareth speaks of "the third fool of their allegory." Lynette refers to "The second brother in their fool's parable," and Gareth answers: "Parables? Hear / A parable of the knave." The only other employment of "allegory" in Tennyson's poetry is the description of *The Palace of Art* as "a sort of allegory" in the poetic preface to the poem. There is no other poetic occurrence of "parable." Tennyson refers to the parables of the New Testament in *In Memoriam* (XXXVI): "For Wisdom dealt with mortal powers, / Where truth in closest words shall fail, / When truth embodied in a tale / Shall enter in at lowly doors." For the biblical parables, Tennyson had "a measureless admiration"; he called them "perfection, beyond compare" (*Memoir*, I, 325).
14 Tennyson regarded the parable as a literary form of wide accessibility: "in this instance as in others involving the supreme meaning and guidance of life, a parable is perhaps the teacher that can most surely enter in at all doors" (*Memoir*, I, 249). In a note on *The Coming of Arthur*, Hallam Tennyson stated: "In this Idyll the poet lays bare the main lines of his story and of his parable" (Eversley edition, V, 451-452).
15 *Memoir*, I, 166.
16 "He would not call his 'Idylls of the King' 'an Epic' on the title page because according to strict canons of criticism an epic celebrates only one hero, whereas his 'Idylls of the King' involves not only the tragedy of King Arthur but also the tragedy of Sir Lancelot. His original intention of spelling his 'Idylls of the King' with two 'lls' was to differentiate them from his 'Theocritan Idyls,' since they were to be Idylls woven into a kind of Epic Unity" (*Materials*, I, 237). Hallam Tennyson noted: "If Epic unity is looked for in the 'Idylls,' we find it not in the wrath of an Achilles, nor in the wanderings of an Ulysses, but in the unending war of humanity in all ages,—the world-wide war of Sense and Soul, typified in individuals, with the subtle interaction of character upon character, the central dominant figure being the pure, generous, tender, brave, human-hearted Arthur,—so that the links (with here and there symbolic accessories) which bind the 'Idylls' into an artistic whole, are perhaps somewhat intricate" (*Memoir*, II, 130).
17 See Chapter 1, footnote 15.
18 *Memoir*, II, 203.

resemblance to the final work. The *Idylls of the King* is a panoramic study of the spirituality of man, a study which focuses on Arthur, a man conscious of his complete nature and committed to its highest calling. Arthur's birth is a mystery; his death is a mystery; in the midst comes the Round Table, ten idylls which depict "the tableland of life, and its struggles and performances."

For Tennyson, man must search for the Ideal, and his success lies in the continuation of the search: "It is motive, it is the great purpose which consecrates life."[19] The spiritual is the only reality; man must understand and move beyond physical reality in order to see that physical reality is also spiritual reality. Aided by such an understanding, man may face the one question: "How can I in my little life, in my small measure, and in my limited sphere reflect the highest Ideal?" For Arthur the answer is the creation of the Order of the Round Table; the dissolution of the Order indicates the spiritual blindness of the knights and their wilful abdication of the responsibility of asking themselves that one question. For Tennyson the answer to the question lies in the social purpose of his poetry, in the *Idylls of the King* which is meant to teach his generation "the need of the Ideal." Tennyson saw the spiritual blindness of his time:

> This is a terrible age of unfaith ... I hate utter unfaith, I cannot endure that men should sacrifice everything at the cold altar of what with their imperfect knowledge they choose to call truth and reason. One can easily lose all belief, through giving up the continual thought and care for spiritual things.[20]

Victorian England's failure to alter its dedication to materialism and self-gratification prompted an elder Tennyson to lament: "I tried in my *Idylls* to teach these things, and the need of the Ideal. But I feel sometimes as if my life had been a very useless life."[21] Like King Arthur, Tennyson saw his own society crumbling, and he employed the Arthurian legends to show that society the importance of the Ideal. Arthur stands at the centre of the *Idylls* as the vision of the Ideal, and Guinevere stands beside him as a vision of the Real, unaware of the crucial need for a personal commitment to the Ideal. Like the young Guinevere, Victorian society seemed unwilling or unable to look beyond the base desires of its struggling humanity. The *Idylls of the King* stands, ultimately, as Tennyson's own Camelot, his legacy to his generation, an indictment of his society through a vindication of his idealism.

19 Ibid., I, 318.
20 Ibid., I, 309.
21 Ibid., II, 337.

Epilogue

Alfred Tennyson and Victorian Arthuriana

The second half of the nineteenth century saw the emergence of unprecedented interest in the stories of King Arthur and the Round Table. Painters, writers, and literary scholars turned to the medieval world of Camelot with intense dedication. Tennyson's poetry did not stand behind all the Arthurian art and literature of Victorian England, but it did serve to raise the subject-matter to a new level of literary respectability. The neglect and abuse of the Arthurian legends which characterized the romantic and early Victorian attitudes gave way to the literary eminence of the world of Camelot by the end of the nineteenth century. Though a complete analysis of the Arthurian art and literature of the period remains outside the realm of this study, a survey of the major Arthurian works does reveal the pervasive influence of Tennyson.

In the world of painting, Dante Gabriel Rossetti and his Pre-Raphaelite associates often turned to the Middle Ages for their subject-matter. Rossetti found in Malory incidents which would serve as objective correlatives for his own feelings. His Arthurian paintings usually present two episodes from the legends: the relationship of Lancelot and Guinevere or the quest of the Holy Grail. For Rossetti, the earthly and the spiritual were opposing forces vying for man's soul. In Lancelot's love for the Queen, he saw his own passion for womanly beauty; in the Grail quest, he saw the mystical experience that he and Lancelot would never attain.

Though it is impossible to date Rossetti's first encounter with Malory,[1] his admiration of Tennyson's early poetry may have been his

---

1 In *Dante Gabriel Rossetti—His Family Letters with a Memoir* (London, 1895), William Michael Rossetti commented about his brother's plans for the Oxford Union: "He thought the bays of the Debating-room would be suitable for wall-paintings and suggested that they should be covered with tempera-pictures from the Romance of King Arthur. This was not a specifically appropriate theme, but Rossetti had not at

first introduction to Arthurian stories.[2] The Pre-Raphaelite Brotherhood was aware of Tennyson's plan to write an Arthurian epic a decade before the appearance of the first volume of the *Idylls*.[3] When Rossetti turned to Malory in the early eighteen-fifties, he knew that Tennyson, now Poet Laureate, had established the literary stature of the Arthurian legends. Tennyson provided Rossetti with his first extended employment of Arthurian material. For the 1857 illustrated edition of Tennyson's *Poems*, Rossetti contributed five illustrations; three of them depicted Arthurian episodes.[4] The Arthurian trio did not prompt Rossetti to consult Malory; indeed, he used Tennyson's poetry only as a suggestion for the illustrations.[5]

In 1858 Rossetti began *God's Graal*, his only attempt to write an Arthurian poem. He was unable to complete it at that time. The publication of Tennyson's *The Holy Grail* prompted Rossetti's return to his unfinished poem.[6] In 1870, however, his understanding of the polarity of

that time any clear notion of the purpose which the room was to serve. Malory's *Morte d'Arthur* is a book to which, so far as memory serves me, he had not paid any marked attention in earlier years. Perhaps Mr. Morris, rather than his self-directed readings, had impressed its interest upon him, and Morris, at the same time as Rossetti, offered to paint something in the Union Room. At any rate my brother was now in a vigorously Arthurian mood, which lasted some years, and never left him entirely'' (I, 196).

2   '' 'If any man has any poetry in him,' he [Rossetti] said to Burne-Jones again and again that summer, 'he should paint, for it has all been said and written, and they have scarcely begun to paint it.' The feeling which Morris had shared with his contemporaries at Oxford, that Tennyson represented the end of all things in poetry, no doubt received a powerful stimulus or revival from this doctrine of Rossetti's'' (J. W. Mackail, *The Life of William Morris* [London, 1899], I, 110-111).

3   The Pre-Raphaelite journal recorded on December 18, 1849: ''His [Tennyson's] poem of King Arthur is not yet commenced, though he has been for years past maturing the conception of it; and he intends that it should occupy him some fifteen years'' (*Preraphaelite Diaries and Letters,* edited by W. M. Rossetti [London: Hurst and Blackett, 1900], pp. 238-239).

4   For Moxon's 1859 edition Rossetti contributed *The Lady of Shalott* (Lancelot descending into the barge where the Lady's body lies), *King Arthur and the Weeping Queens* (an illustration of the lines describing Arthur in *The Palace of Art*), and *Sir Galahad* (an illustration of the third stanza of the poem). In *Tennyson and His Pre-Raphaelite Illustrators* (London: E. Stock, 1894), G. S. Layard noted Rossetti's intention to make another illustration of Sir Galahad, which he never created (p. 49). For a description of Rossetti's Arthurian paintings, see Virginia Surtees, *The Paintings and Drawings of Dante Gabriel Rossetti* (Oxford: The Clarendon Press, 1971).

5   ''It must be said also that himself only, and not Tennyson, was his guide. He drew just what he chose, taking from his author's text nothing more than a hint and an opportunity... As to our great poet Tennyson—who also ought to have counted for something in the whole affair—I gather that he really liked Rossetti's designs when he saw them, and he was not without a perceptible liking and regard for Rossetti himself, so far as he knew him'' (*Dante Gabriel Rossetti—His Family Letters with a Memoir,* I, 189).

6   Rossetti wrote to Swinburne on December 21, 1869: ''One thing is that I shall proceed with additional zest to my projected poem of *God's Graal* (Lancelot losing the Sancgrail), wherein God and Guenevere will be weighed against each other by another table of weights and measures'' (*Letters of Dante Gabriel Rossetti,* edited by Oswald Doughty and John Robert Wahl [Oxford: The Clarendon Press, 1965-1967], II, 779).

the earthly and the spiritual was changing so that Lancelot's quest became an example of the superiority of the earthly.[7] To re-create Malory so that Lancelot's failure was not essentially tragic perplexed Rossetti and the poem remained incomplete.[8]

Tennyson's early Arthurian poetry may have fostered Rossetti's initial interest in the Arthurian legends; his later poetry did prompt Rossetti to return to his only effort at an Arthurian poem. And the *Idylls* may have caused Rossetti's increasing hesitation to employ Arthurian themes. When the 1859 volume of the *Idylls of the King* appeared, Rossetti read about an Arthurian world which bore little relationship to his more passionate Camelot. The moral tone of Tennyson's account of the Grail story influenced his decision to attempt a different version, yet the popularity of Tennyson's Arthurian poetry may have been the final factor in his inability to create his own Arthurian world.

Rossetti's associates showed similar fascination with Arthurian themes, and they too entered the world of Camelot through the guidance of Tennyson. Their Arthurian paintings were either illustrations of Tennyson's poems[9] or depictions of incidents which originated in Tennyson's Arthurian world.[10] As a consequence, Tennyson became the source of their understanding of the legends. Their medievalism owed more to Tennyson than to the medieval world and the *Idylls of the King* came to hold the inspirational force that Malory occupied for Tennyson.

Among the Pre-Raphaelite associates, Edward Burne-Jones was the most devoted disciple of the Arthurian legends. When he first read Malory in 1855, he discovered a world that would become his natural

7   Rossetti wrote to Swinburne on March 9, 1870: "The poem I shall do (if any) will be, I believe, *God's Graal*—i.e. the loss of the Sangraal by Lancelot—a theme chosen to emphasize the marked superiority of Guenevere over God" (*Letters*, II, 812).

8   On March 22, 1870 Rossetti wrote to Swinburne: "If I do anything else it will be *God's Graal*, the Lancelot poem, but this baffled me rather on taking it up, owing to the limitations of the burden I had adopted. However I may tackle it yet, but the time runs short" (*Letters*, II, 824). The unfinished poem was first published in *The Works of Dante Gabriel Rossetti*, edited by William Michael Rossetti (London: Ellis, 1911), p. 239.

9   Holman Hunt made one illustration of *The Lady of Shalott* for the 1857 edition; his later painting of the same title took the illustration for its basis. Daniel Maclise made two illustrations of Tennyson's *Morte d'Arthur* for the same edition. For both Hunt and Maclise, Tennyson's poetry provided the inspiration for their only attempts at paintings with Arthurian subjects. The only extant work by John Everett Millais on an Arthurian subject is a pen-and-ink drawing, *The Lady of Shalott*, dated 1854, an illustration of the third stanza of the fourth section of Tennyson's poem.

10 F. G. Stephens found inspiration in Tennyson's *Morte d'Arthur* for his unfinished painting of the same title. The painting, his only Arthurian work, dated 1849, showed its indebtedness to Tennyson, not only by its title, but by its figures, one knight trying to carry a dying Arthur. Stephens followed Tennyson in reducing Malory's presentation of two knights to one attendant in the final scene. Arthur Hughes turned to Tennyson's poetry for his three Arthurian paintings: *The Lady of Shalott, Sir Galahad,* and *Enid and Geraint*. G. F. Watts made two Arthurian paintings: *Sir Galahad* and *Enid and Geraint*.

and perpetual haunt;[11] like Tennyson he made his artistic career an attempt to re-create the beauty and the power of the legends.[12] Yet his endless re-creation of the medieval world found its initial inspiration in Tennyson. Burne-Jones first encountered Arthurian characters in Tennyson's early poetry. He never realized his early plan to form a "small conventual society," but his plan emphasized his admiration for Tennyson and especially for his early Arthurian poetry.[13] When he discovered Malory, he found further inspiration, "reading the Morte d'Arthur, the chapters about the death of Percival's sister and the Shalott lady."[14] His first Arthurian painting, *Sir Galahad*, was his entrance into the world of Camelot and his unconscious acknowledgement of his debt to Tennyson.[15] For Burne-Jones and his Pre-Raphaelite associates, Tennyson opened the door to the wealth of the Arthurian legends.

Tennyson's re-creation of the Arthurian legends precipitated an abundance of literary treatments of the story of Camelot.[16] The three major literary figures who also employed Arthurian material shared both an interest in the subject-matter and a dislike of Tennyson's re-creation.

11   "It was Southey's reprint of Malory's Morte d'Arthur: and sometimes I think that the book never can have been loved as it was by those two men. With Edward it became literally a part of himself. Its strength and beauty, its mystical religion and noble chivalry of action, the world of lost history and romance in the names of people and places—it was his own birthright upon which he entered" (Georgiana Burne-Jones, *Memorials of Edward Burne-Jones* [London: Macmillan, 1904], I, 116). Burne-Jones described his affinity with the story of Camelot: "I can't expect people to feel about the subject as I do, and have always. It is such a sacred land to me that nothing in the world touches it in comparison" (*Memorials*, II, 247); "nothing was ever like Morte d'Arthur—I don't mean any one book or any one poem, something that never can be written I mean, and can never go out of the heart" (*Memorials*, II, 168).

12   Burne-Jones completed ten paintings with Arthurian subjects. In addition, he left a series of unfinished Arthurian paintings and some Arthurian cartoons for stained glass. For a complete listing of his works, see Malcolm Bell, *Sir Edward Burne-Jones* (London, 1898).

13   "Remember, I have set my heart on our founding a Brotherhood. Learn Sir Galahad by heart. He is to be the patron of our Order. I have enlisted *one* in the project up here, heart and soul. You shall have a copy of the canons some day. (Signed) General of the Order of Sir Galahad" (*Memorials,* I, 77). On May 1, 1853 Burne-Jones wrote to Morris: "I am well pleased that our taste in poetics is concurrent. If Tennyson affords you as many hours of unmitigated happiness—I speak without affectation here—as he has to me, you will look with gratitude to any who helped you to appreciate him. When I take up the works of any other poet, save Shakespeare only, I seem to have fallen from the only guide worth following far into dreamland" (*Memorials,* I, 76).

14   *Memorials*, I, 117. It is significant that Burne-Jones came to refer to Elaine as "the Shalott lady," an appellation indicative of his debt to Tennyson since Malory referred to her home as Astolat.

15   Malcolm Bell described Burne-Jones's first Arthurian painting as "one of the few traces in the artist's work of the influence exercised by Tennyson over the school to which he was affiliated. Even this is rather an expression of the feeling of the poem than an illustration to it, since it depicts no actual incident therein" (p. 21).

16   For a listing of the major Arthurian writings of the nineteenth century with commentary on specific works related to Tennyson's poetry, see Eggers, pp. 215-252.

Despite their criticism and their own Arthurian works, Tennyson's poetry continued to exert enormous influence in Victorian England.

Matthew Arnold did not approve of Tennyson's medieval characters:

> The fault I find with Tennyson in his *Idylls of the King* is that the peculiar charm and aroma of the Middle Age he does not give in them. There is something magical about it, and I will do something with it before I have done. The real truth is that Tennyson, with all his temperament and artistic skill, is deficient in intellectual power; and no modern poet can make very much of his business unless he is pre-eminently strong in this.[17]

Arnold's only Arthurian poem, *Tristram and Iseult,* never satisfied its author; his revisions and additions only served to emphasize his artistic failure.[18] As an Arthurian work his poem became isolated in its own time. The fact that no other writer followed his originality in the depiction of the second Iseult as a mother of two children is final proof of the curious unimportance of the first modern English treatment of the Tristram story in the history of Arthurian literature. Despite his criticism of Tennyson's Arthurian poetry and his vow to "do something with it before I have done," Arnold never returned to the Arthurian legends.

William Morris shared Arnold's appreciation of the Middle Ages and his dislike of Tennyson's treatment of the legends. His first volume of poetry, *The Defence of Guenevere and Other Poems*, begins with four Arthurian poems; each of them is a distinct, dramatic, and vividly realized incident borrowed from Malory with varying degrees of fidelity.[19] Morris employs personal names, the basic structure of certain incidents, and the general portrait of the *Morte d'Arthur*, but closer examination reveals the dissimilarities, the distinctly Pre-Raphaelite intensity of depiction and the sense of heightened passion which he imposed upon basic beginnings offered to him by Malory. Morris continued to study the medieval Arthurian world, but later years found him increasingly suspicious of his own ability to employ that world effectively. He disapproved of "the transfusion of modern sentiment into an

17 "Letter to Miss Arnold, December 17, 1860," *Letters of Matthew Arnold 1848-1888,* edited by George W. E. Russell (London, 1895), I, 127.

18 Arnold's poem was first published in 1852; the following year he brought out a second edition which included a long preface about Tristram's history from Dunlop's *History of Prose Fiction.* In a letter to Clough of May 1, 1853, he admitted: "I wish I had you with me to put marks against the places where something is wanted. The whole affair is by no means thoroughly successful" (*The Letters of Matthew Arnold to Arthur Hugh Clough,* edited by H. F. Lowry [London: Oxford University Press, 1932], p. 136).

19 The four poems are *The Defence of Guenevere, King Arthur's Tomb, Sir Galahad: A Christmas Mystery,* and *The Chapel in Lyoness.* For a detailed study of Morris' employment of his Arthurian sources, see my essay, "Morris' Treatment of His Medieval Sources in *The Defence of Guenevere and Other Poems*," *Studies in Philology,* 70 (1973), 439-464.

ancient story,"[20] which he observed in the *Idylls of the King*; he did not
attempt, however, to realize his original plan of an Arthurian cycle. His
early idolatry of Malory and the popularity of Tennyson's achievement
seemed to unite in preventing him from employing Malory in his own
literary efforts.

Like Morris, Swinburne turned to the Arthurian world and re-
created Malory according to the Pre-Raphaelite devotion to pictorial
intensity. His earliest Arthurian poem, *Queen Yseult*, is an unsatisfying
combination of medieval narrative romance and Pre-Raphaelite detailed
depiction. His other early Arthurian efforts are further attempts to
create some kind of Arthurian cycle.[21] His rejection of the Pre-
Raphaelite creed marked the end of Morris' influence upon his treatment of Malory, yet he never abandoned his interest in the legends.
Tristram of Lyonesse and *The Tale of Balen*, his major Arthurian poems,
are deliberate reactions against Tennyson's Arthurian world. In each he
tries to retell the medieval story without any embellishments. *Tristram
of Lyonesse* is more than a retelling; it is a re-creation that becomes a
celebration of love. In *The Tale of Balen* Swinburne observes such close
fidelity to Malory that the poem is his most unoriginal Arthurian work; it
is little more than a dramatic paraphrase. His explicit denunciations of
Tennyson's treatment of the legends[22] make him adhere closely to his
source; such adherence dictates the form of his final employment of
Arthurian material. It is ironic that *The Tale of Balen* employs the stanza
of *The Lady of Shalott*[23] and achieves a degree of structural and verbal
fidelity to Malory that Tennyson never sought after his early *Morte
d'Arthur*. Swinburne's rejection of Tennyson's method of handling the
legends led him to a method of retelling them that is both a direct

20 Mackail, I, 299.
21 In addition to *Queen Yseult* his early Arthurian poems were *Joyeuse Garde*, a short
narrative about the love of Tristram and Yseult when they are at Joyeuse Garde; *King
Ban*, a lamentation by Ban; *The Day Before the Trial*, a soliloquy by Arthur on the day
before Guenevere's trial; *Lancelot*, the title figure's soliloquy about his mystical aims
and his earthly love. For a detailed study of Swinburne's Arthurian poetry, see my
essay, "Swinburne's Arthurian World: Swinburne's Arthurian Poetry and Its
Medieval Sources," *Studia Neophilologica*, 50 (1978), 53-70.
22 Swinburne's most explicit attack on the *Idylls* was published in 1872 in his essay,
"Under the Microscope." In a similar vein he wrote to Theodore Watts on August 29,
1874: "If the mystery of our redemption is thus to be associated by ribald writers with
the badge of cuckledom, what wonder that our Laureate should find in the ideal
cuckold his type of the ideal man?" (*The Swinburne Letters*, edited by Cecil Y. Lang
[New Haven: Yale University Press, 1959-1962], II, 335). A further instance of
Swinburne's dislike of Tennyson's Arthurian world was a notice in the "Weekly
Gossip" column of the *Athenaeum* of March 14, 1868: "Mr. Algernon Swinburne is
composing a poem on Tristram and Yseult; and is also to write, next year,—if rumour
is not mistaken,—an essay on the Women of Arthurian Romance, for the Early
English Text Society's edition of Malory's 'Morte Darthur'; in which Mr. Tennyson's
view of Guinevere, Vivien, &c., will not be adopted" (p. 394).
23 Swinburne borrowed the stanza from Tennyson's poem, although he added a syllable
to the fifth line and he did not attempt to create a refrain in the final line of each stanza.

criticism of Tennyson's method and an acknowledgement of the influence and popularity of Tennyson's poetry.

The final testimony of Tennyson's importance to the development of
interest in the Arthurian legends is the sudden emergence in the latter
half of the nineteenth century of scholarly commitment to Malory.
Whereas the first half of the century saw the publication of three editions
of Malory which were not reprinted, the second half witnessed the
appearance of several new editions.[24] More significantly, in 1862 James
Knowles compiled *The Story of King Arthur and His Knights of the
Round Table,* the first modernization of Malory and a volume destined
to pass through seven separate editions before 1900. Knowles dedicated
his book to Tennyson: "This attempt at a popular version of the Arthur
legends is by his permission dedicated, as a tribute of the sincerest and
warmest respect."[25] Five more modernizations appeared before the end
of the century and each of them noted the importance of Tennyson in the
steadily growing interest in Arthurian stories.[26]

24 Thomas Wright brought out a three-volume edition of *La Mort d'Arthure* in 1858; a
    second edition appeared in 1866, and a third in 1889; the third edition was reprinted in
    1893 and 1897. In 1868 Edward Strachey published a one-volume edition of the *Morte
    Darthur*; published in March, the edition was followed by a second edition in August
    of the same year. The latter edition with an added index was published in 1869 and
    reprinted in 1871, 1876, 1879, 1882, 1884, 1886, and 1889. Another edition by Strachey
    appeared in 1891 and was reprinted in 1893, 1897, 1898, and 1899. Ernest Rhys edited a
    series of small editions of selections from Malory: *Malory's History of King Arthur
    and the Quest of the Holy Grail* (London, 1886); *The Book of Marvellous Adventures
    and Other Books of the Morte D'Arthur* (London, 1893); *The Noble and Joyous
    History of King Arthur* (London, 1894). Between 1889 and 1891 H. O. Sommer's
    three-volume edition of the *Morte Darthur* appeared. Israel Gollancz edited a four-
    volume edition of Malory (London, 1897); the first edition, brought out in May, was
    followed by a second edition in November of the following year and a third edition in
    August, 1899. A. T. Martin edited *Selections from Malory's Le Morte D'Arthur*
    (London, 1896), and W. E. Mead edited *Selections from Sir Thomas Malory's Le
    Morte D'Arthur* (London, 1897).
25 James T. Knowles, *The Story of King Arthur and His Knights of the Round Table*
    (London, 1862). The volume ends with Arthur's disappearance on the barge; no final
    scenes from Malory are retained. Knowles accepted Tennyson's ending as an appro-
    priate conclusion to his modernization. Though Knowles became Tennyson's close
    friend, he had not met the poet at the time of this edition. In his third edition (London,
    1868), he noted: "The revival of the Arthur legends, under the influence of the 'Idylls
    of the King' has interested so many in the subject, that an outline of the noble story has
    almost become a necessary item of general information" (p. iii).
26 *La Morte D'Arthur. The History of King Arthur,* abridged and revised by Edward
    Conybeare (London, 1868); Conybeare did retain Malory's ending. The other moder-
    nizations were *La Mort D'Arthur,* edited by B. Montgomerie Ranking (London, 1871),
    the subtitle being "The Old Prose Stories whence the 'Idylls of the King' have been
    taken by Alfred Tennyson," even though appropriate material from the *Mabinogion*
    was included; *The Life and Exploits of King Arthur and His Knights of the Round
    Table: A Legendary Romance,* edited anonymously (London, 1878), a volume which
    returned to Tennyson's ending; *The Boy's King Arthur,* edited by Sidney Lanier
    (London, 1880); *King Arthur and the Knights of the Round Table. A Modernized
    Version of the Morte Darthur,* edited by Charles Morris (London, 1892).

By the beginning of the twentieth century the Arthurian legends attained the literary stature they had commanded in the Middle Ages and in the Renaissance.[27] The story of Camelot inspired many artists in Victorian England. Behind this revival of interest in the material stood the august figure of the Poet Laureate, who first employed the legends when they seemed to lack proper respectability for artistic consideration. At the same time that his lifelong commitment to the material created the *Idylls of the King*, which, "regarded as a whole, gives his innermost being more fully, though not more truly, than 'In Memoriam,' "[28] his Arthurian poetry created the Arthurian renaissance of the nineteenth century. The *Idylls* presented Victorian England with an avenue into the medieval accounts of Camelot. Some contemporaries employed Tennyson's poetry as a medieval document and failed to study the original legends. Others turned to Malory as a rebuttal of Tennyson's treatment of the material. In any event, Tennyson's pervasive presence and influence are evident.

Tennyson never answered Coleridge's question about King Arthur: "What have *we* to do with him?" He re-created the medieval legends to present a "mundane" rather than "national" poem. At the same time the *Idylls of the King* raised Arthur to a stature which made him assume epic dimensions within English literary tradition. Tennyson brought the Arthurian legends to the consciousness of the English people; his poetry re-established their literary eminence. Though Tennyson made no attempt to answer Coleridge's question, many of his contemporaries would agree with Edward Strachey's assertion: "it was well that the old order should yield place to the new, or at least make room for it at its side. And such are the thoughts and sentiments with which the lover of the old Morte Arthur will, if he be also a student of the growth of our national character, read the new *Idylls of the King*."[29] Tennyson re-created the medieval legends according to his own idealistic philosophy so that the Arthurian world of his creation stands both after and beside the Arthurian world of medieval England.

27 For the development of Arthurian literature in the early twentieth century, see Nathan C. Starr, *King Arthur Today* (Gainesville: University of Florida Press, 1954).
28 *Memoir*, II, 128.
29 *Le Morte Darthur*, edited by Edward Strachey (London, 1891), p. xxvi.

Appendix 1

Morte d'Arthur

A comparison of Tennyson's account of the final moments of Arthur's life in the *Morte d'Arthur* (1842) and the relevant passages from Malory's account in the 1816 Wilks edition:

Malory:
Vol. III, ch. clxvii[i],
unless otherwise indicated

Tennyson:

(And therewith Sir Mordred fell down stark dead to the earth, and the noble King Arthur fell in a swoon to the earth. And there he swooned often times. And Sir Lucan and Sir Bedivere often times heaved him up, and so weakly they led him between them both unto a little chapel not far from the sea side. – clxvii)

So all day long the noise of battle roll'd
Among the mountains by the winter sea,
Until King Arthur's table, man by man,
Had fall'n in Lyonness about their Lord,
King Arthur: then, because his wound was deep,
The bold Sir Bedivere uplifted him,
Sir Bedivere, the last of all his knights,
And bore him to a chapel nigh the field,
A broken chancel with a broken cross,
That stood on a dark strait of barren land.
On one side lay the Ocean, and on one
Lay a great water, and the moon was full.

Then spake King Arthur to Sir Bedivere:

("Alas, that ever I bear any crown upon my head, for I have now lost the

"The sequel of to-day unsolders all

fairest fellowship of noble Knights that ever held christian King together. Alas, my good Knights be slain away from me, now within these two days have I lost forty Knights, and also the noble fellowship of Sir Launcelot and his blood, for now I may never more hold them together with my worship. Alas, that ever this war began." – cl)

(Some men yet say in many parts of England that King Arthur is not dead, but by the will of our Lord in another place. And men say that he will come again. – clxx)

"But my time hieth fast, therefore take you Excalibur, my good sword,

(So they rode till they came to a lake, which was a fair water, and abroad, and in the midst of the lake King Arthur was ware of an arm, clothed in white samite, that held a fair sword in the hand ... said the damsel, "go ye into yonder barge and row yourself unto the sword, and take it and the scabbard with you, and I will ask my gift when I see my time." – I, xxiii)

and go with it unto yonder water side, and when thou comest there, I charge thee throw my sword into that water, and come again and tell me what thou shalt see there."

"My lord," said Sir Bedivere, "your command shall be done, and lightly bring you word again."

The goodliest fellowship of famous knights
Whereof this world holds record. Such a sleep
They sleep—the men I loved. I think that we
Shall nevermore, at any future time,
Delight our souls with talk of knightly deeds,
Walking about the gardens and the halls
Of Camelot, as in the days that were.
I perish by this people which I made,—
Though Merlin sware that I should come again
To rule once more—but let what will be, be,
I am so deeply smitten through the helm
That without help I cannot last till morn.
Thou therefore take my brand Excalibur,
Which was my pride: for thou rememberest how
In those old days, one summer noon, an arm
Rose up from out the bosom of the lake,
Clothed in white samite, mystic, wonderful,
Holding the sword—and how I row'd across
And took it, and have worn it, like a king:
And, wheresoever I am sung or told
In aftertime, this also shall be known:
But now delay not: take Excalibur,
And fling him far into the middle meer:
Watch what thou seëst, and lightly bring me word."

To him replied the bold Sir Bedivere:
"It is not meet, Sir King, to leave thee thus,
Aidless, alone, and smitten through the helm.
A little thing may harm a wounded man.

Yet I thy hest will all perform at full,
Watch what I see, and lightly bring
　thee word.''

And so Sir Bedivere departed,

　　　So saying, from the ruin'd
　shrine he stepp'd,
And in the moon athwart the place of
　tombs,
Where lay the mighty bones of
　ancient men,
Old knights, and over them the
　sea-wind sang
Shrill, chill, with flakes of foam. He,
　stepping down
By zigzag paths, and juts of pointed
　rock,
Came on the shining levels of the
　lake.
　　　There drew he forth the brand
　Excalibur,
And o'er him, drawing it, the winter
　moon,
Brightening the skirts of a long cloud,
　ran forth

and by the way he beheld that noble
sword, where the pomel and the haft
were all of precious stones, and then
he said to himself: ''If I throw this
rich sword into the water, thereof
shall never come good, but harm and
loss.''

And sparkled keen with frost against
　the hilt:
For all the haft twinkled with
　diamond studs,
Myriads of topaz-lights, and
　jacinth-work
Of subtlest jewellery. He gazed so
　long
That both his eyes were dazzled, as
　he stood,
This way and that dividing the swift
　mind,
In act to throw: but at the last it
　seem'd

And then Sir Bedivere hid Excalibur
under a tree, and as soon as he might
he came again unto King Arthur, and
said he had been at the water, and
had thrown the sword into the water.

Better to leave Excalibur conceal'd
There in the many-knotted
　waterflags,
That whistled stiff and dry about the
　marge.
So strode he back slow to the
　wounded king.

　　　Then spake King Arthur to Sir
　Bedivere:
''Hast thou perform'd my mission
　which I gave?
What is it thou hast seen? or what
　hast heard?''

''What sawest thou there?'' said the
King.

"Sir, said he, "I saw nothing but waves and wind."

And answer made the bold Sir Bedivere:
"I heard the ripple washing in the reeds,
And the wild water lapping on the crag."

"That is untruly said of thee," said King Arthur,

To whom replied King Arthur, faint and pale:
"Thou hast betray'd thy nature and thy name,
Not rendering true answer, as beseem'd
Thy fëalty, nor like a noble knight:
For surer sign had follow'd, either hand,
Or voice, or else a motion of the meer.
This is a shameful thing for men to lie.

"therefore go thou lightly and do my command, as thou art to me life and dear, spare not but throw it in."

Yet now, I charge thee, quickly go again
As thou art lief and dear, and do the thing
I bad thee, watch, and lightly bring me word."

Then Sir Bedivere returned again, and took the sword in his hand; and then he thought it sin and shame to throw away that noble sword.

Then went Sir Bedivere the second time,
Counting the dewy pebbles, fix'd in thought;
But when he saw the wonder of the hilt,
How curiously and strangely chased, he smote
His palms together, and he cried aloud.

"And if indeed I cast the brand away,
Surely a precious thing, one worthy note,
Should thus be lost for ever from the earth,
Which might have pleased the eyes of many men.
What good should follow this, if this were done?
What harm, undone? deep harm to disobey,
Seeing obedience is the bond of rule.
Were it well to obey then, if a king demand

("That is the *Lady of the Lake*," said Merlin, "and within that lake is a rock, and therein is as fair a place as any is on earth, and richly beseen."
– I, xxiii)

And so after he hid the sword, and returned again, and told to the King that he had been at the water, and done his command. "What saw ye there," said the King.

"Sir," said he, "I saw nothing but the water wap and the waves wan."

"Ah traitor, untrue," said King Arthur, "now hast thou betrayed me two times, who would have wend that thou hast been unto me so self and dear, and thou art named a noble Knight,

An act unprofitable, against himself?
The King is sick, and knows not what
  he does.
What record, or what relic of my lord
Should be to aftertime, but empty
  breath
And rumours of a doubt? but were
  this kept,
Stored in some treasure-house of
  mighty kings,
Some one might show it at a joust of
  arms,
Saying, 'King Arthur's sword,
  Excalibur,
Wrought by the lonely maiden of the
  Lake.
Nine years she wrought it, sitting in
  the deeps
Upon the hidden bases of the hills.'
So might some old man speak in the
  aftertime
To all the people, winning reverence.
But now much honour and much
  fame were lost."

  So spake he, clouded with his
  own conceit,
And hid Excalibur the second time,
And so strode back slow to the
  wounded King.

  Then spoke King Arthur,
  breathing heavily:
"What is it thou hast seen? or what
  hast heard?"

  And answer made the bold Sir
  Bedivere:
"I heard the water lapping on the
  crag,
And the long ripple washing in the
  reeds."

  To whom replied King
  Arthur, much in wrath:
"Ah, miserable and unkind, untrue,
Unknightly, traitor-hearted! Woe is
  me!
Authority forgets a dying king,
Laid widowed of the power in his eye
That bowed the will. I see thee what
  thou art.

and wouldest betray me for the rich sword. But now, go again lightly, for thy long tarrying putteth me in great jeopardy of my life, for I have taken cold. And but if thou do as I command thee, and if ever I may see thee, I shall slay thee with mine own hands, for thou wouldest for my rich sword see me dead.''

Then Sir Bedivere departed, and went to the sword, and lightly took it up, and went to the water side, and there he bound the girdle about the hilt. And then he threw the sword into the water as far as he might,

and there came an arm and an hand above the water, and met it and caught it, and so shook it thrice and brandished.

And then the hand vanished away with the sword in the water. So Sir Bedivere came again to the King and told him what he had seen.

For thou, the latest-left of all my
   knights,
In whom should meet the offices of
   all,
Thou wouldst betray me for the
   precious hilt;
Either from lust of gold, or like a girl
Valuing the giddy pleasure of the
   eyes.
Yet, for a man may fail in duty twice,
And the third time may prosper, get
   thee hence:
But, if thou spare to fling Excalibur,
I will arise and slay thee with my
   hands.''

   Then quickly rose Sir
   Bedivere, and ran,
And, leaping down the ridges lightly,
   plunged
Among the bulrush-beds, and
   clutch'd the sword,
And strongly wheel'd and threw it.
   The great brand
Made lightnings in the splendour of
   the moon,
And flashing round and round, and
   whirled in an arch,
Shot like a streamer of the northern
   morn,
Seen where the moving isles of
   winter shock
By night, with noises of the northern
   sea.
So flash'd and fell the brand
   Excalibur:
But ere he dipt the surface, rose an
   arm
Clothed in white samite, mystic,
   wonderful,
And caught him by the hilt, and
   brandish'd him
Three times, and drew him under in
   the meer,
And lightly went the other to the
   King.

   Then spoke King Arthur,
   drawing thicker breath:
''Now see I by thine eyes that this is
   done.
Speak out: what is it thou hast heard,
   or seen!''

And answer made the bold
Sir Bedivere:
"Sir King, I closed mine eyelids, lest
the gems
Should blind my purpose, for I never
saw,
Nor shall see, here or elsewhere, till I
die,
Not though I live three lives of mortal
men,
So great a miracle as yonder hilt.
Then with both hands I flung him,
wheeling him,
But when I look'd again, behold an
arm,
Clothed in white samite, mystic,
wonderful,
That caught him by the hilt, and
brandish'd him
Three times, and drew him under in
the meer."

"Alas," said the King, "help me
from hence, for I dread me I have
tarried over long."

And answer made King
Arthur, breathing hard:
"My end draws nigh; 'tis time that I
were gone.
Make broad thy shoulders to receive
my weight,
And bear me to the margin; yet I fear
My wound hath taken cold, and I
shall die."

So saying, from the pavement
he half rose,
Slowly, with pain, reclining on his
arm,
And looking wistfully with wide blue
eyes
As in a picture. Him Sir Bedivere
Remorsefully regarded thro' his
tears,
And would have spoken, but he
found not words,
Then took with care, and kneeling on
one knee,
O'er both his shoulders drew the
languid hands,

Then Sir Bedivere took King Arthur
upon his back, and so went with him
to the water's side.

And rising bore him thro' the place of
tombs.

But, as he walk'd, King
Arthur panted hard,

Like one that feels a nightmare on his
bed
When all the house is mute. So sigh'd
the King,
Muttering and murmuring at his ear
"Quick, quick!
I fear it is too late, and I shall die."
But the other swiftly strode from
ridge to ridge,
Clothed with his breath, and looking,
as he walk'd,
Larger than human on the frozen
hills.
He heard the deep behind him, and a
cry
Before. His own thought drove him
like a goad.
Dry clash'd his harness in the icy
caves
And barren chasms, and all to left
and right
The bare black cliff clang'd round
him, as he based
His feet on juts of slippery crag that
rang
Sharp-smitten with the dint of armed
heels—
And on a sudden, lo! the level lake,
And the long glories of the winter
moon.

And when they were at the water's
side, even fast by the bank, hoved a
little barge, with many fair ladies in
it, and among them all was a Queen,
and all they had black hoods, and
they wept and shrieked when they
saw King Arthur.

Then saw they how there
hove a dusky barge,
Dark as a funeral scarf from stem to
stern,
Beneath them; and descending they
were ware
That all the decks were dense with
stately forms
Black-stoled, black-hooded, like a
dream—by these
Three Queens with crowns of
gold—and from them rose
A cry that shiver'd to the tingling
stars,
And, as it were one voice, an agony
Of lamentation, like a wind, that
shrills
All night in a waste land, where no
one comes,
Or hath come, since the making of
the world.

"Now put me into the barge," said the King. And so he did softly, and there received him three Queens with great mourning, and so these three Queens set him down, and in one of their laps King Arthur laid his head. And then that Queen said: "Ah, dear brother, why have ye tarried so long from me. Alas, this wound on your head hath taken over much cold."

Then murmur'd Arthur,
    "Place me in the barge,"
And to the barge they came. There
    those three Queens
Put forth their hands, and took the
    King, and wept.
But she, that rose the tallest of them
    all
And fairest, laid his head upon her
    lap,
And loosed the shatter'd casque, and
    chafed his hands,
And call'd him by his name,
    complaining loud,
And dropping bitter tears against his
    brow
Striped with dark blood: for all his
    face was white
And colourless, and like the wither'd
    moon
Smote by the fresh beam of the
    springing east;
And all his greaves and cuisses
    dash'd with drops
Of onset; and the light and lustrous
    curls—
That made his forehead like a rising
    sun
High from the daïs-throne—were
    parch'd with dust,
Or, clotted into points and hanging
    loose,
Mix'd with the knightly growth that
    fringed his lips.
So like a shatter'd column lay the
    King;
Not like that Arthur who, with lance
    in rest,
From spur to plume a star of
    tournament,
Shot thro' the lists at Camelot, and
    charged
Before the eyes of ladies and of
    kings.

And so then they rowed from the land. And Sir Bedivere beheld all those ladies go from him, then Sir Bedivere cried: "Ah, my lord Arthur, what shall become of me now ye go from me, and leave me here alone among mine enemies."

Then loudly cried the bold Sir
    Bedivere,
"Ah! my Lord Arthur, whither shall
    I go?
Where shall I hide my forehead and
    my eyes?
For now I see the true old times are
    dead,

When every morning brought a noble
chance,
And every chance brought out a
noble knight.
Such times have been not since the
light that led
(Also Merlin made the *Round Table*   The holy Elders with the gift of myrrh.
in token of the roundness of the   But now the whole ROUND TABLE
world. For by the *Round Table* is the   is dissolved
world signified by right. – III, 1)   Which was an image of the mighty
world;
And I, the last, go forth
companionless,
And the days darken round me, and
the years,
Among new men, strange faces,
other minds."

And slowly answer'd Arthur
from the barge:
"The old order changeth, yielding
place to new,
And God fulfils himself in many
ways,
Lest one good custom should corrupt
the world.
"Comfort thyself," said King   Comfort thyself: what comfort is in
Arthur, "and do as well as thou   me?
mayest, for in me is no trust for to   I have lived my life, and that which I
trust in, for I will into the vale of   have done
Avilion, for to heal me of my   May He within himself make pure!
grievous wound. And if thou never   but thou—
hear more of me, pray for my soul."   If thou shouldst never see my face
again,
Pray for my soul. More things are
wrought by prayer
Than this world dreams of.
Wherefore, let thy voice
Rise like a fountain for me night and
day.
For what are men better than sheep
or goats
That nourish a blind life within the
brain,
If, knowing God, they lift not hands
of prayer
Both for themselves and those who
call them friend?
For so the whole round earth is every
way
Bound by gold chains about the feet
of God.

But now farewell. I am going a long way
With these thou seëst—if indeed I go—
(For all my mind is clouded with a doubt)   .
To the island-valley of Avilion;
Where falls not hail, or rain, or any snow,
Nor ever wind blows loudly; but it lies
Deep-meadow'd, happy, fair with orchard-lawns
And bowery hollows crown'd with summer sea,
Where I will heal me of my grievous wound.''

But evermore the Queens and the ladies wept and shrieked, that it was pity for to hear them. And as soon as Sir Bedivere had lost sight of the barge, he wept and wailed, and so took the forest, and so he went all the night and in the morning he was ware between two hills of a chapel and an hermitage.

So said he, and the barge with oar and sail
Moved from the brink, like some full-breasted swan
That, fluting a wild carol ere her death,
Ruffles her pure cold plume, and takes the flood
With swarthy webs. Long stood Sir Bedivere
Revolving many memories, till the hull
Look'd one black dot against the verge of dawn,
And on the meer the wailing died away.

Appendix 2

Collinson's Somersetshire

In *Materials for a Life of A.T.*, IV, 462-463, Hallam Tennyson presents the following notes made by his father:

> *Morte d'Arthur* (Extract kept by A.T.)
> Collinson's *"Somersetshire."* Vol. II.
> pp. 240 *et seqq.*[1]

St David Archbp. of Menevia was uncle of the renowned King Arthur, who, in his time, A.D. 542, having been mortally wounded in the rebellion of his cousin Mordred at the battle of Camlan, was carried to this Abbey, Glastonbury, that he might prepare himself for his departure out of life in the society of the religious, and be interred among such a number of saints as reposed there from the beginning of Christianity. He was accordingly here buried, and his bones remained unmolested in the monks' cemetery for 640 years; when, being found in digging a sepulchre, the relics were removed into the presbytery of the Church, and reinterred, with the following inscription by Abbot Swansey.[2]

> "Hic jacet Arthurus, flos regum, gloria regni,
> Quem mores, probitas, commendant laude perenni."

The common tradition was that he suffered only a temporary kind of death, and that he would come again to reassume the sceptre:

> "But for he skaped yᵉ batell yᵉ wys,
> Bretons and Cornysch seyeth thus,
> That he levyth zut perde,
> And schall come and be a kynge aye.
> At Glastyngbury on the queer,
> They made Arter's tombe ther,

---

1   The book from which the poet copied this note is John Collinson's *The History and Antiquities of the County of Somerset* (Bath, 1791).

2   "Henry de Swansey was 40th Abbot of Glastonbury, whence he was promoted to the see of Worcester on the Annexation of Glastonbury to Bath and Wells in consequence of the arrangements made in the matter of the release of Richard I" (*Materials*, IV, 463).

And wrote with Latyn vers thus
'Hic jacet Arthurus, rex quondam, rexque futurus.' ''

Five different epitaphs were attributed to Arthur's tomb.
Queen Guinever, and several Saxon kings and bishops were also buried at
Glastonbury. p. 262.

Appendix 3

The Seduction of Merlin

The following account of Merlin's seduction, recorded in the *Romance of Merlin,* is found in Southey's introduction to his edition of Malory (1817), xliv-xlvi:

When Merlin related all this to his master Blaise, who seems to have been his confessor as well as historiographer, Blaise was much troubled, and censured him greatly, and gave him good advice; but good advice was lost upon Merlin, who saw his own fate, and with all his wisdom was unable to avoid it. Accordingly one day the enchanter took leave of his old master, telling him "it was the last time he would ever see him, for from thenceforth he must abide with his mistress, and should never more have the power of leaving her, nor of going and coming at his pleasure. When Blaise heard this, he said to him full sorrowfully, Since then it is so that you will not be able to depart when once you shall have gone there, fair friend go not there at all, for you well know the thing that must happen to you. Certes, answered Merlin, I needs must go, for so I have covenanted and promised; and even if I had not covenanted, I am so taken with her love that I could not forbear going. All this have I done myself, for I have taught her great part of what I know, and she will still learn more from me, for I have no power to withhold myself. With that Merlin departed from Blaise his master, and travelled so long in few hours, that he came to Viviane his mistress." This was good travelling, for Blaise lived in Northumberland, and Viviane in France. They dwelt a long while together, and "she showed him greater semblance of love than she had ever done before, as one who knew so many enchantments that never other woman knew so much. So she devised within herself how she might detain him for ever more; but never could she compass nor achieve this: then was she full sorrowful and vexed, and cast about how she might discover it. Then began she to fawn and to flatter Merlin more than before; and she said to him, My sweet friend, I do not yet know one thing which I would fain know, I pray you teach me it. And Merlin, who well knew what it was, and to what she tended, said to her, Mistress, what is it? Sir, said Viviane, I would have you teach and show me how to inclose and imprison a man without a tower, without walls, without chains, but by enchantments alone, in such manner that he may never be able to go out, except by me. When Merlin heard her he shook his head, and began to sigh deeply; and Viviane, when she perceived it, asked of him wherefore he sighed thus. Dame, said Merlin, I will tell you. Well I know

177

that you are devising how you may detain me; but I am so taken, that perforce will I or not, it behoves me to do your will. When Viviane heard this, for her great treason, and the better to delude and deceive him, she put her arms round his neck, and began to kiss him, saying, that he might well be hers, seeing that she was his: You well know, said she, that the great love which I have in you, has made me leave father and mother that I may have you in my arms day and night. All my desire and thought is in you; without you I have neither joy nor good. I have placed all my hope upon you, and I never look to have joy or good except from you. Seeing then that I love you, and you love me, is it not right that you should do my will and I yours? Certes, lady, yes, said Merlin, and I will do it; tell me what you would have. Sir, said she, I would that we should make a fair place and a suitable, so contrived by art and by cunning, that it might never be undone, and that you and I should be there in joy and in solace. My lady, said Merlin, I will perform all this. Sir, said she, I would not have you do it, but you shall teach me, and I will do it, and then it will be more to my will. I grant you this, said Merlin. Then he began to devise, and the damsel put it all in writing. And when he had devised the whole, then had the damsel full great joy, and showed him greater semblance of loving him than she had ever before made; and they sojourned together a long while. At length it fell out that as they were going one day hand in hand through the forest of Broceliande, they found a bush of white thorn which was laden with flowers; and they seated themselves under the shade of this white thorn upon the green grass, and they disported together and took their solace, and Merlin laid his head upon the damsel's lap, and then she began to feel if he were asleep. Then the damsel rose and made a ring with her wimple round the bush and round Merlin, and began her enchantments such as he himself had taught her; and nine times she made the ring, and nine times she made the enchantment; and then she went and sate down by him, and placed his head again upon her lap; and when he awoke and looked round him, it seemed to him that he was inclosed in the strongest tower in the world, and laid upon a fair bed; then said he to the dame, My lady, you have deceived me unless you abide with me, for no one hath power to unmake this tower, save you alone. Fair friend, she replied, I shall often be here, and you shall hold me in your arms, and I will hold you in mine. And in this she held her covenant to him, for afterwards there was never night nor day in which she was not there. And Merlin never went out of that tower where his mistress Viviane had inclosed him. But she entered and went out again when she listed; and often time she regretted what she had done, for she had thought that the thing which he taught her could not be true, and willingly would she have let him out if she could." T.2.f.134.

The writer very properly remarks upon Merlin, for having taught his mistress so much, *quil en fut depuis, et est encore tenu pour fol.*

Appendix 4

The Prose Drafts of the
Idylls of the King

The *Idylls of the King* is a cumulative literary achievement. The completed poem is the union of two different modes of composition. The *Morte d'Arthur* and the first quartet of *Idylls* were first written out in poetic drafts. The ten-year delay in the progress of his Arthurian poem seemed to lead to a new form of composition. For many of the remaining idylls, Tennyson wrote out his first drafts in prose. The prose drafts offer an important perspective on the poet's method of composition. They reveal the central ideas that form the nucleus of the idyll; they exhibit a closer dependence upon source material than the final poetic form suggests; they present the poet experimenting with different approaches to the stories he selects.

With the exception of the two fragmentary prose drafts of *Gareth and Lynette* in the Tennyson collection of the University of Texas, all the extant prose drafts of the *Idylls of the King* are found in the Harvard College Library collection of Tennyson's Notebooks. In the reproduction of these drafts, the system of transcription employed throughout is as follows: all deletions in the manuscript appear within pointed brackets; additions above the lines in the manuscript appear in italics; the transcription of each folio ends with the folio number on the right hand side of the passage; an asterisk after the folio number indicates that the poet inverted the Notebook when he wrote the passage.

The Holy Grail

Harvard Notebook 38 (watermarked 1863) is devoted entirely to the Grail idyll. The first half of the Notebook contains a long prose draft of

179

the idyll with only a few short poetic passages interspersed throughout the narrative. The second half of the Notebook contains an early poetic rendering of the prose account. Near the end of the Notebook is a short prose account of the quest of Sir Bors.

Now when Sir Percivale had come back from the Quest of the Holy Grail, he would have no more to do with tilt & tournament but entered into a monastery & presently after died.

But ere this one of the holy fathers who was his chief friend in the monastery, would often ask him about this Quest of the Grail, & how it all came about, & one day Sir Percivale told him all he could remember.

O brother, this holy Grail, is the cup out of which our blessed lord drank at the last supper. Joseph of Arimathea brought it to Glastonbury & it healed many of their diseases & wrought faith in their hearts: but the times grew so wicked that it ⟨pa⟩ was caught up to heaven & disappeared.

O brother, I had a sister a nun in the nunnery at Camelot. No holier being ever wore the pavement with her knee. Shut out as she was from the world, the noise of an adulterous race beat thro' the gratings of her cell, & she prayd & fasted the more.

Now her confessor, a holy Father, a hundred winters old, told her this legend of the Holy Grail, which had been handed down from the times of our Lord, by six or seven old men, each a hundred winters old. If the Holy Grail (he said) should reappear, there might yet be hope for the world. O father she said would it appear to me if I pray'd & fasted? & he answered, 'Yea, daughter,   1r

---

who knows but it might, if thy heart be as pure as snow. & she prayd & fasted till the sun shone thro' her & the wind blew thro' her.

Then on a day she sent to me to speak with her: & I went to the nunnery, & behold her eyes were wonderful in the light of her holiness & she told me that she had seen the holy vessel. In the dead night, she had been waked by a strain of sweet music, & there came in a long beam of light, brighter than any sunbeam & down this beam slowly past the Holy Grail & the white walls of her cell were dyed in rose-colour, & the Grail past & the beam, & the rosecolour slowly faded away. Lo now, my brother, she said, fast thou also & pray & tell thy brother knights to fast & pray that peradventure the holy thing may come to you also, & the world be healed of its wickedness.

And I went away & spake of all this to my brother knights & many among us pray'd & fasted. Now there was a young man among us, Galahad, whom Arthur had knighted, & there never was so young a man knighted before—some said he was a son of Lancelot, some that he was begotten by enchantment—but when I spake with him of the Grail, his eyes look'd so like my sister's that I could have thought he was her brother.

And there stood a seat in our great Hall which   2r

Merlin had fashioned long ago before he past away; & it was carved with strange figures & in & out the figures there were letters in a tongue no man could read; &

Merlin call'd the seat The Siege Perilous for he said No man can sit there but he shall lose himself & Galahad said If I lose myself I shall save myself.

And it chanced one night when the banquet was spread in the Hall that Galahad would sit in the chair of Merlin.

And immediately there was cracking & riving & rending of the rafters, & there entered in a beam seven times more clear than day, & in the midst of the light the Holy Grail past thro' the Hall, *but it was hidden in a luminous cloud* & every man looked at his neighbour & behold his face was glorious, & we stared at one another like dumb men.

Then I arose among the knights & bound myself by a strong vow that because I had *not* seen the Holy Grail when it past I would go forth to the end of the world till I found it. And Galahad & most of the knights swore with me: & even Gawain swore.

> Then said the monk to Sir Percivale
> And what said Arthur? did he allow your vows?   3r

And Percivale answer'd

The King was not there albeit he had willed to be there: he was sacking a bandit-hold over the hills: howbeit he saw something of the marvel, for as he returned from the sacking, having slain the robbers, when the land was darkening he looked up & he cried aloud Behold the roofs of our great Hall are roll'd in thundersmoke: pray heaven they be not smitten by the thunderbolt: for the roofs of the Hall seemed to smoke & the Hall was dear to him seeing it is the costliest in the world.

> O brother had you known our mighty hall
> Which Merlin built for Arthur long ago.
> For four great zones of sculpture, set betwixt
> With many a mystic symbol, gird the Hall
> And in the lowest beasts are slaying men,
> And in the second men are slaying beasts
> And in the third are warriors perfect men
> And in the fourth are men with growing wings
> And on the top a statue in the mould
> Of Arthur, made by Merlin with a crown
> And peakd wings pointed to the Northern Star.

& the statue faces the East & the crown & the wings are golden & shine far over the land at sunrise.   4r

---

The great King & his company rode swiftly up to the Hall. And the King rode into the hall & I looked up & saw the golden dragon blaze on his head.

And he spoke to me O Percivale / for there was a tumult among us / what is this

And I told him what had chanced & his face darkened & he said had I been here ye would not sworn & he said O Percivale didst thou see the Grail

Nay Lord I said I heard the sound & I saw the light but the Grail was covered with a cloud.

And the King spoke again & asked us knight by knight whether any had seen the holy Grail

And they answer'd & said Nay Lord for the Grail was hidden & therefore we have taken our vows
⟨For⟩ And Galahad cried out in a shrill voice
    But I Sir Arthur saw the Holy Grail
    I saw the Holy Grail & heard a cry
    O Galahad & O Galahad follow me!

Ah Gawain, Gawain said the king. Is this vision for thee? but now O Percivale thou & the holy nun, thy sister, have broken up the fair order of my Table Round which I founded for pure life, & the redressing of human wrong. For many among you have taken this vow, who will never see this vision, & many among you will follow wandering fires & be lost in the quagmire, & this same goodly company of knights will never meet again in my hall.   5r

Wherefore my heart is sad unto death: but since I may not disallow the vows ye have taken, lo now, let us come together in the morning for one last tilt & tourney of gracious pastime that I may see you once more all together & rejoice in your prowess & the order which I have made.

Then we met together in the morning & I & Sir Galahad overthrew most of the knights for the strength of the Vision was in us.

And when this was over the King & the Queen & many Ladies rode with us to the gates, & the women wept & the men, & rich & poor wept, & the King could scarce speak for weeping & the Queen shrieked & waild & said Alas for our sins this has come upon us.

Then we parted & went each his own way: & I was glad at heart, & I thought of my prowess in my lists & how I had beaten down ⟨the⟩ *many* knights, & the sun never seemed so bright, nor the sky so blue, nor the earth so green, & I felt that I should come upon the Holy Grail.

Then after awhile my mind was darkened & every evil word I had spoken, & every evil thought I had thought, & every evil deed I had done stood round about me like fiends & cried aloud The Holy Grail is not for thee. And I lifted up my eyes & I was in a land of sand & thorns, & I was athirst even unto swooning & I said 'This quest is not for thee!   6r

And I thought my thirst would have slain me: when behold as I rode on I saw lawns of deep grass, & a running brook which made a sound among the stones, & great appletrees with golden apples on either side of the brook & among the lawns. and I said I will rest here: I am not worthy of the quest. And I began to drink of the brook & to eat of the golden apples, & while I was eating, it all fell away into dust, & I was again among the sand & the thorns.

And again I rode on & suddenly I was aware of a fair woman, & she sat by the door of a house: & the house was fair & pleasant to look upon, & the eyes of the woman were kind & innocent & her ways were gracious & she opened out her arms to me, as tho' she would say rest here & I went up & touched her & lo she fell into dust & the house became a ruined shed & in it there was a dead babe, & I was again among the sand & the thorns

And again I rode forward & there fell a yellow gleam over the world, & it past over the plough'd field & the plowman left his plough & fell down before it & the milkmaid left milking her kine & fell down before it & I thought it was the rising sun but the Sun had risen & I turned & behold a giant with a jewelld helmet & in golden armour & his horse in golden armour studded with jewels. & he seemed the Lord of all the world he was so huge & I thought he would slain me & I made ready to do battle with him & behold he opened his arms wide to embrace me & I touchd him & he fell into dust, & I was among the sand & the thorns   7r

And again I rode onward & far off behold there was a city on the top of a great hill: & the towers & pinnacles ⟨thereof⟩ were unbelieavable for the height thereof, for they pierced thro' the clouds of heaven. And as I drew near I saw a great company before the gates of the city & they cried out to me as I clomb the hill Come up Sir Percivale welcome thou greatest knight among men. But when I came to the top there was no man there & I went into the city & it was waste & desolate & there was only one man in it of an exceeding old age & I spake to him where is that great company that cried out ⟨to me⟩ upon me. and he had scarce any voice to answer but he said Whence art thou & who art thou & even while he was speaking he fell into dust & disappeared & I cried out

Lo if I find the Holy Grail itself & touch it it also will crumble to dust

Then I went down into valley on the other side of the hill & the valley was as low as the hill was high & in at the bottom was a little chapel & a hermitage & a hermit & when I had told him all that chanced to me he answered me & said

> O Son thou hast not true humility
> The highest virtue, mother of them all,
> For when the Lord of all things made himself
> Naked of Godhead for his mortal change
> Take thou my robe O lord she said tis pure
> And all her form shone forth in sudden light
> So that the angels were amazed & she   8r

> Follow'd him down & like a flying star
> Led on the grayhaired wisdom of the East
> But her thou hast not known: for what is this
> Thou thoughtest of thy prowess & thy sins
> Thou hast not lost thyself to save thyself
> As Galahad. And Sir Galahad as he spake

Rode up to the chapel: & when I lookd on the bright *faced* boy knight his eye had power upon me, & I believed ⟨what⟩ *as* he believed & my fear left me. And the Holy man took away my burning thirst, & at the sacring of the mass, & I saw but the blessed Elements but he said

> I saw the fiery face as of a child
> That smote itself into the bread & went

And we left our horses with the hermit for there was a mountain before us which none could climb but man. And as we clomb the mountain I told Sir Galahad all that I had told the hermit & he said Care not thou for thou shall see the Grail even tho far away & I go to be a crowned king in the Spiritual city.' And when we came to the top of the mountain there brake on us a thunder & a lightening so that I never saw the like of it; & as we went down again, the lightening was so fierce it struck here & there to the left & to the right, & the old trunks & stems of trees that were dead brake into fire; & at the bottom of the mountain there was a foul & black swamp, & by the lightening I saw that in it there ⟨were⟩ *lay* the bones of men. And there were seven piers built across the marsh & seven light bridges from pier to pier. & every one of the bridges was veiled in with   9r

---

roses. ⟨And Gal⟩ and at the end of the piers was a boat and beyond it the Great Sea.

And Galahad ran along them bridge by bridge
And every bridge as soon as he had past
Sprang into fire & vanished

& he leapt into the boat & I was alone for I would not follow. and the boat went with an exceeding swiftness & thrice over him the Heavens opened & blazed with thunder like the shoutings of all the sons of God. and when first they opened I beheld him far out on the Great sea & over his head was the holy vessel clothed in white samite or a luminous cloud. & when they blazed I beheld him very far away & over him the holy vessel redder than any rose whereby I knew that the veil had been withdrawn from it: & when the Heavens opened & blazed the third time I saw him no bigger than the point over an i & far away behind him in a clear spot of sky I saw the gates of the Spiritual City no larger than a pearl & over it a tiny bloodred spark, *& dwelt there* & I knew it it was the Holy Grail. Then the Heavens came down as tho they would drown the world & I saw no more *& I was glad at heart* & I went back to the Hermitage & took my charger & so rode back to the Court of the King, & I had been from him twelvemonth & a day.

And there sat the King in his hall which Merlin & all his knights were before him, they that ⟨nev⟩ had not gone out on the Holy Quest, & they had gone; & of these not ten had returned, but among them were Sir Gawain & Sir Lancelot 10r

---

Then Ambrosius askd him again. O brother for in our old books I find many such marvels & ⟨like⟩ miracles like unto these— only I find not this Holy Grail; & when I have read til my eyes are dazed & my head swims, & when our holy offices have been accomplish'd, then I go forth into our little thorpe & stand in the market, & have joy in the chaffering & chattering of the men & the women, & I gossip with them about all things, delighting myself yea ⟨not⟩ even with their hens & their eggs. O brother, didst not thou also find men & women in thy quest, or ⟨did⟩ phantoms only

O brother, said Percivale, to one so bound by vow as I was women & men are but as phantoms. Why wilt thou shame me to make me confess to thee that I faltered in *my* quest & my vow. ⟨for the Vision had not come to me, &⟩ *for* I had lain many nights in the thicket, & I ⟨had⟩ was lean & meagre & the Vision had not come: & happened one night that I drew near a goodly town with a great dwelling in midst of it, & I went into it & I was disarmed by fair maidens & when I came into the banquet hall, behold the Princess of the Castle, was the one & that one only which had *ever* made my heart leap. For I was a slender page in her father's hall & she a slender damsel & my heart went after with longing.   9v

---

But we never had kissd lips or claspt hands. & lo I had found her again & one had wedded *her* & ⟨s⟩ he was dead & she had all his possessions and I dwelt there & she gave her me banquet each richer than before, for her longing was to me; & one day when I sat under the castle in an orchard she came toward me *& embraced me & call'd me the greatest of all the knights* & gave herself with all her wealth to me, & I remembered Arthur's words & the Quest faded in my heart. And her people came to us & said we have heard of thee, do thou wed our lady, & rule over us & be as Arthur in the land. But one night I arose for I remember'd the vow I had sworn, & past from her but I waild & wept & I hated myself & the Holy Grail to which I had sworn.

> I walking in her orchard underneath
> The castle walls, she came upon there
> Lo now I came upon her once again
> And one had wedded her & he was dead
> And all his wealth & land & state was hers.
>
> And calling me the greatest of all knights
> Embraced me & so kiss'd me the first time
> And gave herself and all her wealth to me
> And I remember'd Arthurs warning to us
> That most of us would follow wandering fires
> And the Quest faded in my heart. Anon
> The heads of all her people came to me
> Rejoicing
> And there I dwelt & everyday she ⟨set⟩ made
> A banquet richer than the day before,
> For all *her* longing after many years
> Was toward me, as before.
>
> Wed thou with her, & rule thou over us
> And show sh   10v

Then spake the King to Sir Gawain   O Gawain was this quest for thee?

Nay, Lord, said Sir Gawain, & I spake with a holy man & he told me: This quest is not for thee, & I was weary of the quest but I chanced upon merry maidens & the twelvemonth & a day were pleasant to me.

And the King bow'd his head nor answered him but turned to me & ⟨spake⟩ ask'd me   O Percivale, pure knight & true, what hath chanced to thee?

And I told him all that chanced & the King bowed his head toward me, but answered *me* not & spake to Sir Lancelot

Thou also, Sir Lancelot, in whom I have most love & most affiance, hast thou seen the holy vision.

And Sir Lancelot dropt his head upon his breast, & his colour wanned upon his face & till after a while he spake not, & then he groaned & said

O king, my friend—happier are those that welter in their sin & are covered like the swine with the mud of the ditches: but my sin was of so strange a kind that all that was noble in me, & all that was knightly ⟨at⟩ grew to it & twined about it till the wholesome flower & the poisonous flower were each as either & could not be rent asunder. And I therefore took my vow with the rest, that peradventure, if I might see & touch the Holy Vessel, they would be rent asunder. And I went forth & I too spake with a holy man & he told me that save I could rend them asunder my Quest was in vain: & I swore to him to do according to all that he   11r

willed: & I past forth from him & in striving to rend them asunder I fell into my madness as of old: & my madness drove me into waste fields where I was beaten down by mean knights, who should have fallen before the whiff of my sword & the shadow of my lance: & I came to the naked sea-shore, & the land was flat & barren & nothing grew on the banks of the sea but a little coarse grass but a blast blew along the sea & the shore.

    & heap'd in mounds & ridges all the sea
Drove like a cataract & all the sand
Swept like a river & the cloudy sun
Was shaken with the motion & the sound

& there was a little boat tossing, brimful of seafoam, anchored with chain; & I said to myself in my madness I will embark & wash away my sin in the great sea

      Seven days I drove along the dreary deep
And with me drove the moon & all the stars
And the wind fell & on the seventh day
I heard the shingle grinding in the surge
          & behold
A castle like a rock upon a rock
With mighty portals open to the sea
And steps that met the breaker. There was none
Stood near it but a lion on each side
That kept the entry. & the moon was full.   12r

      And from the boat I leapt & up the stairs
Those two great beasts rose upward like a man
Each seized a shoulder & I stood between
And when I would stricken them came a voice
Doubt not, go forward if thou doubt the beasts
Will tear thee piecemeal; & with violence
It smote the sword out of my hand & went.
And up into the sounding hall I saw
No bench nor table, painting on the wall
Nor shield of knight only the rounded moon
Thro' the tall oriel on the rolling sea.
But always in the quiet house I heard
Clear as a lark, high oer me as a lark
A sweet voice singing in the topmost tower
To the eastward: up I clomb a thousand steps
With pain: as in a dream I seem'd to climb
For ever: but I reach'd a little door
A light was in the crannies & I heard
Then in my madness I essay'd the door

& it yielded, & there came out a light 7 times more clear & therewithal a heat w[h] blasted my eyesight so that I swooned away: but thro' the light & the heat methought I saw the Holy Grail—all pall'd in crimson samite & around

Great Angels, awful shapes & wings & eyes
And but for my madness & my swooning & my sin I s[d] know that
I saw what I saw: yet what I saw was covered, & I
Count myself as having fail'd in the Quest.   13r

And the king said. O Lancelot thou hast erred with thy tongue. Never could all that was noble in a man & all that was cling round his one sin whatsoever it be, but there was left a remnant of knighthood & of nobleness, that grew apart. see thou to that.

And said I not well that few of those who went out to the Holy Quest w[d] return: that most of you would follow wandering fires & be lost in the quagmire, & that ever after I should have to look at a barren board & a lean order. and not ten among you have returned & of those to whom the Vision came, he, my greatest knight, holds himself as having failed to see it: & another has seen it afar off, & he will pass away into the Silent life & be lost to me, & another has had the vision face & has past away, & left his place empty here, however otherwise they may crown him.   14v

This marks the end of the major prose draft of the Grail idyll. Folio 15r contains a poetic version of Arthur's final speech to his knights, "And some among you said that if the king." The following folios, with the exception of 29v and 30v, contain a poetic account of the Grail story.

Yea said Percivale for as I rode back thro' a wood that was half stript of the leaf I beheld before me whom afar off I knew for Sir Bors for I knew him by the breadth of shoulder & I rode up to him & we fell into talk & after I had told him all I had seen & besought him also to speak to me of his Quest The colour came into his visage & the water to his eyes & after a while he spake to me.

I went forth with the rest & wandering thro field & forest Sir Lancelot dash'd across me on his great black charger & I feard me that he had fallen into madness wh had seized on him before & made him the talk of the court & I cried out to him to say Ridest thou thus madly after so Holy Quest as ours? & he stayd not for a moment but cried out Withold me not: there is a lion in the way & he galloped on to the Great Sea & I lost him. & I rode on softly nor did I much vex my heart about the Quest, for I thought if it will come it will come & ⟨the⟩ I & the Quest are in the hands of God, but about my brother was I troubled for how should he ever come upon the Vision being as he was

And I rode on even until I came upon the Paynims of the West, our blood & our folk, to whom the message had not come but yet they dwelt in Pagan darkness & made their circles of stone, & struck up a straight stone to fall before it, & call'd it God & knew no God but the Sun. & when they saw a knight of the new faith & from A[s] court   29v

---

they mockd & told me that I followed a wandering fire—believing in the words of Arthur—but our God is no

By whom the blood beats, & the blossom blows
And the sea rolls & everything is done

& it would never be well for this Britain till the Xt were put down & the
Sunworship set up again

Scofed me & beat me & bound me & cast me down
chamber
theft
wickerwork
The 7 cold stars of Arthur's wain
& in a moment all across
The seven cold stars in colour like a hand
Before a burning taper past the Grail
a young damsel
& thro' the cleft
I saw the torn sky & the flying rack   30v

Pelleas and Ettarre

Though Hallam Tennyson referred to a prose draft of *Pelleas and
Ettarre* among his father's manuscripts (*Memoir*, II, 134), there is no
extant prose draft to verify his statement. In Harvard Notebook 39
(watermarked 1863), however, there are five stubs which did contain a
prose draft of the idyll. Only a few folios remain in this Notebook; at the
beginning, there is a poetic draft of a few lines from *The Coming of
Arthur*, a poetic draft of a new addition to *Merlin and Vivien* ("He
walked with dreams"), and a few lines from the new addition to the
Morte d'Arthur. At the back of the Notebook are five stubs which show
that Tennyson inverted the Notebook and began a prose draft here of the
Pelleas idyll. The few words remaining on the stubs show that the draft
extended four-and-one-half pages in length. On the fourth stub, the
seventh last line begins with "Pelle" and the third last line begins with
"Pell." The opening line of the fifth stub begins, "So Gawai." Thus the
stubs are evidence that Tennyson did write a prose draft of at least a
large section of *Pelleas and Ettarre*.

The Passing of Arthur

When Tennyson decided to incorporate his earlier poem, the *Morte
d'Arthur*, as the final idyll in his series, he added an introduction to the
poem. Harvard Notebook 37 (watermarked 1863) contains the following
draft of the addition.

O Sir King shall one sin eat out the memory of all thy noble deeds. Remember thou how many a time we fought the Godless heathen & conquered. how often we drove them on the west & from the Roman wall. & when Rome had grown too weak to drive the heathen to & sent to us for her tribute as of old how we prevailed against her; & now thro' the sin of Launcelot Sir Modred hath brought in the heathen again, & some of their own knights & of the people whom thou hast made vie against thee yet doubt not thou—and go forth & conquer as of old.

> And answer made the bold Sir Bedivere
> O me Sir King let elf & fairy pass
> But thy great name shall ever cleave & cling
> To all high places in this realm of thine. like a golden cloud

> Far other is this fight from *than* those of old
> Wherein we broke the heathen—like mine own death to me
> To fight against my people & the knights   14v

O me but this fight is far other than those wherein we drove the heathen from the West or the Roman wall.
I fight against my people & the knights whom I have made and that is to me even as mine own death
That sweet smile w^h Guinevere & Lancelot smiled in the May woods was cruel as many deaths.
They say that I am no king: they ⟨not⟩ know not nor do I myself whence I came.
Theirs then *is* the blame who fostered me, & spake softly to me, & held me sacred, & drest me delicately, *nor ever let a foul word be spoken before me* & showd me the fields & hills & said this is thy realm for ever they told me that I was a King's son but that I s^d not see my father on earth
And I believed them & believe them still
But arise & go if we can find a way
For ever since I learnt the sin of Guinevere so dense a fog had hidden the world
Nevertheless arise & we will beat these traitors underfoot.   15v

Gareth and Lynette

Two of the Harvard Notebooks contain extended drafts of *Gareth and Lynette* in prose and in poetry. In Notebook 40 (watermarked 1863), the first twenty-three folios contain portions of the idyll; there are a few blank folios in the Notebook and one folio, partially torn out, which contains the poem, "Some pleasure and exceeding pain."

The long prose draft of *Gareth and Lynette,* which occurs at the beginning of Notebook 40, reveals the poet's original plan of composition, namely, a portrait of the adulterous Bellicent.

Lots wife Bellicent, the Queen of Orkney sat in her castle on the sea & she was lost in thought: for there had come to her ⟨a twelvemonth before⟩ a noise that Queen Guinevere was false with Lancelot: & thereupon the Queen who had been long haunted by a passion for *Sir* Lamorack had yielded herself to him & thus dishonoured her house.

But now she said to herself Lo if Guinevere have not sinned & this rumour is untrue I shall be the first woman who have broken the fair order of the Table Round & made a knight forego his vows & so my name shall go down thro' the world for ever: but if Guinevere have sinned the sin will be hers & my shame covered by her shame.

And there came in to her Gareth her son & he said O mother for here my life is spilt & lost among rocks & stones that never heard the sound of a trumpet blowing the knights together in the lists *but* let me have thy leave to go to the halls of Arthur & be made knight by Arthur as my brethren Modred & Gawain are.

And she answered Yea my son Gareth so that thou wilt swear a vow to me to do my will when thou comest to Arthur.

And Gawain swore a vow that he would do her will.

Then the Queen spake & said I have heard for this long time that Queen Guinevere is false to the King & my heart is troubled thereby & my life darkened for I love him.	2r

---

but thou shalt go & be made knight & seek into this scandal & dwell among them & bring me word whether there be truth therein

Then said Gareth O mother shall I ask the Knights of the Table Round whether the King is dishonoured by his wife

Grieved am I that I have taken such a vow.

And the Queen said thou hast taken it & shalt abide by it but think not to ask this of the knights for they hold together by their vows & are sworn to speak no slander & from them wilt thou learn nothing but thou shalt mingle with the thralls of the house & with those that hand the dish across the bar for these are they that know the things of a house & delight in the evils thereof & from them shalt thou learn & bring back the truth of this matter to me thy mother: for it were shame that Arthur should be shamed by his own Queen not knowing, moreover this sin will pass thro all the Table Round & ruin the King's purpose, if ⟨thi⟩ it be not known & put an end to.

And Gareth said An evil vow have I sworn. Are not Modred & Gawain wiser than I?

And the Queen answer'd Modred & Gawain were liars from their youth upward but thou hast ever spoken the truth

So Gareth took two of the house & sware them to silence & disguised himself & came before the King.

And the King was holding the feast of Pentecost at King-Keredon in Wales. 3r

---

And the sides of the hills were green, & the earth quickened with flowers & the birds warbled in the bush for it was the feast of Pentecost.

Then came Gareth unto hill & he was clad like a tiller of the *field* soil but his raiment was without soil & he moved heavily as tho' he were faint & about to fall & he leaned his hands on the shoulders of those twain with whom he came & the

twain were richly beseen like those in the court of a king & his hands were the
largest & fairest that ever man saw.

[And the day was one of driving showers: & as they drew near to Camelot,
sometimes the city gleam'd out at top while the rest of it was hidden, sometimes
only the middle of it was seen, sometimes only the great gate of Arthur at the
bottom & sometimes it disappeared altogether.

And the two that were with Gareth were amazed & said to him Lo now my lord
let us go no further for we have heard that this is a city of enchanters & was built
by Fairy Kings and Queens

And the other said There is no such city: it is a vision.

But Gareth brought them to the great Gate: & there was no gate like it under
heaven: for the deeds of Arthur were sculptured there in strange types & old &
new was mingled together so that it made a man dizzy to look at it.   4r

---

And there came a blast of music from the town & the three started back[1]

& now they have been frightened with this music nor care to go in[2]   4v

---

And the two that were with Gareth stared so long at the figures on the
gateway that it seemed to them that the tails of the dragons & other strange
shapes on the gate began to move & to twine & to curl.

And they caught hold of Gareth saying to him O my lord 'the gate is alive.

And Gareth lookd also so long that the figures seemed to him also to move.

And while they were thus amazed Old Merlin came out from under the gate. & he
saw them staring & askd Who be ye? my sons?

And Gareth answer'd O master we be tillers of the soil & come to see the state of
the King: but these men are feared to go into the city for they have heard it was
built by enchantment & by fairy kings & queens ∧

And Merlin I will speak the truth as thou hast spoken it to me: for truly O son this
city was built by a fairy king & many fairy Queens & they came from out the cleft
of a mountain toward the sunrise; & they built it to the sound of their harps & as
thou sayst it is enchanted & nothing in it is what it seems, saving the King &
many hold the city is real & the King is unreal: & take thou of him for if thou pass
under this gateway thou wilt become subject to this enchantment & the King will
swear thee to vows which it is a shame that a man should not swear, & which 5r

---

yet no man can keep: but if ye *be* afeard to swear pass not beneath the gateway
but abide here among the cattle of the field: for the city is built to music, &
therefore not built at all, & therefore built for ever.

1 This line is intended to follow the line, "And Gareth lookd also so long that the figures
   seemed to him also to move," on folio 5r.
2 This line is intended to follow the passage, "And Gareth answer'd . . . by fairy kings &
   queens," on folio 5r.

And Gareth was angry & answer'd Old master, hast thou no reverence for thine own white beard which is wellnigh as long as thou art tall that thou mockest strangers. Why mockest thou me & my men who have *been* fairspoken to thee?

And Merlin answer'd Have ye never heard the riddling of the bards? I mock thee because thou mockest me & all that look at thee. thou art not what thou seemest but I know thee & who thou art, & thou goest up to mock the Great King.

And Gareth was abashed & said to his men Here sits a white lie like a little ghost on the threshold of our enterprise. But let my good mother—heaven bless her—bear the blame.

And he & his men past up into the city & they had never seen stranger or statelier palaces & they came to the doors of the great Hall & Arthur was speaking to his knights & rendering thanks for such service as they had done him in subduing the heathen: & Gareth saw in the eyes of each of them loyalty & clear honour sparkling like the morning star in heaven, & high promise, & the light of victory, And glory ⟨to be⟩ gain'd & glory yet to be gain'd.   6r

---

Then went Gareth & lived & ate among the grooms; & he heard them talk of the love that was between Lancelot & the King & at times they talked in such fashion that he broke out into whistling & into singing; so that the thralls marvelled at him & at last reverenced him; & he was the best among them at putting the bar & stone; & if there ever chanced to be a tourney he was ever at the barrier & his eyes kindled.

But after a while he tired of their company & on a morning when the great king paced before the Hall alone, he came upon him & said

I am Gareth thy nephew & I bound myself by a foolish vow to one whom I loved that I would live among thy thralls for season; but now am I come to thee for those other two boons which thou hast promised. Make me thy knight in secret & give me the first adventure that comes to thy court that I may spring like flame out of ashes.

And Gareth gave the king secret signs whereby he should know that he was Gareth—& the King granted him what he would, nor revealed his name

Then there came a maiden into hall: & she was of high lineage; & her eye was sharp as a falcon's when he sees his prey beneath him, & her colour clear as a rose, & her nose tilted up at the tip & she spake to the king

O King, for thou hast driven the heathen—but there be thieves & bandits enow *left* to ruin a realm & everyone that has a tower is king for a league round, nor canst thou be verily & indeed King till these be driven as thou hast driven the heathen.   7r

---

Why sit ye there? were I thou I would not rest till the whole land were as free from accursed bloodshed as the altar cloth from the blessed wine which it is a sin to spill

Comfort thyself said Arthur I rest not nor my knights & so they keep their vows but for a year the *whole* realm will be safe as the centre of this hall.

Lo now she answer'd Is it not foul wrong—my sister whom even the heathen spared when they spoilt the land—she hath a great heritage— & rich she is & comely—yea & comlier than I myself—& there ever wails a knight nor lets her stir abroad but vows that he will wed her perforce save that one of thine own knights overthrow him.

Then cried out Sir Gareth. O King thy promise. I can overthrow seventy such: for thou knowest I have been thy kitchen knave, & so am I full of thy meats & drinks & strong as a lion.

Well spoken kitchenboy said Sir Kay. Thou wilt lose nothing for the asking.

But the damsel Linette cried out upon the king Fie on thee: I asked thee for a knight & thou hast given me a kitchen knave. & right so past quickly out of the hall.

     And there were men of Sir Gareth in the city & they brought him his armour & he mounted his horse & rode swiftly down the street & past thro' the gate & found the damsel ⟨in⟩ hardby the tourney-field: & she was inflamed   8r

───────────

with wrath as she looked at the field, saying could not the king have lent me one of the knights that fight in this field rather than a kitchen-knave?   9r

On folio 9v, there is a prose draft of a conversation between Gareth and Bellicent before his departure for Camelot:

     And Gareth knelt by his mother & she blest him laying hand on head & he ask'd her.

Sweet mother know ye the parable of the Golden Goose
And she said thou art a Goose to mind me of so foolish a parable.

And he Foolish enow, sweet Mother for it is the Eagle that lays the golden egg. here is my parable. There was a youth & he was poor but lusty, & he knew that the Eagle had laid a golden egg high up on a—call it a palmtree. & it seemd to him that he would be rich & happy if he could climb the tree & get the egg from the nest. & as he was about to climb one that loved him laid hold on him & prayd him by his love, not to climb less he should break his neck; & many times the youth w^d have climbd save for the love between them but he still longed for the egg day & night, & so sweet mother, he brake not his neck but he brake his heart 9v

On folios 16r and 16v, there is a prose draft of the entrance of Mark's messenger into Arthur's court:

     Now as the King ceased speaking & Gareth stood yet among the crowd there came in a messenger from King Mark of Cornwall & he held in his hand a cloth of gold, & spake to him that Mark was on his way to Arthur, for he had heard that the King had made Tristram *his kinsman* knight of his Table, & that he was of the greater state, being a king, & therefore trusted that Arthur would all the more give him this honour, & to show his reverence to Arthur he sent him this cloth of gold.

And Arthur said 'take it & cast it on the hearth Shall the shield of Mark stand among these? For in the middle of the side of the ⟨great⟩ Hall there rose over the hearth ⟨a mighty pile⟩ a great arch & over that a mighty pile of stone work: & as many knights as made the Table, so many shields were there & *the name & every knight was written thereupon*, in the stone, & *on* some of these ⟨n⟩ the arms were only carven, & some were carven & blazoned, & some were blank. for this was the custom of Arthur. When a knight had achieved one deed of prowess his arms were carven, & when he had achieved twain, they were blazoned & those that had achieved one had their shields blank: & *Gareth saw that* the shield of Gawain was blazoned   16r

---

& that of Modred was *blank*, & there was a vast oak-log smouldering on the hearth, so that the King said Cast it on the log.   16v

On folios 20r and 21r, there is one final piece of prose, a draft of Dagonet's confrontation with Tristram which becomes the germ of *The Last Tournament*. There is a folio torn out of the Notebook immediately before folio 20; the missing folio probably continued the prose passage of folios 16r and 16v where the reference to Tristram would seem to stand behind the meeting between Tristram and Dagonet.

Sir Dagonet, the king's fool, stood before the hall of Arthur. & the wind was blowing & the leaves flying in the wood below.

[And below him there past into the wood Sir Lamorack & his head was down, & his heart darkend for he had heard that Queen Bellicent was dead.]

And ⟨the dwarf skipt.⟩

And below him riding three abreast there past into the wood Sir Gawain Sir Modred & Sir Gaheris: & the face of Gawain was red as tho' with wine; & the face of Modred was white but he had bitten his thin lips till they were bloody: & so they past away.

And about an hour after there rode into the wood Sir Lamorack & his head was down & his heart darkend for his old love Queen Bellicent was dead.

And the dwarf skipt upon the steps before the hall & out of the hall came Tristram & cried to him.
O fool why skippest thou:
And the dwarf pointed to the wood & said
'They are gone to keep the vows of the King'
And Tristram said who are gone.
And he answer'd the sons of the Queen: for Lancelot has kept the vows of the king, & Lamorack has kept the vows of the king & thou also: for ye have all lain by Queens,   20r

---

So that no king knoweth his own son   21r

In Harvard Notebook 32 (watermarked 1822, front flyleaf dated "Oct. 13. – 56" by the poet), there is a series of prose drafts of sections of *Gareth and Lynette*. In "The Manuscripts of Tennyson's 'Gareth and Lynette,'" *Harvard Library Bulletin,* 13 (1959), Joan Hartman has correctly described the poet's use of this Notebook: "Sometimes Tennyson held the notebook right side up, sometimes upside down; sometimes he progressed forward from page to page in a normal fashion, sometimes backward Chinese-style. Here too is verse and prose, though less prose than in Notebook 40. In this disorder and confusion, for the manuscript cannot be read consecutively, are segments that constitute the remainder of "Gareth and Lynette'" [240]. This statement, however, demands some clarification because Notebook 32 had a special function for the poet. The large number of short prose drafts of sections of the idyll and their seemingly scattered position in the Notebook reveal that Tennyson used this Notebook as an exercise pad, a function further suggested by the surviving folios which contain sections from other idylls: passages from *Guinevere, Balin and Balan,* a much altered first draft of *To the Queen,* a few lines from *The Passing of Arthur,* and the sections from *Gareth and Lynette;* the Notebook also contains versions of *The Spiteful Letter, The Lord Has Grown as Commonplace,* and *Guess Well, and That is Well,* and several folios devoted to *Queen Mary.* Thus in this Notebook Tennyson would write a short prose draft of one episode of the Gareth idyll and then he would make a series of poetic renderings of the prose draft. Each prose draft represents the earliest version of the episode and often shows a very close verbal fidelity to Malory's account of the same scene; the poetic renderings show the poet's continuing expansion and clarification of the prose passages. The major prose draft follows Gareth's adventures from his departure from Camelot until his departure from the Baron's castle.

Now these two entries into the great hall, one, whereinto a man c^d walk only, & there was also, a side-entry, huge & lofty whereinto a man c^d. And Gareth past to the side entry: & there stood a great & goodly charger given by the King, & there likewise were those twain who had come with Gareth one whereof held a helmet & a shield & one the horse; & Gareth when he came without threw off a rough dress that veil'd him from head to foot, & shone forth all in complete armour; & there was a tumult in the street. And he took shield & put on helm & *mounted horse*, & all the thralls ran into the street & when they saw their fellow whom they loved, everyone threw up his cap & rejoiced in him & the King & cried out God ⟨sa⟩ bless the King & all his fair fellowship & the people mingled with the cry of the thralls & Gareth rode down between the shouters & so past down by the gate

But Sir Kay stood by the door & was wroth with the thralls & the people & Gareth; & said *My kitchen k sent on a quest* Of a surety that old wound on the head w^h the king got in Badon battle hath broken out again—this is madness Thralls to your work! why—now let the good sun roll backward let there be dawn in west & Eve in East. The boy was tame enow when I had him in keeping. Now will I after my kitchen knave & see whether he know me for the better man. but of the smoke hath he come & into the mere he shall go, & thence into the smoke again

But Lancelot said Told I thee not there was a mystery. Abide: the lad is great lusty & knowing of sword & lance & thou art past thy force; & moreover thou goest against the King's will & that did never he whom ye rail at.

But Sir Kay armed & rode down the street & The people gazed him at silence. 15v*

So, till it darken'd after evensong,
The two rode on, reviler & reviled.
Then after climbing a great slope they saw
⟨a glo⟩ Bowl-shaped, a gloomy gladed hollow sink
To westward, & beneath, a rounded mere
Red as the round eye of an Eagle-owl
Under the half-dead sunset glared in gloom.

And from the mere came shrieks & cries

Then from the black wood came a serving man
Flying & crying 'They have bound my lord
Six robbers & will cast him in the mere'
That some may know

I may not leave thee alone in the black wood
I am bound to right the wrong
The damsel a   spake contemptuously
Lead & I follow & Gareth cried again
Follow I lead & plunged into the wood.
And three with blows he quieted & three
Fled thro' the pines & Gareth loosed his bonds

& so set him upright on his feet whereon he said I owe thee my life & ask for what reward I may give thee w^h is in my power

And Gareth I will no reward have. I have my deed for the deeds sake & in uttermost obedience to the King but an thou wilt give this gentle damsel & myself harbourage for this night, then were I well-rewarded.

And the damsel said

Weenest thou that I have joy of thee *a shepherd thresher with a*[3] for this deed thou hast done it hath but mishappened thee for these were all craven thieves. fie how ye smell after your exercise of the tallowgrease! but if my lord the Baron will yield me harbourage then I grateful

So when they came to his castle w^h was hard at hand, the Baron made them ⟨the⟩ great cheer & goodly; & there was set a peacock in his pride before the damsel, & the lord set Gareth before the damsel but she arose & cried fie fie Sir Baron ye are uncourteous to set a kitchen-page beside me. I went this morning to King Arthur 18r*

I have ever warred on these thieves & my manner was when I had overcome them to tie a stone round their necks & drown them in this mere—& there be many rotting under this wan water[4]

3 "thresher" is written above "shepherd" on the page.
4 This passage is intended to follow the line, "ask for what reward I may give thee w^h is in my power," on folio 18r*.

to ask him for a knight who w^d do battle with Night & Day—yea & none but Lancelot c^d do it, then this kitchen knave cries out 'thy promise, king give me the quest; & the king having gone mad, gives it to him, to him—a fellow fitter to stick a swine than sit beside a noble gentlewoman.[5]   17v*

& the Baron was half amazed & half ashamed & ⟨set Ga⟩ left the damsel with the peacock in his pride before her & set Gareth at a sideboard & set himself beside him. & said

Friend whether thou beest kitchen knave or not Thou art a strong man & a goodly & I owe thee my life & therefore bethink thee as to this quest; for here be four of the mightiest knights living, tho' they be but the scum of Uther's time. & these in their fantastic fashion call themselves the Day, the morning star, the noonday sun & the evening star, & the fourth calls himself the night, & sometimes Death for he hath a skeleton painted on his harness & his helmet is fashion'd like a scull, whereby he have men know that even if any s^d overthrow the three he will be at last slain by himself & pass into eternal night. Wherefore I beseech thee bethink thyself whether thou wilt not return with the lady Linette that she may choose another champion for by my faith if thou pass on I count thee but as lost, & all this I say for thy *avail* ⟨benefit⟩ & because thou hast saved my life.

And Gareth said whether I be kitchen knave or not ⟨The I⟩ will be shown hereafter: but the King has granted me this quest & I follow it to the death 20r*

On the folios opposite these prose drafts are their corresponding poetic versions; 16r* corresponds to 15v*, 17r* to 18r*, and 19v* to 20r*. In addition to this extended prose passage, there are brief prose drafts of later episodes of the idyll; each of these drafts is surrounded by poetic renderings of the episode.

And lifting up the torch she show'd him on the cavern-walls painted figures of Day & Night & Death & evil custom pursuing the soul drest like a bride—the work of the hermit who had lived there—& to whom the four w^d confess themselves, & while he lived they restrained themselves & fear'd the king, & now they care not for the king but fear the cave—& from these walls these unfurnished fools—said I not they were fools have suckd their allegory. 26v*

W^d God had made us tongueless. all the day I riled & reviled thee; & now have I got Sir L. to give thee his shield & horse & let thee fight in his stead; & now I repent me yet again, for thou hast gaind thee glory enough in overthrowing those three knights but before this last thou wilt surely go down: for he is the mightiest living: & he will slay thee, for ⟨his squire⟩ he hath spared not man nor woman nor babe; & some say he hath eaten childs flesh—a monster. And I know not his face, but it is *too* horrible be looked upon & never have I seen it, nor heard him speak but ever his squire spoke for him, & the squire was sore sick when I left, & like to die   25v*

---

5 This passage is intended to follow the passage, "And the damsel said," on folio 18r*.

So when they had eaten the baken venison & drank in much as they w^d of the red wine of Southland, Gareth disarmed himself & lay down & slept. Then the damsel Lynette said to Lancelot. 'Wilt thou do me a grace? I sware to the black knight that I w^d *bring* thee to fight him. Wilt thou fight him in the lieu of Sir Gareth? Nay fair damsel, for therein w^d be too much discourtesy but an he overthrows Sir Gareth then shall he not scape *me*. 'Yet she said, an thou refuse me this thou wilt yield me another grace? *so that my sister's heart may be comforted & I may not seem forsworn at first sight* Willingly fair damsel, so that I may' Thou shalt let Gareth have thine armour, & he shall take thine. Willingly said Lancelot so that Gareth agree thereto

And when Gareth had awaked he was mighty again as any lion, & he sware that an he had Lancelots harness on him he w^d have tenfold might from the touch thereof, & tenfold might from the thought that he w^d never disgrace the shadow of Lancelot in the arms of Lancelot.

And so it was done: & Gareth said ⟨Shall we not fall⟩ let us go on the instant. Fair Sir said the damsel it yet wanteth 6 hours to the sunrise. Care not for that we will be there to fall on him when it dawneth.

Then they rode thence & when they gained the space before the castle, they ware of a huge black pavilion under the stars, & the harp of Arthur bickered over it, & a great black horn hung by the side of the pavilion. And Gareth was so fresh & eager that ere Lancelot or the damsel c^d stay him he blew it. & in the black night horribly brayed the horn. & a light flashd in a tower & past away; & Gareth once more winded the great horn & there were many lights but when he had blown it thrice, the castle doors were flung open & there came out two & two men bearing torches till all was as light as day.

Then the great black pavilion opend & yielded up Night on a huge black horse, & he was ghastly to gaze upon, & he rode like a bare-ribb'd Death & the scull grinn'd over him   22r*

And when he saw Gareth he cried out Art thou Sir Lancelot & he said I am all that thou wilt find for him   21v*

In addition to the prose drafts of *Gareth and Lynette* in the Harvard collection, there are two fragmentary prose drafts of the idyll in the Tennyson collection of the University of Texas. Both fragments are written on plain blue laid paper similar to the paper of Harvard Notebook 40; both present scenes which should occur between folio 6r and folio 7r of Notebook 40; there is no evidence, however, of a torn folio here in the Notebook.

And Gareth came before Arthur & said

O King deem ye not that I must fain be faint & weary when ye behold me trailing my feet along thy hall & leaning on the shoulders of these twain? wherefore I pray thee, grant me a boon for to grant it will be neither against thyself nor thy realm nor thy Table Round, & the boon I beg thee to grant is this that I may live & eat among thy thralls & those that hand the dish across the bar, for as long as I will

---

And Arthur said Thou seemest the goodliest boy I ever look'd on, yet grant I thy request: hast thou ought else *to ask* for this request of thine is below thee, & my heart warms toward thee.

And Gawain: yea, King, there be two other boons which I would fain have thee grant me & they are neither against thyself nor thy realm nor thy Table Round: but I ask them *not* now, but when the time comes.

And the king said If these be not against me nor my state nor my Round Table & provided they be nobler in their nature than eating & drinking they are granted to thee.

Balin and Balan

Harvard Notebook 37 contains a prose draft of the story of Pellam, an episode which occurs before the story of Balin since Garlon is now withholding the tribute. In this account, Vivien's introduction would occur in Mark's court, a scene ultimately placed in the final introduction to *Merlin and Vivien.*

Pellam the King who held & lost with Lot had his realm render'd tributary, & he had no child, but Sir Garlon, his heir, was his nephew. and Sir Garlon hated K.A. because the King had refused to make him of his Round Table, knowing him & many times in his anger he had sworn that come what might come he w^d pay the tribute no more.

And it chanced on a time that he sat drinking red wine in Lyonesse with King Mark for these were close friends; & they spoke of the great King, who promised to bring the world right by swearing his knights to vows of perfect obedience & perfect purity: & either laugh'd & scorned at the phantasy of so many knights being pure.

And there was with him a damsel of that court *battlefield* who bewitched men with her beauty. & she said What will thou wager, Sir king with me that I do not go to the court of this & bring back love-tokens from these pure ones, yea, even were it curl from the golden beard of Arthur. Have we not heard that this Lancelot worships no unwedded damsel but the Queen herself, to show forsooth, his utter selflessness, swears by her, & fights in her name. here be snakes in the grass, w^h methinks I can stir till they sting.

Go as thou wilt said Mark the King & an thou canst make a mischief among them there is nothing I will not give thee.   5r

---

Then spake Sir Garlon. I ride on the tomorrow back to the castle of King Pellam on the way to Arthur. Ride now with me. ⟨but when they came⟩ & she took with her a squire whom now she treated as a lover & now she mocked as a child. & the boy was besotted with her. But King Pellam thrust her from the gates. & there she dwelt among the woods awhile waiting Sir Garlon to go with her. And Garlon ever kept the tribute from being paid.   5v

Later in the same Notebook is a brief prose draft of the description of Pellam's court.

So Balan, added to their table, stood
Before the King, to whom one day there came
An ancient Baron sent from him to claim
Tribute of Pelles, one who took the side
Of Lot, when Arthur winning, took his realm
Gave it again but made it tributary.

We got the tribute with much ado, for the king is old & hath fallen into dreams, & his brother, Sir Garlon rules him & his & he would fain be holier than thou art & so hath put his wife away, & lets not dame or damsel enter his castle, holding them a pollution, & hath let all things to to wrack & we past into his chapel, & saw

Thorns of the crown & shivers of the cross
Rich arcs with precious bones of martyrdom
& Sir Garlon hates thee & thine, & cried out against the tribute.

& there we saw the spear wherewith the soldier Longus pierced our Lord & which he said was inherited from his ancestor Joseph of Aromat. so deep is he in his foulness.

But I will tell thee another thing. In the woods nigh Pelles castle we found a knight of thine speared thro' the back & again another whom we buried & whether this be the work of a bandit or Sir Garlon it behoves thee to look to it. 11v*

In Harvard Notebook 33 (watermarked 1870), there is a poetic draft of an account of Vivien's arrival at Camelot, which the poet rejected as an introduction for Vivien into the series. For further discussion, see Chapter 5.

'Better' she said 'I love this garden.rose
Deep-hued & many-folded. See thy hand
Is kindled with the glowing dust of these!
Thy maiden emblems have a heart as warm
As other maids who look as white as they.
All white is rare in aught that lives: in snow
We find it, but the firstlings of the snow—
Fair-maids of February, as we say—
Flare in them, look'd to close, a spark of fire:
And this a damsel, seven small summers old,
Show'd me at Cameliarde—where first we met.   4r

Meanwhile in open sun the royal crown
Sparkled, & swaying in the breezes lured
An errant damsel, Vivien & her squire.   6r

So Vivien spake, & with the dead mens hair
The batter'd shield, & the besotted boy
Fled lightly back to Mark & Lyonesse.   10r

Stealthily sped she then to Arthur's hall,
Took the dead hair, & the besotted boy
And batter'd shield, & came before the Queen;
Knelt lowly then, & bidden rise arose,
And stood with folded hands & downward eyes
Of glancing corner and all meekly said

'My father died in battle for thy king
My mother on his body in open field
Brake her true heart. An orphan maid am I,
For what small share of beauty may be mine
Pursued by Mark the king;—yea—& by one
Sir Tristram—of the Table—nay perchance
I wrong him, being fearful, full of shame;
The Cornish manners be so rough; but lo
I bring thee here a message from the dead.
And therewithal showing Sir Balan's hair
Know ye not this? not so, belike; but this
A most strange red, is easier known. The Queen
Took the dead hair & slightly shuddering ask'd
Sir Balin's? is he slain? Yea, noble Queen
Likewise his brother, Balan: for they fought,
Not knowing—some misprision of their shields—
I know not what. I found them side by side
And wounded to the death, unlaced their helms,   12r

And gave them air & water, held their heads,
Wept with them; & thy Balin joy'd my heart
Calling thee stainless wife & perfect Queen
Heaven's white Earth-angel; then they bad me clip
A tress from either head, & bring it thee,
Proof that my message is not feign'd; and pray'd
King Arthur would despatch some holy man,
As these had lain together in one womb,
To give them burial in a single grave—
Sent their last blessings to their king & thee,
And therewithal their dying wish, that thou,
For that good service I had done thy knights,
Wouldst yield me shelter for mine innocency.
To whom the Queen made answer 'We must hear
Thy story further; thou shalt bide the while.'
And when she saw Sir Lancelot askt him saying
Know ye the stranger woman?' Let her be'
Said Lancelot; half-forgotten by the Queen
Thro' the still court with wistful eyes she crept
And whisper'd: then as Arthur in the highest
Leaven'd the world, so Vivien in the lowest,
Arriving in a time of golden rest,
When no quest came, but all was joust & play
And all the heathen lay at Arthur's feet
Leaven'd his hall. They heard & let her be.   14r

Among thy maidens 'Damsel' said the Queen
I know no more of thee than that thy tale
Hath chill'd me to the heart. Ghastly mischance,
Enough to make all childless motherhood
Fain so to bide for ever! Where do they lie?
And Vivien's voice was broken answering her.
Dead in a nameless corner of the woods
Each lockd in either's arms. I know the place,
But scarce can word it plain for thee to know.'
And therefore damsel shalt thou ride at once
With Arthur's knights & guide them thro' the woods
Thy wish, & these dead men's, if such were theirs
Must bide mine answer till we meet again.'

After when Vivien on returning came
To Guinevere & spake I saw the twain
Buried; I wept above their woodland grave
But grant me now my wish and theirs' the Queen
All-glittering like may-sunshine among leaves
In green & gold, & plumed with green, replied

A moiety of thy tale is proven true;
Yet must we test thee more; but even now
We ride on-hawking with Sir Lancelot.
He hath given me a fair falcon which he traind
We go to fly her. Bide thou here the while.'   15r

But when she rode with Lancelot down the plain
Their talk was all of training, terms of art,
Feeding, & diet, leash & lure.
She is too noble' he said 'to check at pies,
Nor will she rake: there is no baseness in her.'
Here when the Queen demanded as by chance
'Know ye this stranger woman?' 'Let her be'
Said Lancelot, & unhooded casting from him
The goodly falcon loose; she tower'd; her bells
Tone under tone, shrill'd; & they lifted up
Their eager faces, wondering at the strength
Boldness & royal knighthood of the bird
Who pounced her quarry & slew it many a time.
They rode; & half-forgotten of the Queen
Among her maidens broidering Vivien sat
And whisper'd;   16r

Bibliography

1. The Poetry of Tennyson

Poems. London: Edward Moxon, 1833.
Poems. London: Edward Moxon, 1842.
Poems. London: Edward Moxon, 1857.
Idylls of the King. London: Strahan, 1859.
The Holy Grail and Other Poems. London: Strahan, 1870.
Idylls of the King. London: Strahan, 1869.
"The Last Tournament." *Contemporary Review*, 19, 1871, 1-22.
Gareth and Lynette Etc. London: Strahan, 1872.
The Works of Alfred Tennyson, Imperial Library Edition, 6 Vols. London: Strahan, 1872-1873.
The Works of Alfred Tennyson, Cabinet Edition, 10 Vols. London: Henry S. King, 1874-1875.
Tiresias and Other Poems. London: Macmillan, 1885.
The Poetical Works of Alfred Lord Tennyson, New Miniature Edition, 12 Vols. London: Macmillan, 1886-1891.
The Poetical Works of Alfred, Lord Tennyson. London: Macmillan, 1890.
The Life and Works of Alfred, Lord Tennyson, 12 Vols. Edited by Hallam, Lord Tennyson. London: Macmillan, 1898-1899.
The Works of Tennyson, Eversley Edition, 9 Vols. Annotated by Alfred, Lord Tennyson. Edited by Hallam, Lord Tennyson. London: Macmillan, 1907-1908.
The Poems of Tennyson. Edited by Christopher Ricks. London: Longmans, 1969.
A Variorum Edition of Tennyson's Idylls of the King. Edited by John Pfordresher. New York: Columbia University Press, 1973.

2. Tennysonian Scholarship

Adicks, Richard. "The Lily Maid and the Scarlet Sleeve: White and Red in Tennyson's *Idylls*." *University Review*, 34, 1967, 65-71.
————. "Structure and Meaning in Tennyson's *Idylls of the King*." Unpublished Dissertation, Tulane University, 1965.

203

Alaya, Flavia M. "Tennyson's 'The Lady of Shalott': The Triumph of Art." *Victorian Poetry*, 8, 1970, 273-289.

Baker, Arthur E. *A Concordance to the Poetical and Dramatic Works of Alfred, Lord Tennyson*. London: Kegan Paul, Trench, Trübner, 1914.

Baum, Paull F. *Tennyson Sixty Years After*. Chapel Hill, North Carolina: University of North Carolina Press, 1948.

Bausenwein, Joseph. *Die Poetischen Bearbeitungen der Balin- und Balansage von Tennyson und Swinburne und ihr Verhältnis zu Malory*. Würzburg: Bucher, 1914.

Bernstein, Ethel. "Victorian Morality in the *Idylls of the King*." Unpublished Dissertation, Cornell University, 1939.

Brashear, William. "Tennyson's Tragic Vitalism: *Idylls of the King*." *Victorian Poetry*, 6, 1968, 29-49.

_____. *The Living Will*. The Hague: Mouton, 1969.

Buckley, Jerome H. *Tennyson: The Growth of a Poet*. Cambridge, Mass.: Harvard University Press, 1960.

Burchell, S. C. "Tennyson's 'Allegory in the Distance.'" *Publications of the Modern Language Association of America*, 68, 1953, 418-424.

Campbell, Nancie, ed. *Tennyson in Lincoln*, 2 Vols. Lincoln, England: Keyworth and Fry, 1971-1973.

Cannon, Garland. "The Lady of Shalott and the Arabian Nights' Tales." *Victorian Poetry*, 8, 1970, 344-346.

Chambers, D. Laurance. "Tennysoniana." *Modern Language Notes*, 18, 1903, 227-233.

Cross, Tom Peete. "Alfred Tennyson as a Celticist." *Modern Philology*, 18, 1921, 485-492.

Culler, A. Dwight. *The Poetry of Tennyson*. New Haven: Yale University Press, 1977.

Donahue, Mary Joan. "The Revision of Tennyson's 'Sir Galahad.'" *Philological Quarterly*, 28, 1949, 326-329.

Eggers, J. Phillip. *King Arthur's Laureate*. New York: New York University Press, 1971.

_____. "The Weeding of the Garden: Tennyson's Geraint Idylls and the *Mabinogion*." *Victorian Poetry*, 4, 1966, 45-51.

Elliott, Philip L. "Imagery and Unity in the *Idylls of the King*." *Furman Studies*, 15, 1968, 22-28.

Engbretsen, Nancy M. "The Thematic Evolution of the *Idylls of the King*." *Victorian Newsletter*, 26, 1964, 1-5.

Engelberg, Edward. "The Beast Image in Tennyson's *Idylls of the King*." *English Literary History*, 22, 1955, 287-292.

Furnivall, F. J. "Mr. Hutton and Tennyson's King Arthur." *Notes and Queries*, Series Four, 11, 1873, 3-4.

Gossman, Ann and Whiting, George W. "King Arthur's Farewell to Guinevere." *Notes and Queries*, New Series, 6, 1959, 446-448.

Gray, J. M. "The Creation of Excalibur: An Apparent Inconsistency in the *Idylls*." *Victorian Poetry*, 6, 1968, 68-69.

_____. "Fact, Form, and Fiction in Tennyson's 'Balin and Balan.'" *Renaissance and Modern Studies*, 12, 1968, 91-107.

_____. "A Feature Characterizing Lancelot in Tennyson's 'Lancelot and Elaine.'" *Notes and Queries*, New Series, 17, 1970, 15.

_____. "Knightly Combats in Malory's Tale of Sir Gareth and Tennyson's 'Gareth and Lynette.'" *Notes and Queries*, New Series, 16, 1969, 207-208.

_____ . " 'The Lady of Shalott' and Tennyson's Readings in the Super-natural." *Notes and Queries,* New Series, 12, 1965, 298-300.

_____ . *Man and Myth in Victorian England: Tennyson's The Coming of Arthur.* Lincoln, England: Keyworth and Fry, 1969.

_____ . *Organicism in the Evolution of Tennyson's Idylls.* Lincoln, England: Keyworth and Fry, 1973.

_____ . "An Origin for Tennyson's Characterization of Percivale in 'The Holy Grail.' " *Notes and Queries,* New Series, 18, 1971, 416-417.

_____ . "The Purpose of an Epic List in 'The Coming of Arthur.' " *Victorian Poetry,* 8, 1970, 339-341.

_____ . *Serial and Cyclical Characterization in Tennyson's Idylls.* Lincoln, England: Keyworth and Fry, 1973.

_____ . "Source and Symbol in 'Geraint and Enid': Tennyson's Doorm and Limours." *Victorian Poetry,* 4, 1966, 131-132.

_____ . "A Study in Idyl: Tennyson's 'The Coming of Arthur.' " *Renaissance and Modern Studies,* 14, 1970, 111-150.

_____ . "Tennyson and Geoffrey of Monmouth." *Notes and Queries,* New Series, 14, 1967, 52-53.

_____ . "Tennyson and Layamon." *Notes and Queries,* New Series, 15, 1968, 176-178.

_____ . "Tennyson and Nennius." *Notes and Queries,* New Series, 13, 1966, 341-342.

_____ . *Tennyson's Doppelgänger: Balin and Balan.* Lincoln, England: Keyworth and Fry, 1971.

_____ . "Two Transcendental Ladies of Tennyson's *Idylls:* The Lady of the Lake and Vivien." *Tennyson Research Bulletin,*1, 4, 1970, 104-105.

Gridley, Roy. "Confusion of the Seasons in Tennyson's 'The Last Tournament.' " *Victorian Newsletter,* 22, 1962, 14-16.

Haight, G. S. "Tennyson's Merlin." *Studies in Philology,* 44, 1947, 549-566.

Hartman, Joan E. "The Manuscripts of Tennyson's 'Gareth and Lynette.' " *Harvard Library Bulletin,* 13, 1959, 239-264.

Hellstrom, Ward. *On the Poems of Tennyson.* Gainesville: University of Florida Press, 1972.

Hill, James L. "Tennyson's 'The Lady of Shalott': The Ambiguity of Commitment." *Centennial Review of Arts and Science,* 12, 1968, 415-429.

Hume, Robert D. and Olshin, Toby A. "Ambrosius in 'The Holy Grail': Source and Function." *Notes and Queries,* New Series, 16, 1969, 208-209.

Hunt, John Dixon. "The Poetry of Distance: Tennyson's *Idylls of the King.*" *Victorian Poetry.* Edited by Malcolm Bradbury and David Palmer. London: Edward Arnold, 1972, pp. 89-121.

Jones, Richard. *The Growth of the Idylls of the King.* Philadelphia, 1895.

Joseph, Gerhard. *Tennysonian Love: The Strange Diagonal.* Minneapolis: University of Minnesota Press, 1969.

Kaplan, Fred. "Woven Paces and Waving Hands: Tennyson's Merlin as Fallen Artist." *Victorian Poetry,* 7, 1969, 285-298.

Killham, John. "Tennyson and the Sinful Queen: A Corrected Impression." *Notes and Queries,* New Series, 5, 1958, 507-511.

Killham, John, ed. *Critical Essays on the Poetry of Tennyson.* London: Routledge and Kegan Paul, 1960.

Kincaid, James R. *Tennyson's Major Poems: The Comic and Ironic Patterns.* New Haven: Yale University Press, 1975.

Knowles, Sir James. "Aspects of Tennyson." *Nineteenth Century*, 191, 1893, 164-188.

Kozicki, Henry. "Tennyson's *Idylls of the King* as Tragic Drama." *Victorian Poetry*, 4, 1966, 15-20.

————. "Wave and Fire Imagery in Tennyson's *Idylls*." *Victorian Newsletter*, 43, 1973, 21-23.

Lawry, J. S. "Tennyson's 'The Epic': A Gesture of Recovered Faith." *Modern Language Notes*, 74, 1959, 400-403.

Layard, G. S. *Tennyson and His Pre-Raphaelite Illustrators*. London, 1894.

Lewin, Lois. "The Blameless King? The Conceptual Flaw in Tennyson's Arthur." *Ball State University Forum*, 10, 1969, 32-41.

Littledale, Harold. *Essays on Lord Tennyson's Idylls of the King*. London, 1893.

Litzinger, Boyd. "The Structure of Tennyson's 'The Last Tournament.'" *Victorian Poetry*, 1, 1963, 53-60.

MacCallum, M. W. *Tennyson's Idylls of the King and the Arthurian Story from the XVIth Century*. Glasgow, 1894.

Marshall, George O., Jr. *A Tennyson Handbook*. New York: Twayne, 1963.

Meinhold, George D. "The *Idylls of the King* and the *Mabinogion*." *Tennyson Research Bulletin*, 1, 3, 1969, 61-63.

[Mill, John Stuart.] "Tennyson's Poems." *London Review*, 1, 1835, 402-424.

Miller, Betty. "Tennyson and the Sinful Queen." *Twentieth Century*, 158, 1955, 355-363.

Nicolson, Harold. *Tennyson: Aspects of His Life, Character, and Poetry*. New York: Houghton Mifflin, 1923.

Packer, Iona Mosk. "Sun and Shadow: The Nature of Experience in Tennyson's 'The Lady of Shalott.'" *Victorian Newsletter*, 25, 1964, 4-8.

Pallen, Condé B. *The Meaning of the Idylls of the King*. New York: American Book Company, 1904.

Pfordresher, John. "A Bibliographical History of Alfred Tennyson's *Idylls of the King*." *Studies in Bibliography*, 26, 1973, 192-218.

Pitt, Valerie. *Tennyson Laureate*. Toronto: University of Toronto Press, 1962.

Poston, Lawrence, III. "The Argument of the Geraint-Enid Books in *Idylls of the King*." *Victorian Poetry*, 2, 1964, 269-275.

————. "'Pelleas and Ettarre': Tennyson's 'Troilus.'" *Victorian Poetry*, 4, 1966, 199-204.

————. "The Two Provinces of Tennyson's *Idylls*." *Criticism*, 9, 1967, 372-382.

Potwin, L. S. "The Sources of Tennyson's The Lady of Shalott." *Modern Language Notes*, 17, 1902, 473-477.

Priestley, F. E. L. *Language and Structure in Tennyson's Poetry*. London: André Deutsch, 1973.

Reed, John R. *Perception and Design in Tennyson's Idylls of the King*. Athens, Ohio: Ohio University Press, 1969.

Richardson, Joanna. *The Pre-Eminent Victorian: A Study of Tennyson*. London: Jonathan Cape, 1962.

Richardson, Robert E., Jr. "A Critical Introduction to the *Idylls of the King* (1859)." Unpublished Dissertation, Princeton University, 1967.

Ricks, Christopher. *Tennyson*. New York: Collier Books, 1972.

Ritchie, Anne Thackeray. "Alfred Tennyson." *Harper's New Monthly Magazine*, 68, 1883, 21-41.

Rosenberg, John D. *The Fall of Camelot: A Study of Tennyson's Idylls of the King*. Cambridge, Mass.: The Belknap Press, 1973.

Ryals, Clyde de L. *From the Great Deep*. Athens, Ohio: Ohio University Press, 1967.

Scott, P. G. "Tennyson's Celtic Reading." *Tennyson Research Bulletin*, 1, 2, 1968, 4-8.

Shannon, Edgar F., Jr. "The Proofs of 'Gareth and Lynette' in the Widener Collection." *Papers of the Bibliographical Society of America*, 41, 1947, 321-340.

————. *Tennyson and the Reviewers*. Cambridge, Mass.: Harvard University Press, 1952.

Shannon, Edgar F., Jr. and Bond, W. H. "Literary Manuscripts of Alfred Tennyson in the Harvard College Library." *Harvard Library Bulletin*, 10, 1956, 254-274.

Shaw, W. David. "Gareth's Four Antagonists: A Biblical Source." *Victorian Newsletter*, 34, 1968, 34-35.

————. "The Idealist's Dilemma in *Idylls of the King*." *Victorian Poetry*, 5, 1967, 41-53.

————. "*Idylls of the King*: A Dialectical Reading." *Victorian Poetry*, 7, 1969, 175-190.

————. *Tennyson's Style*. Ithaca: Cornell University Press, 1976.

Solimine, Joseph, Jr. "The *Idylls of the King*: The Rise, Decline, and Fall of the State." *The Personalist*, 50, 1969, 105-116.

Solomon, Stanley. "Tennyson's Paradoxical King." *Victorian Poetry*, 1, 1963, 258-271.

Staines, David. "The Prose Drafts of Tennyson's *Idylls of the King*." *Harvard Library Bulletin*, 22, 1974, 280-308.

————. "Tennyson's 'The Holy Grail': The Tragedy of Percivale." *Modern Language Review*, 69, 1974, 745-756.

————. "Tennyson's Mysticism: A Personal Testimony." *Notes and Queries*, New Series, 24, 1977, 404-405.

Tennyson, Sir Charles. *Alfred Tennyson*. London: Macmillan, 1949.

————. "The Dream in Tennyson's Poetry." *Virginia Quarterly Review*, 40, 1964, 228-248.

————. "The *Idylls of the King*." *Twentieth Century*, 161, 1957, 277-286.

————. *Six Tennyson Essays*. London: Cassell, 1954.

Tennyson, Sir Charles and Fall, Christine, eds. *Alfred Tennyson: An Annotated Bibliography*. Athens, Georgia: University of Georgia Press, 1967.

Tennyson, Hallam, Lord. *Alfred Lord Tennyson: A Memoir*, 2 Vols. New York, 1897.

————. *Materials for a Life of A.T.*, 4 Vols. Privately printed, no date.

————, ed. *Tennyson and His Friends*. London: Macmillan, 1911.

Tillotson, Kathleen. "Tennyson's Serial Poem." *Mid-Victorian Studies*. Edited by Geoffrey and Kathleen Tillotson. London: The Athlone Press, 1965, pp. 80-109.

Turner, Paul. *Tennyson*. London: Routledge and Kegan Paul, 1976.

Waterston, Elizabeth H. "Symbolism in Tennyson's Minor Poems." *University of Toronto Quarterly*, 20, 1951, 369-380.

Wilkenfield, R. B. "Tennyson's Camelot: The Kingdom of Folly." *University of Toronto Quarterly*, 37, 1968, 281-294.

Wilson, Hugh. "Tennyson: Unscholarly Arthurian." *Victorian Newsletter*, 32, 1967, 5-11.

Wise, T. J. *A Bibliography of the Writings of Alfred, Lord Tennyson*, 2 Vols. London: privately printed, 1908.

Wright, H. G. "Tennyson and Wales." *Essays and Studies*, 14, 1929, 71-103.
Wüllenweber, W. "Tennysons Konigsidylle The Coming of Arthur." *Archiv für das Studium der Neueren Sprachen und Litteraturen*, 83, 1889, 1-66.

3. Contemporary Reviews of Tennyson's Arthurian Poetry
(Unless an author is named, a review appeared anonymously.)

A. Poems (1842)

"Poems. By Alfred Tennyson." *Examiner*, May 28, 1842, pp. 340-341.
"Tennyson's Poems." *London Evening Sun*, May 28, 1842, p. 4.
"Tennyson's Collected Poems." *Spectator*, June 4, 1842, p. 544.
"Poems. By Alfred Tennyson." *Monthly Review*, 2, July 1842, 369-375.
"Poetry of the Year 1842." *Christian Remembrancer*, 4, July 1842, 42-58.
"Poems. By Alfred Tennyson." *Athenaeum*, August 6, 1842, pp. 700-702.
"Poems. By Alfred Tennyson." *Morning Post*, August 9, 1842, p. 6.
"Poems. By Alfred Tennyson." *Weekly Dispatch*, August 21, 1842, p. 406.
"Tennyson's Poems." *Tait's Edinburgh Magazine*, 9, August 1842, 502-508.
"Poems by Alfred Tennyson." *Quarterly Review*, 70, September 1842, 385-416.
"Poems. By Alfred Tennyson." *Westminster Review*, 38, October 1842, 371-390.
"Tennyson's Poems." *Christian Teacher*, New Series 4, October 1842, 414-423.
"Poems, by Alfred Tennyson, in Two Volumes." *Cambridge University Magazine*, 2, October 1842, 629-639.
"Poems by Alfred Tennyson." *Church of England Quarterly Review*, XII, October 1842, 361-376.
"Poems. By Alfred Tennyson." *Literary Gazette*, November 12, 1842, pp. 788-789.
C., W. A. "Poems, by Alfred Tennyson." *London University Magazine*, 1, December 1842, 286-314.
"Poems by Alfred Tennyson." *Edinburgh Review*, 57, April 1843, 373-391.
"Poems by Alfred Tennyson." *Foreign and Colonial Quarterly Review*, 3, 1844, 207-209.
"The Poetry of Alfred Tennyson." *Chambers's Edinburgh Journal*, New Series 4, July 12, 1845, 25-29.
"Poems. By Alfred Tennyson." *British Quarterly Review*, 2, August 1845, 46-71.
Gilfillan, George. "Alfred Tennyson." *Tait's Edinburgh Magazine*, 14, April 1847, 229-234.
"Alfred Tennyson." *Hogg's Weekly Instructor*, 6, December 25, 1847, 281-284.
Sutton, Henry. "The Poet's Mission." *Howitt's Journal*, 3, 1848, 39-42.

B. Idylls of the King (1859)

"Idylls of the King." *Athenaeum*, July 16, 1859, pp. 73-76.
"The Laureate's New Poem." *Critic*, 19, July 16, 1859, 52-54.
"Idylls of the King." *Examiner*, July 16, 1859, p. 452.
"Idylls of the King." *Saturday Review*, 8, July 16, 1859, 75-76.
"Idylls of the King." *Literary Gazette*, 3, July 23, 1859, 81-82.
"Tennyson's Idylls of the King." *Spectator*, July 23, 1859, pp. 764-766.
"Four Idylls of the King." *Edinburgh Review*, 110, July 1859, 247-263.

"The Idylls of the King." *Chambers's Journal*, 12, August 20, 1859, 121-124.
"Idylls of the King." *North British Review*, 13, August 1859, 148-174.
"Poets and Poetry." *Tait's Edinburgh Magazine*, 26, August 1859, 464-470.
"Idylls of the King." *London Times*, September 10, 1859, 5.
"Idylls of the King." *Fraser's Magazine*, 9, September 1859, 301-314.
"Tennyson's 'Idylls of the King.' " *Eclectic Review*, New Series, 2, September 1859, 287-294.
"Tennyson—Idylls of the King." *Bentley's Quarterly Review*, 2, October 1859, 159-194.
"Idylls of the King." *British Quarterly Review*, 30, October 1859, 481-510.
"Idylls of the King." *London Review*, 13, October 1859, 62-80.
"Tennyson's Idylls." *National Review*, 9, October 1859, 368-394.
"Tennyson's Poems." *Quarterly Review*, 106, October 1859, 454-485.
"Tennyson's Idylls of the King." *Westminster Review*, New Series, 16, October 1859, 503-526.
"The Idylls of the King." *Blackwood's Edinburgh Magazine*, 49, November 1859, 608-627.
Ludlow, J. M. "Moral Aspects of Mr. Tennyson's 'Idylls of the King.' " *Macmillan's Magazine*, 1, November 1859, 63-72.
"Idylls of the King." *Irish Quarterly Review*, 9, 1859, 834-859.
"Mr. Tennyson." *New Quarterly Review*, 8, 1859, 336-351.
"Idyls of the King." *Scottish Review*, 7, 1859, 327-339.
"The Poet Laureate." *Christian Observer*, April 1860, pp. 244-257.
"Tennyson's Poems." *Meliora: A Quarterly Review of Social Science*, 2, 1860, 225-248.
A Country Parson. "Religious Aspects of Mr. Tennyson's Poetry." *Dublin University Magazine*, 55, 1860, 353-356.
"Living English Poets." *Dublin Review*, 49, 1861, 513-518.
Cheetham, S. "The Arthurian Legends in Tennyson." *Contemporary Review*, 7, 1868, 497-514.

C. The Holy Grail and Other Poems (1869)

"The Holy Grail, and other Poems." *Athenaeum*, December 18, 1869, pp. 809-810.
"The Poet Laureate's New Poem." *London Times*, December 23, 1869, p. 4.
"Mr. Tennyson's New Poems." *Spectator*, December 25, 1869, pp. 1530-1533.
A Subscriber. "Tennyson's Arthurian Poem." *Spectator*, January 1, 1870, pp. 15-17.
Lawrenny, H. "The Holy Grail and other Poems." *Academy*, 1, January 8, 1870, 91-94.
"Mr. Tennyson and the Round Table." *British Quarterly Review*, 51, January 1870, 200-214.
Alford, Henry. "The Idylls of the King." *Contemporary Review*, 13, January 1870, 104-125.
"The Holy Grail and other Poems." *Quarterly Review*, 128, January 1870, 1-17.
"The Holy Grail and other Poems." *Chambers's Journal*, 7, February 26, 1870, 137-140.
"The Holy Grail and other Poems." *Victoria Magazine*, 14, February 1870, 376-383.
"Mr. Tennyson's Arthurian Poems." *Dublin Review*, 66, April 1870, 418-429.
"The Epic of Arthur." *Edinburgh Review*, 131, April 1870, 502-539.

"The Laureate and His 'Arthuriad.'" *London Quarterly Review*, 34, April 1870, 154-186.

"The Quest of the Sancgreal." *St. James' Magazine*, New Series, 4, April 1870, 785-814.

"New Books." *Blackwood's Edinburgh Magazine*, 107, May 1870, 640.

"Old Romance and Modern Poetry." *All the Year Round*, New Series, 4, September 17, 1870, 373-379.

"Tennyson and the Holy Vision." *Intellectual Repository and New Jerusalem Magazine*, 202, October 1870, 472-476.

D. Gareth and Lynette Etc. (1872)

Leary, T. H. L. "Tennyson and the 'Quarterly Review.'" *Gentleman's Magazine*, New Series, 8, April 1872, 423-430.

"Mr. Tennyson's New Poem, 'Gareth and Lynette.'" *London Times*, October 24, 1872, p. 6.

"Mr. Tennyson's King Arthur." *Athenaeum*, October 26, 1872, pp. 521-524.

"Gareth and Lynette." *Spectator*, October 26, 1872, pp. 1363-1365.

"The Last of the Arthurian Legends." *Chambers's Journal*, 49, December 21, 1872, 813-816.

"New Books." *Blackwood's Edinburgh Magazine*, 112, December 1872, 760-765.

Hutton, Richard H. "Tennyson." *Macmillan's Magazine*, 27, December 1872, 143-167.

"Gareth and Lynette." *London Quarterly Review*, 39, January 1873, 394-405.

"Belles Lettres." *Westminster Review*, 43, January 1873, 326-328.

G., C. A. L. "Gareth and Lynette." *Victoria Magazine*, 20, February 1873, 308-313.

"The Meaning of Mr. Tennyson's 'King Arthur.'" *Contemporary Review*, 21, May 1873, 938-948.

E. Tiresias and Other Poems (1885)

"Lord Tennyson's New Poems." *London Times*, December 9, 1885, p. 8.

"The Poet Laureate's New Poems." *Spectator*, 58, December 12, 1885, 1649-1651.

Caine, T. Hall. "Tiresias, and other Poems." *Academy*, December 19, 1885, pp. 403-405.

"Tiresias and other Poems." *Saturday Review*, December 19, 1885, pp. 810-811.

"Tiresias, and other Poems." *Athenaeum*, December 26, 1885, pp. 831-834.

"Tennyson: The Conservative." *Atlantic Monthly*, 57, March 1886, 423-426.

"Tiresias and other Poems." *British Quarterly Review*, 165, April 1886, 210-211.

Ker, W. P. "Poetry." *Contemporary Review*, 49, April 1886, 598-600.

"Tiresias and other Poems." *Edinburgh Review*, 163, April 1886, 466-498.

"Belles Lettres." *Westminster Review*, 125, April 1886, 581-582.

4. Related Medieval and Later English Arthurian Literature

Alberic. "Chronicle." *Accessiones Historicae*. Edited by G. W. Leibniz. Lipsiae, 1698.

Bulwer-Lytton, Edward. *King Arthur*, 2 Vols. London, 1849.

Ellis, George, ed. *Specimens of Early English Metrical Romances*, 3 Vols. London, 1811.

Giles, J. A. *Six Old English Chronicles*. London, 1848.

Guest, Lady Charlotte, trans. The *Mabinogion*, 3 Vols. London, 1840.

Hawker, R. S. *The Quest of the Sangraal*. Exeter, 1864.

Knowles, James. *The Story of King Arthur and His Knights of the Round Table*. London, 1862; third edition, 1868; eighth edition, 1912.

Layamon. *Layamon's Brut*, 3 Vols. Edited by Sir Frederick Madden. London, 1847.

Lovelich, Henry. *Seynt Graal, or the Sank Ryal: The History of the Holy Graal*, 2 Vols. Edited by F. J. Furnivall. London, 1861-1863.

MacDonald, George. "The Sangreal." *Good Words*, 4, 1863, 454-455.

Malory, Thomas. *The Most Ancient and Famous History of the Renowned Prince Arthur*. Edited by William Stansby. London, 1634.

_____ . *The History of the Renowned Prince Arthur and His Knights of the Round Table*, 2 Vols. Edited by Walker and Edwards. London, 1816.

_____ . *La Mort D'Arthur*, 3 Vols. Edited by R. Wilks. London, 1816.

_____ . *The Byrth, Lyf and Actes of Kyng Arthur*, 2 Vols. Edited by Robert Southey. London, 1817.

_____ . *La Mort d'Arthure*, 3 Vols. Edited by Thomas Wright. London, 1856.

_____ . *La Morte D'Arthure. The History of King Arthur*. Abridged and revised by Edward Conybeare. London, 1868.

_____ . *Morte Darthur*. Edited by Edward Strachey. London, 1868.

_____ . *La Mort D'Arthur*. Edited by B. Montgomerie Ranking. London, 1871.

_____ . *The Life and Exploits of King Arthur and His Knights of the Round Table: A Legendary Romance*. Edited anonymously. London, 1878.

_____ . *The Boy's King Arthur*. Edited by Sidney Lanier. London, 1880.

_____ . *Malory's History of King Arthur and the Quest of the Holy Grail*. Edited by Ernest Rhys. London, 1886.

_____ . *Morte Darthur*, 3 vols. Edited by H. O. Sommer. London, 1889-1891.

_____ . *Le Morte Darthur*. Edited by Edward Strachey. London, 1891.

_____ . *King Arthur and the Knights of the Round Table. A Modernized Version of the Morte Darthur*. Edited by Charles Morris. London, 1892.

_____ . *The Book of Marvellous Adventures and Other Books of the Morte D'Arthur*. Edited by Ernest Rhys. London, 1893.

_____ . *The Noble and Joyous History of King Arthur*. Edited by Ernest Rhys. London, 1894.

_____ . *Selections from Malory's Le Morte D'Arthur*. Edited by A. T. Martin. London, 1896.

_____ . *Selections from Sir Thomas Malory's Le Morte D'Arthur*. Edited by W. E. Mead. London, 1897.

_____ . *Le Morte Darthur*, 4 Vols. Edited by Israel Gollancz. London, 1897.

Map, Walter. *La Queste del Saint Graal*. Edited by F. J. Furnivall. London, 1864.

Percy, Thomas, ed. *Reliques of Ancient English Poetry*, 3 Vols. London, 1765.

Price, Thomas. *Hanes Cymru*. Crughywel, 1842.

Ritson, Joseph, ed. *The Life of King Arthur*. London, 1825.

_____ . *Ancient English Metrical Romances*, 3 Vols. London, 1802.

Scott, Walter, ed. *Sir Tristrem*. Edinburgh, 1806.

Turner, Sharon. *The History of the Anglo-Saxons*, 3 Vols. London, 1836.

Westwood, Thomas. *The Quest of the Sancgreall, The Sword of the Kingship, and Other Poems*. London, 1868.

5. Select Bibliography of Arthurian Criticism

App, A. J. *Lancelot in English Literature*. Washington: Catholic University of America Press, 1929.

Benson, Larry D. "Sir Thomas Malory's *Le Morte Darthur*." In *Critical Approaches to Six Major English Works*. Edited by R. M. Lumiansky and Herschel Baker. Philadelphia: University of Pennsylvania Press, 1968, pp. 81-131.

Brinkley, R. F. *Arthurian Legends in the Seventeenth Century*. Baltimore: The Johns Hopkins Press, 1932.

Bruce, James Douglas. *The Evolution of Arthurian Romance*, 2 Vols. Baltimore: The Johns Hopkins Press, 1928.

Brugger, E. "'Der Schöne Feigling' in der arthurischen Literatur." *Zeitschrift für romanische Philologie*, 61, 1941, 1-44; 63, 1943, 123-173, 275-328; 65, 1945, 121-192, 289-433.

Gutbier, Elisabeth. *Psychologisisch-ästhetische Studien zu Tristandichtungen der neuren englischen Literatur*. Erlangen: K. Döres, 1932.

Halperin, Maurice. *Le Roman de Tristran et Iseut*. Paris: Jouve et cie, 1931.

Hibbard, Laura A. "Malory's 'Book of Balin.'" In *Medieval Studies in Memory of Gertrude Schoepperle Loomis*. Edited by Roger S. Loomis. New York: Columbia University Press, 1927, pp. 175-195.

Loomis, Roger S., ed. *Arthurian Literature in the Middle Ages*. Oxford: The Clarendon Press, 1959.

Löseth, Eilert. *Le Roman en prose de Tristan, le Roman de Palamède, et la compilation de Rusticien de Pise*. Paris, 1891.

Maynadier, Howard. *The Arthur of the English Poets*. Boston: Houghton Mifflin, 1907.

Merriman, James Douglas. *The Flower of Kings*. Lawrence, Kansas: The University Press of Kansas, 1973.

Moorman, Charles. "'The Tale of the Sankgreall': Human Frailty." In *Malory's Originality*. Edited by R. M. Lumiansky. Baltimore: The Johns Hopkins Press, 1964, pp. 184-204.

Reid, Margaret J. C. *The Arthurian Legend*. London: Methuen, 1938.

Rumble, Thomas C. "Malory's 'Balin' and the Question of Unity in the *Morte Darthur*." *Speculum*, 41, 1966, 68-85.

_____ . "'The Tale of Tristram': Development by Analogy." In *Malory's Originality*. Edited by R. M. Lumiansky. Baltimore: The Johns Hopkins Press, 1964, pp. 118-183.

Schueler, Donald G. "The Tristram Section of Malory's *Morte Darthur*." *Studies in Philology*, 65, 1968, 51-66.

Schüler, Meier. *Sir Thomas Malorys Le Morte d'Arthur, und die englische Arthurdichtung des XIX. jahrhunderts*. Strassburg: Singer, 1900.

Staines, David. "King Arthur in Victorian Fiction." *Harvard English Studies*, 6, 1975, 267-293.

_____ . "Morris' Treatment of His Medieval Sources in *The Defence of Guenevere and Other Poems*." *Studies in Philology*, 70, 1973, 439-464.

_____ . "Swinburne's Arthurian World: Swinburne's Arthurian Poetry and Its Medieval Sources." *Studia Neophilologica*, 50, 1978, 53-70.

Starr, Nathan C. *King Arthur Today*. Gainesville: University of Florida Press, 1954.

Thearle, Beatrice J. "Malory in the Nineteenth Century." Unpublished Dissertation, University of Maryland, 1958.

Ven-ten Bensel, E. F. Van der. *The Character of King Arthur in English Literature*. Amsterdam: H. J. Paris, 1925.
Vettermann, Ella. *Die Balen-Dichtungen und Ihre Quelle*. Halle: Karras, 1914.
Vinaver, Eugène. *Etudes sur le Tristan en Prose*. Paris: Champion, 1925.
_____. *Le Roman de Tristan et Iseut dans l'Oeuvre de Thomas Malory*. Paris: Champion, 1925.
Whitehead, F. "On Certain Episodes in the Fourth Book of Malory's *Morte Darthur*." *Medium Aevum*, 2, 1933, 199-216.
Whiting, B. J. "Gawain: His Reputation, His Courtesy, and His Appearance in Chaucer's 'Squire's Tale.'" *Mediaeval Studies*, 9, 1947, 189-234.
Wilson, R. H. "The 'Fair Unknown' in Malory." *Publications of the Modern Language Association of America*, 58, 1943, 1-21.

6. Other Works Relevant to this Study

Allingham, William. *William Allingham: A Diary*. Edited by H. Allingham and D. Radford. London: Macmillan, 1907.
Altick, Richard D. *Victorian People and Ideas*. New York: Norton, 1973.
Arnold, Matthew. *Letters of Matthew Arnold 1848-1888*, 2 Vols. Edited by George W. E. Russell. London, 1895.
_____. *The Letters of Matthew Arnold to Arthur Hugh Clough*. Edited by H. F. Lowry. London: Oxford University Press, 1932.
_____. *The Poems of Matthew Arnold*. Edited by Kenneth Allott. London: Longmans, 1965.
Bell, Malcolm. *Sir Edward Burne-Jones*. London, 1898.
Buckley, Jerome H. *The Victorian Temper*. Cambridge, Mass.: Harvard University Press, 1951.
Burne-Jones, Georgiana. *Memorials of Edward Burne-Jones*, 2 Vols. London: Macmillan, 1904.
Carter, John and Pollard, Graham. *An Enquiry into the Nature of Certain Nineteenth Century Pamphlets*. London: Constable, 1934.
Chandler, Alice. *A Dream of Order*. Lincoln, Nebraska: University of Nebraska Press, 1970.
Coleridge, S. T. *The Table Talk and Omniana of Samuel Taylor Coleridge*. London: G. Bell and Sons, 1923.
Collinson, John. *The History and Antiquities of the County of Somerset*, 3 Vols. Bath, 1791.
De Reul, Paul. *L'Oeuvre de Swinburne*. Bruxelles: Robert Sand, 1922.
Domett, Alfred. *The Diary of Alfred Domett, 1872-1885*. Edited by E. A. Horsman. London: Oxford University Press, 1953.
Doughty, Oswald. *Dante Gabriel Rossetti: A Victorian Romantic*. New Haven: Yale University Press, 1949.
Dunlop, John Colin. *History of Prose Fiction*, 3 Vols. London, 1814.
Ferrario, G., ed. *Raccolta di Novelle*. Milan, 1804.
FitzGerald, Edward. *Letters and Literary Remains of Edward FitzGerald*, 7 Vols. London: Macmillan, 1902-1903.
Fredeman, William E. *Pre-Raphaelitism: A Bibliographical Study*. Cambridge: Mass.: Harvard University Press, 1965.
Houghton, Walter E., ed. *The Wellesley Index to Victorian Periodicals 1824-1900*, 2 Vols. Toronto: University of Toronto Press, 1966-1972.
Hunt, W. Holman. *Pre-Raphaelitism and the Pre-Raphaelite Brotherhood*, 2 Vols. New York: Macmillan, 1906.

————— . *The Story of the Painting of the Pictures on the Walls and the Decorations on the Ceiling of the Old Debating Hall.* Oxford: Oxford University Press, 1906.

Johnson, E. D. H. *The Alien Vision of Victorian Poetry.* Princeton: Princeton University Press, 1952.

Johnston, Arthur. *Enchanted Ground.* London: The Athlone Press, 1964.

Lafourcade, Georges. *La Jeunesse de Swinburne 1837-1867*, 2 Vols. Paris: Société d'édition Les Belles lettres, 1928.

Mackail, J. W. *The Life of William Morris,* 2 Vols. London, 1899.

Marillier, H. C. *Dante Gabriel Rossetti: An Illustrated Memorial of His Art and Life.* London, 1899.

Millais, John Guille. *The Life and Letters of Sir John Everett Millais,* 2 Vols. London, 1899.

Morris, William. *The Collected Works of William Morris,* 24 Vols. Introductions by May Morris. New York: Russell and Russell, 1966.

Roscoe, Thomas. *The Italian Novelists*, 4 Vols. London, 1825.

Rossetti, Dante Gabriel. *The Letters of Dante Gabriel Rossetti*, 4 Vols. Edited by Oswald Doughty and J. R. Wahl. Oxford: The Clarendon Press, 1965-1967.

————— . *The Works of Dante Gabriel Rossetti.* Edited by William Michael Rossetti. London: Ellis, 1911.

Rossetti, William Michael, ed. *Dante Gabriel Rossetti: His Family-Letters with a Memoir*, 2 Vols. London, 1895.

————— . *Preraphaelite Diaries and Letters.* London: Hurst and Blackett, 1900.

————— . *Rossetti Papers 1862-1870.* New York: Charles Scribner's, 1903.

Scott, Walter. *The Letters of Sir Walter Scott*, 12 Vols. Edited by H. J. C. Grierson. London: Constable, 1932-1937.

————— . *Miscellaneous Prose Works*, 6 Vols. Edinburgh, 1827.

Shakespeare, William. *The Plays of William Shakespeare*, 10 Vols. Notes by Samuel Johnson and George Steevens. London, 1785.

Surtees, Virginia. *The Paintings and Drawings of Dante Gabriel Rossetti*, 2 Vols. Oxford: The Clarendon Press, 1971.

Swinburne, A. C. *Complete Works*, 20 Vols. Edited by Edmund Gosse and Thomas J. Wise. New York: G. Wells, 1925-1927.

————— . *The Swinburne Letters*, 6 Vols. Edited by Cecil Y. Lang. New Haven: Yale University Press, 1959-1962.

————— . *Swinburne Replies.* Edited by C. K. Hyder. Syracuse: Syracuse University Press, 1966.

Warton, Thomas. *The History of English Poetry*, 4 Vols. London, 1824.

Welsford, Enid. *The Fool: His Social and Literary History.* London: Faber and Faber, 1935.

Westwood, Thomas. *A Literary Friendship.* London: John Murray, 1914.

Woolner, Amy. *Thomas Woolner R.A. Sculptor and Poet: His Life in Letters.* London: Chapman and Hall, 1917.

INDEX

General Index

215

Index to Arthurian Characters